P9-BIC-852

DANGEROUS LIAISONS

How to Recognize and Escape from Psychopathic Seduction

Claudia Moscovici

Hamilton Books
A member of
The Rowman & Littlefield Publishing Group
Lanham · Boulder · New York · Toronto · Plymouth, UK

Copyright © 2011 by
Hamilton Books
4501 Forbes Boulevard
Suite 200
Lanham, Maryland 20706
Hamilton Books Acquisitions Department (301) 459-3366

Estover Road
Plymouth PL6 7PY
United Kingdom

All rights reserved
Printed in the United States of America
British Library Cataloging in Publication Information Available

Library of Congress Control Number: 2011935400
ISBN: 978-0-7618-5569-9 (paperback : alk. paper)
eISBN: 978-0-7618-5570-5

♾™ The paper used in this publication meets the minimum
requirements of American National Standard for Information
Sciences—Permanence of Paper for Printed Library Materials,
ANSI Z39.48-1992

Advance Praise for Claudia Moscovici's *Dangerous Liaisons: How To Recognize and Escape from Psychopathic Seduction*

As a clinical specialist in the narcissistic spectrum personality disorders, I find that nobody addresses this subject matter more trenchantly, and with more penetrating insight, than Claudia Moscovici does in her consistently illuminating work. Hers is a clinically keen, lucid mind, indeed. In *Dangerous Liaisons*, Moscovici presents the reader with the rare opportunity, if he or she dares, to enter and understand the mind and twisted machinations of psychopathic personalities. With dangerously deficient consciences, psychopaths are highly inclined to perpetrate sundry disturbing violations against others, remorselessly. In her examination of the dynamics of this puzzling, chilling personality, and in applying her insights to real-life, modern examples of classic psychopaths, Moscovici has written a book from which anyone (curious lay person or seasoned clinician) interested in how psychopaths insinuate themselves into others' lives, leaving trails of often hard-to-imagine devastation, will benefit immensely. With *Dangerous Liaisons*, Moscovici makes an invaluable, genuinely distinguished contribution to the literature on psychopathy.

Steve Becker, MSW, LCSW LoveFraud.com feature columnist, Expert/ Consultant on Narcissism and Psychopathy

The Institute has long said that what is shocking is not that pathology exists, but that there is so little public and survivor education about the most dangerous relationships on the planet. Claudia Moscovici's *Dangerous Liaisons* is a needed perspective about the invisible tyranny and death grip of pathological love relationships and what they do to those who love psychopaths. We can't avoid what we can't spot, and we can't heal from what we don't identify. This book helps to highlight the unique strength and lure of pathology, the devastating outcomes to the survivor, and an understanding of what pathology is and does. Not merely another 'I-Fell-In-Love-With-A-Psychopath' memoir, *Dangerous Liaisons* dives into recent information by the leading experts about the most disordered and dangerous person alive."

Sandra L. Brown, M.A. is a psychopathologist, the CEO The Institute for Relational Harm Reduction & Public Pathology Education, and author of Women Who Love Psychopaths (2nd Ed.), How to Spot a Dangerous Man, and Counseling Victims of Violence.

To my husband, Dan Troyka,
who taught me the meaning of true love

"I don't want my past to become anyone else's future."
– Elie Wiesel

Contents

Introduction

Sometimes truth can be stranger than fiction. Consider the following true story, which sounds so fantastic that it could have been lifted off the pages of an Agatha Christie mystery. One October evening in 1998, a despondent Englishman named John Allan rushes into the hotel lobby of the New Winter Palace Hotel in Luxor, Egypt. He appears to be very distressed. He announces in a panic-stricken voice that his wife is dying in their hotel room. Pamela Black, a guest who happens to be trained in administering first aid, goes with him to try to help his wife. She finds Cheryl Lewis sprawled out naked on the bed. A ring of sweat surrounds her limp body. She's frothing at the mouth. Unwilling to risk her own life for a stranger, Black tells Allan that she'll instruct him on how to give his dying wife mouth-to-mouth. Strangely, the man refuses to help. He paces back and forth by the foot of the bed while his partner is dying. To make matters worse, the doctor called to the scene also refuses to aid the sick woman because she's a foreigner. The hospital staff can't save her either. Cheryl Lewis, a seemingly healthy woman, expires at the age of 43.

The Egyptian doctors declared in their report that Cheryl Lewis died of natural causes. But in England detectives decided to investigate the matter further. John Allan's bizarre behavior aroused their suspicion. Only days after his partner's death, he kept company with prostitutes. A few weeks later, he courted Jennifer Hughes, one of Cheryl's close friends. He flattered her, cooked for her, pampered her and made her feel special, just as he had his previous girlfriend. Like Cheryl, she also believed that she had finally found her soulmate. However, when Jennifer refused to move in with him in a church where, strangely, his previous lover was supposed to be buried, Allan turned on her. That day Jennifer ended up sick. She was hospitalized for severe nausea and stomach cramps. The cause of her illness turned out to be cyanide poisoning. Police also discovered large doses of cyanide in Cheryl's car. During the trial it came to light that Allan had used cyanide to kill off his butterfly collection. Detective Superintendent Dave Smith, who investigated Cheryl Lewis's homicide, concluded that John Allan had poisoned his girlfriends. Yet both women had been very enamored with him, considered him to be their life partner and trusted him fully. "He opens car doors for them, has their drinks when they come home, cooks their meals and just pampers them," Detective Smith explained Allan's magnetic hold on women.

Those who had not fallen victim to Allan's seduction skills, however, saw another, more menacing, side of him. Close friends of Cheryl have described him as a "first-rate parasite" and "pure evil." Eric Lewis, Cheryl's father, stated in an interview that Allan was "a confessed liar, a confessed forger. He's extremely devious. He's a skillful manipulator and a very, very dangerous man." Lewis admitted that he never liked Allan. He didn't see what his daughter, who was wealthy, successful and attractive, ever saw in him. Yet before the misfortunate turn of events, even he couldn't predict just how dangerous John Allan would be.

On the surface, Allan's motive for killing Cheryl Lewis, his companion of seven years, appeared to be money. Police discovered that he had forged part of her will, declaring himself the main beneficiary of her $690,000 estate. But this motive doesn't even begin to explain the sordid mind games he played with women. It doesn't quite capture the lies he told his girlfriend when he claimed to be involved in illegal arms deals in the Middle East and pursued by terrorists. It doesn't fully explain why he tried to extort money from Cheryl for a topaz ring her mother had given her, demanding more than $3000 for its return. Later, his DNA was found on the stamp placed on the anonymous letter sent by the blackmailer. It also doesn't explain why he attempted to shoot his previous wife, Sima, the mother of his three children. And it doesn't explain why he asked his newest girlfriend to live in the church where Cheryl's body was supposed to be buried. In other words, no rational explanation or comprehensible motive can even begin to explain this dangerous seducer's severe personality disorder, which led him to pathological lying, malicious manipulation, sexual perversion, theft, blackmail and eventually the cold-blooded murder of the woman he called the love of his life.

My native country, Romania, is best known for a fictional character, Dracula, which is only loosely based on a historical fact: the infamous legend of Vlad Tepes. Novels that draw upon this legend—ranging from Anne Rice's genre fiction, to the popular *Twilight* series, to Elizabeth Kostova's erudite *The Historian*—continue to be best sellers. Yet, ultimately, no matter how much they may thrill us, the "undead" vampires we encounter in novels are harmless fictional characters that play upon our fascination with evil. However, real-life vampires, or individuals who relish destroying the lives of others, do exist. We see them constantly featured in the news and, if we don't know how to recognize them, sometimes we even welcome them into our lives.

What do Scott Peterson, Neil Entwistle and the timeless seducers of literature epitomized by the figures of Don Juan and Casanova have in common? They are charming, charismatic, glib and seductive men who also embody some of the most dangerous human qualities: a breathtaking callousness, shallowness of emotion and the fundamental incapacity to love. To such men, other people, including their own family members, friends and lovers, are mere objects or pawns to be used for their own gratification and sometimes quite literally discarded when no longer useful or exciting. In other words, these men are *psychopaths*.

If there's one thing helpful to learn from psychology it's the dangerous characteristics of these social predators, so that we can recognize them more easily and avoid them whenever possible. By definition, a predator is "one that preys, destroys or devours." Not exactly boyfriend or spouse material, yet psychopaths manage to lure numerous partners into their nets. Most of us are used to hearing the largely interchangeable terms "psychopath" and "sociopath" applied only to serial killers such as Ted Bundy or to murderers such as Scott Peterson. These men made national headlines for remorselessly killing strangers or family members. However, as Robert D. Hare documents in *Without Conscience*, only a very small percentage of psychopaths actually murder. Whether or not they do is not what makes them psychopathic or dangerous to others. Most psychopaths wreak havoc in our daily lives in more subtle yet sometimes equally destructive "subcriminal" ways. They may engage in a pattern of deception and betrayal, an endless string of seductions, emotional and psychological abuse of their loved ones, domestic violence or the financial exploitation of others.

As *lovefraud.com*, the website started by Donna Andersen to help victims indicates, psychopaths are exceptionally selfish individuals who lack empathy. Consequently, they're incapable of forming real love bonds with others. They establish instead dominance bonds, claiming possession of those closest to them rather than genuinely caring for family members, lovers and friends. Their top goal is control, their principal weapon is deceit and their main means is seduction: sometimes physical, but most often psychological in nature. Moreover, it's not just the naïve and the gullible that get taken in by them. Anybody can fall prey to the psychopathic charm. As Martha Stout illustrates in *The Sociopath Next Door*, psychopaths tend to be extremely charismatic. They say all the right things to reel you in. They're also supremely self-confident, highly sexual, have low impulse control and are amazingly good liars. Like real-life vampires, they feed upon people's dreams, vulnerabilities and emotions. They move from person to person, always for their personal advantage, no matter under what otherregarding pretext or guise. Only the most notorious cases make it into the news or get profiled by popular shows such as *Forensic Files*, *Cold Case Files* and *Dateline*. But there are millions of psychopaths in this country alone who poison, in one way or another, tens of millions of lives.

Unfortunately, their personality disorder often passes unnoticed until they commit a horrific crime. Some psychopaths, like Charles Manson, would appear crazy to a normal person even from miles away. In those cases, psychopathy is probably compounded by psychotic tendencies which render the disorder much more obvious to others. But most psychopaths move among us undetected. Scott Peterson, Mark Hacking and Neil Entwistle appeared to be normal young men even to those who thought they knew them best, such as their spouses, parents, in-laws and friends. In fact, in some respects, they seemed better than normal. According to their family members and friends, they could be exceptionally charming. Nothing in particular led them to kill their wives and babies. The media has ascribed traditional motives to their crimes, such as financial distress, girlfriends on the side and the desire for freedom or promiscuous sex. But these motives don't even begin to explain the viciousness, gratuitousness and callousness of their acts. Perhaps one can understand, even if not condone, lack of empathy towards strangers. As history has shown time and time again, it may be easier, in certain circumstances, to dehumanize those one doesn't know more intimately. But these men killed those who loved them most, trusted them fully and were closest to them. They murdered their innocent babies and wives who were either pregnant or had just given birth to their children. They didn't become "crazy" all of a sudden due to a crisis. In some cases, marital squabbles or financial distress may have functioned as a catalyst. But the underlying personality disorder that enabled these men to commit such vicious crimes was present before, during and after the gruesome murders that rendered it visible to the public eye.

What distinguishes a psychopath who commits murder from one who doesn't isn't his conscience, since all psychopaths lack it. What makes the difference may be nothing more than his desires, opportunities, whims and short-term objectives. Most psychopaths choose to dispose of an inconvenient wife or girlfriend in the traditional manner. They divorce or break up with her. A few, like Scott Peterson, Mark Hacking and Neil Entwistle, decide that murder is the better route for them. Such men believe that they're clever enough to fool the police and get away with their crimes. They commit murder to appear to be grieving spouses rather than risk being unmasked for what they really are even before the crimes: empty souls hiding behind a façade of lies. What a psychopath is capable of doing in order to protect his phony good image or to fulfill his deviant desires can't be predicted in advance.

For normal people, it's difficult to imagine such a disordered human being. To most of us, the psychopath represents a distant danger or an abstraction. It's a concept we can comprehend intellectually, but not on an emotional level. Yet this is precisely what Martha Stout asks us to envision: "Imagine—if you can—not having a conscience, none at all, no feelings of guilt or remorse no matter what you do, no limiting sense of concern for the well-being of strangers, friends or even family members. Imagine no struggles with shame, not a single one in your whole life, no matter what kind of selfish, lazy, harmful, or immoral action you have taken…" (*The Sociopath Next Door*, 1). Her conclusion to this thought exercise is clear. Without a conscience, one can do anything at all. No evil act is beneath a psychopath. Once his crime is discovered, people tend to say that they never knew such evil existed. Unfortunately, it does. What's worse, it's common and well hidden enough to present a danger to us all.

Dr. Robert Hare, author of *Without Conscience*, *Snakes in Suits* and of the *Psychopathy Checklist*, which is administered in prisons and psychiatric institutions, estimates that between 1 and 4 percent of the population is psychopathic. Because this personality disorder ties into aggression and the drive for dominance, the percentage tends to be higher in men than in women. What do psychopaths look like? They look, and superficially even behave, like the rest of us.

They come from every class, every race, every ethnicity, every nationality, every social background and upbringing. They tend to be smarter than average. Some become successful businessmen, lawyers, doctors, psychiatrists, writers, teachers, artists and scholars. They can be exceptionally charming. They say all the right things to get what they want, without fumbling or sounding artificial. Lacking any real emotional ties to preoccupy them, they're easily bored and crave constant excitement. Having no conscience yet being glib, they're compelling pathological liars. They rationalize everything they do, including rape and murder. Consequently, they fail to accept responsibility for anything they do wrong. Since they know no loyalty to anything or anyone but themselves, they don't play by the rules. Like the Joker in the blockbuster movie, *The Dark Knight*, they don't even bond with other outlaws. Even that would require having some loyalty and abiding by some subversive principles. Psychopaths, however, are rebels without a cause. Once they reach adulthood, their character solidifies and their personality disorder becomes unfixable.

They vary, however, in what motivates them. Some psychopaths want money, power or fame. Others are sex addicts who have innumerable liaisons and may commit rape and even murder. Yet others are compulsive gamblers, scam artists or crooks. But they all share one thing: a quest for power. To control others, psychopaths seduce them. Seduction doesn't have to be sexual in nature. The narrow definition of "seduce" is, indeed, "to persuade to have sexual intercourse." Many psychopaths enjoy this form of seduction because it naturally combines physical pleasure with control over another person's body and emotions. But the etymological root of "seduction" signifies, more broadly, "to lead away from duty, accepted principles, or proper conduct." In this sense of the term, psychopaths enjoy exercising power not only over their sexual partners, but also over their parents, their siblings, their children, their so-called friends, their employees and their colleagues. Some of them become leaders of cults, luring members with their charisma, false promises, isolation and mind-control. Through a fatal combination of opportunity and machination, a few become leaders of entire nations. They take over the minds and wills of the masses. Their lack of principles and disordered mentality are contagious. It spreads like a virus throughout the country.

As a scholar whose writing focuses on totalitarian movements and as someone who's experienced first-hand, as a child, life under the psychopathic dictator Nicolae Ceausescu in communist Romania, I've studied ruthless leaders of totalitarian regimes. What I find most remarkable about such individuals is not only the vastness of their destruction of healthy social institutions and of fellow human beings, but also their unscrupulous and opportunistic methods. Because psychopaths lack any underlying convictions and loyalties, they're willing to get power by whatever means necessary. To give an example from my field, Allan Bullock shows in *Hitler and Stalin: Parallel Lives* that Stalin only appeared to have a solid allegiance to the Bolshevik movement and to Lenin's political legacy. In reality, however, he used communist rhetoric to gain control over Russia, then over the countries and territories that became the Soviet Union and eventually

over the entire Eastern Europe. To him, the means—shifty allegiances, mass indoctrination, staged show trials, forced confessions as well as torture and murder
of unprecedented proportions—justified the ends, which was absolute control.
This goal was only instrumentally related to communist ideology, as Stalin's
temporary alliance with Hitler, his archenemy, would prove.

Nor did Stalin exhibit any loyalty towards his supposed friends and allies. He
switched political and personal alliances, turning first against the left wing of the
communist party (Trotsky, Zinoviev and Kamenev), then against its right wing
(Bukharin, Rykov and Tomsky). In his insatiable quest for power, Stalin constantly forged alliances and broke them. He imprisoned, tortured and murdered
former allies. He shrewdly reversed his position and retreated when necessary,
only to charge forward again at a more optimal moment. Because he was a psychopath, Stalin could be more ideologically flexible than his dogmatic rivals,
such as Trotsky (on the left) and Bukharin (on the right). He took everyone by
surprise with the extent of his duplicity and ruthlessness. For psychopathic leaders like Hitler and Stalin, other people existed only as tools to be used in their
quest for control or as obstacles to be removed from their path. As Bullock observes:

> Stalin and Hitler were materialists not only in their dismissal of religion but
> also in their insensitivity to humanity as well. The only human beings who ex-
> isted for them were themselves. The rest of the human race was seen either as
> instruments with which to accomplish their purposes or as obstacles to be
> eliminated... Both men were remarkable only for the roles they assumed. Out-
> side those, their private lives were insignificant and impoverished. And each of
> the roles was consecrated to a vision of a world that, however great the differ-
> ences between them, was equally inhuman—a world in which whole popula-
> tions could be moved about; whole classes could be eliminated; races enslaved
> or exterminated; millions of lives sacrificed in war and even in time of peace...
> (*Hitler and Stalin*, 382).

Having done extensive research on the psychopathic dictator Nicolae
Ceausescu for my book on communist Romania, *Velvet Totalitarianism: Post-
Stalinist Romania*, I've arrived at the conclusion that, given the choice between
ruling over a nation of strong individuals and ruling over a nation of slaves, psychopathic leaders would much rather take the latter. This is the only way to explain the malice with which such dictators propose policies intended to ruin the
country economically, isolate its people from the rest of the world and destroy
any sign of individuality. To use my own childhood experience as an example,
conditions in Romania during the so-called "Epoch of Light" were notoriously
miserable. People had to wait in long lines for meager supplies of food, clothing
and household goods. There was limited heat and hot water. By the late 1970's,
the Secret Police, colloquially called the Securitate, had installed microphones in
virtually every home and apartment. The whole population lived in fear. As a
Romanian citizen said to a French journalist following the fall of the Ceausescu
regime, "It was a system that didn't destroy people physically—not many were

actually killed; but it was a system that condemned us to a fight for the lowest possible level of physical and spiritual nourishment. Under Ceausescu, some people died violently, but an entire population was dying." Strong, healthy individuals in a prosperous nation would pose a potential threat to psychopathic rulers. They might be confident enough to challenge their regimes. When people are reduced to fighting for survival and deprived of power, however, they're much more likely to relinquish their rights and freedoms without putting up a fight. While Ceausescu preferred to rule over a nation of beggars, Stalin chose to govern a nation of slaves. His Reign of Terror not only undermined people's spirit and independent thought, but also claimed many of their lives.

The human cost of psychopathic dictators, especially during the Hitler-Stalin era, is one of staggering proportions and unimaginable suffering. Bullock documents, "Not counting the millions who were wounded or permanently maimed, the estimated number of premature deaths between 1930 and 1953 reached a figure in the order of forty to fifty million men, women and children. Suffering on such a scale is beyond the imagination's power to comprehend or respond to" (*Hitler and Stalin*, 969). What makes such suffering particularly reprehensible, at least from a moral perspective, is that unlike natural disasters such as floods, earthquakes and epidemics, the harm was deliberately inflicted, unnecessary and man-made. Granted, the mass murder of tens of millions of innocent civilians can't be attributed solely to the psychopathic leaders in charge. The wrongdoing of many individuals made it possible. As Hannah Arendt demonstrates in *The Origins of Totalitarianism*, totalitarian dictators are a necessary, but not sufficient, explanation of complex historical, economic and social phenomena. Yet without a Hitler, a Stalin, a Mao or a Ceausescu—which is to say, without psychopathic leaders who attain almost total control of a country—this suffering wouldn't have occurred, at least not on such a massive scale.

A few psychopaths, like Hitler and Stalin, want to control and destroy whole nations, entire ethnicities: perhaps even humanity itself. Their hunger for power knows no bounds. Most psychopaths, however, lack the historical opportunities for mass destruction that these evil dictators had at their disposal. They become instead little tyrants in their own homes by controlling the lives of their partners and children. Psychologically speaking, there's very little difference between a psychopath who wants to control and destroy the lives of many and one who wants to control and destroy the lives of few. Both are power-hungry individuals who lack conscience. Both are incapable of caring about anyone but themselves. What separates them is chance, opportunity, their capacity for manipulation and, perhaps above all, the magnitude of their ambition.

I can say this with confidence because I have not only researched this matter in scholarly books, but also witnessed both kinds of psychopaths at work, firsthand. The irony of my life has been that, as a child, I escaped life under a psychopathic ruler in Romania only to voluntarily place myself as an adult into the hands of a psychopathic partner here, in the United States. This man came into my life at a moment when I was vulnerable because my husband and I were experiencing difficulties in our marriage. Initially, the psychopath behaved far better than any man I had ever met. This in itself should have aroused my suspicion, but it didn't. Because he showered me with constant affection at a moment when I craved it, I was temporarily blinded by the illusion of perfect love. I didn't heed the warning signals when he relentlessly pushed for the violation of trust and moral principles and isolated me from my family and friends. I mistakenly attributed his zest for seducing me to the intensity of his love. Admittedly, I played an active role in the process of psychopathic seduction. I was not just his passive pawn. My vulnerability at the time, my weakened moral and sexual boundaries, my willful blindness, as well as my preference for an idealized fantasy rather than tackling the real (yet surmountable) problems in my marriage, made me susceptible to this social predator and complicit with his wrongdoings.

I didn't open my eyes until his mask of sanity started to crack. Then I began to recognize in him the psychological profile I had studied in the maleficent dictators I wrote about in my scholarship and fiction. As soon as I gave in to his unrelenting pressure and agreed to divorce in order to marry him, the seducer proposed that we post our profiles on dating websites. It became apparent that his professed love for me and attempt to break up my marriage had only been a game of conquest to him. When normal people do something wrong or hurt their loved ones, they feel guilty about it. By way of contrast, when psychopaths harm others they experience an immense surge of satisfaction. They gloat about it, congratulating themselves for fooling yet another person and damaging yet another life. Throughout the entire process, they tend to leave behind a trail of evidence of their wrongdoings. This enables them to play a game of catch-me-if-you-can with their victims. It also allows them to experience over and over the pleasure of betrayal, as they repeatedly return to its traces. The more power emotional predators exercise over a given target, and the less value that person has for them, the more brazen they become in leaving behind clues. They wave signs of their infidelity, lies, scams and other kinds of wrongdoings under their victims' noses.

As I picked up on some of the seducer's clues, our relationship began to unravel. Concerned about the personality traits I noticed in him, I fell back upon what I usually do as a scholar: I researched them. I then recognized in him the main characteristics of antisocial personality disorder, or psychopathy: his penchant for constant intrigue and manipulation; his complete insensitivity to the needs and feelings of those he claimed to love; a facile detachment from everyone close to him as soon as he got bored with them or when they no longer served his immediate needs; the pleasure he took in causing others pain and, the icing on the cake, an insatiable and perverse sex addiction, which I initially mistook for sensuality and passion. By the end of our relationship, I came to grips with the disheartening fact that, psychologically speaking, my dream partner was no different from the nightmare dictator my family had struggled to escape in Romania. What made this situation in some ways worse is that I had chosen this psychopath of my own volition, with all the negative implications that stem from making such a bad decision.

In reading my description of this disturbed individual, you might wonder what I saw in him: why I exercised such poor judgment and what that says about me. Once I opened my eyes, I asked myself the same thing. Another way of framing these questions is what I didn't see and why I failed to see it. Because until the seducer's mask of sanity cracked, I bought into the illusion this man conveyed to me. For awhile, I believed that he was a warm, generous, attractive and sensitive man who was stuck in the wrong marriage with a cold and frigid woman. I also believed him when he told me, time and time again, that he had been looking for a partner like me all of his adult life. From an external perspective, this may sound like exactly what it was: a bunch of cheesy lines sleazy men feed needy women to hook up with them. But the delivery, as well as the daily attention and affection the seducer lavished upon me for well over a year, seemed to give substance to these hollow words. Predictably, my case didn't prove to be the one exception to the rule. I didn't turn out to be the only woman to miraculously transform a psychopath into a faithful, loving and caring partner. It become quite clear to me that, as a *lovefraud.com* participant once said, when involved with a psychopath you have only two options: losing a whole lot and losing everything. In disengaging from him for good, I chose not to lose everything.

Yet as I was experiencing our love affair, this conclusion didn't become obvious to me until the end. When living under the rule of a psychopathic tyrant, the disorder of the dictator and the dysfunction of the country are usually quite glaring, at least to those enduring the daily hardships of such a regime. When you're involved with a psychopathic individual, however, his personality disorder can be well masked. It's especially hard to see for those who are blinded by a potent mixture of love, wishful thinking and denial. In extreme cases, some women can even be married to serial killers for many years without seeing the monsters inside the cherished husbands they live with and care about.

Hare and Babiak call the psychopath "the perfect invisible predator. Like chameleons, psychopaths can hide who they really are and mask their true intentions from their victims for extended periods" (*Snakes in Suits*, 39). If you have any doubts about that, all you have to do is glance at the news. As I was writing this book on psychopathy, I could barely keep up with the frequent headlines about individuals who have committed unthinkable crimes, for no apparent reason other than to cause harm. For awhile, the story about Phillip Garrido, a sexual predator who is accused of kidnapping 11-year-old Jaycee Lee Dugard, turning her into his sex slave and forcing her to have children with him, dominated the national headlines. While humiliating Jaycee and locking her and their children in shacks at the back of his house, he also regarded her as his beautiful trophy. Neighbors report that Garrido handed out a card featuring the kidnapped young woman listed as a model. His second wife seems to have been complicit with his evil deeds. By way of contrast, Christine Murphy, Garrido's first wife, ran away from him. She told the show *Inside Edition* that her ex-husband is a monster, who is "capable of doing anything." Murphy also reported that he once tried to gouge out her eyes with a safety pin when another man flirted with her. Some of his neighbors described Garrido as "strange." But many social predators appear to be normal and fit right in.

To offer another example, several months ago Philip Markoff was arrested on the charge of being the alleged Craigslist killer. Markoff was a 22-year old medical student at Boston University. He's accused of murdering Julissa Brisman, whom he met on Craigslist, and of kidnapping several other women. The evidence found on Markoff's computer, the "trophies" or "souvenirs" he kept from his victims to relive his crimes, as well as the testimony offered by some of the surviving victims, lead police to feel quite confident that they caught the right guy. But you wouldn't know it from talking to his fiancée and friends. Markoff appeared to be a very likable, clean-cut, charming and well-adjusted person. His fiancée, Megan McAllister, who's obviously deeply in love with him, described him in an email to ABC news as "a beautiful person inside and out." Strangely, and no doubt unwittingly, she also echoed the famous last words of Hitchcock's *Psycho* in stating that Markoff "wouldn't hurt a fly."

This is what I would have said as well about the dangerous man I was involved with until his phony image of perfection began to deteriorate and I glimpsed at its seedy, and deeply disturbing, underside. Even now, in retrospect, the whole experience of falling in love with a psychopath appears dichotomous, disorienting and, in some ways, surreal. It's as if from the beginning to the end of the relationship, I was involved with two different, even opposite, individuals: a Dr. Jekyll and a Mr. Hyde, coexisting in the same man. Some disillusionment occurs even in normal romantic relationships. Once the honeymoon phase ends, so does the unrealistic mutual idealization. When we get to know a new partner better, we usually discover some characteristics that we don't like about him or her and have to work through together. But with a psychopathic partner, the switch is far more dramatic and extreme. What was white ends up being black. What felt right begins to feel horribly wrong. What seemed good turns out to be inconceivably bad. My research on psychopathy and related personality disorders confirms this unsettling personal observation. It suggests that whatever appears good in a psychopath is an act intended to attract potential targets and win their trust in order to use and harm them.

Building a romantic relationship with a psychopath is like building a house on a foundation of quicksand. Everything shifts and sinks in a relatively short period of time. Seemingly caring, and often flattering, attention turns into jealousy, domination and control. Enjoying time together becomes isolation from others. Romantic gifts are replaced with requests, then with demands. Apparent selflessness and other-regarding gestures turn into the most brutal selfishness one can possibly imagine. Confidential exchanges and mutual honesty turn out to be filled with lies about everything: the past, the present as well as the hollow promises for the future. The niceness that initially seemed to be a part of the seducer's character is exposed as strategic and manipulative, conditional upon acts of submission to his will. Tenderness diminishes and is eventually displaced by a perversion that hints at an underlying, and menacing, sadism. Mutuality, equality and respect—everything you thought the relationship was founded upon—becomes replaced with hierarchies and double standards in his favor. You can bet that if you're involved with a psychopath, particularly if he's also a sex addict, the fidelity he expects of you is not what he's willing to offer you or any other person. Fidelity becomes nothing more than a one-way street, as he secretly prowls around for innumerable other sexual conquests. As the relationship with the psychopath unfolds, Dr. Jekyll morphs into Mr. Hyde.

Like all human beings, psychopaths may have some real qualities. They may be physically attractive. They tend to be extraordinarily charming, spontaneous and fun. They can be cultured, talented, intelligent and successful. But none of these qualities are related to their *character*: which is to say, to their capacity to care about others, to respect their boundaries and needs, to regard them as equals, to be loyal to them and to abide by moral principles. In those respects, psychopaths exhibit pathological deficiencies. Yet those are precisely the qualities that make or break human relationships. Liane Leedom explains in *Just Like His Father?* that adult psychopaths constitutionally lack the three capacities that are necessary for creating meaningful social bonds with others: impulse control, the ability to love and moral reasoning. I have seen with my own eyes the emptiness that results from lacking these essential human qualities. Reading the testimonials of dozens of (mostly female) victims on the website *lovefraud.com* has helped confirm this personal discovery. In many respects, learning about other people's experiences with psychopaths made me feel as if I was re-reading my own life story, no matter what differences of circumstances, age and personality traits may have distinguished us. We shared the same intense and addictive love bonds with the psychopaths. We felt the same hypnotic attraction to them. We underwent a similar deterioration of our identities and boundaries. Last, but certainly not least, we experienced the same devastating sense that we had fallen in love with Prince Charming only to end up with Jack the Ripper.

Just as *lovefraud.com* and the psychology books I read shed light upon the relationship with the psychopath in my life, I hope that this book can help other individuals in similar situations. Despite its personal angle and tone, however, *Dangerous liaisons* is not a memoir. I do not recount here all the details of my personal experience. Instead, I draw upon that experience, reinforced by extensive psychology research, to describe how psychopathic seduction (both literal and figurative) takes place, by whom and of whom and, above all, to suggest the road to recovery through information and lucidity. Sandra L. Brown, M.A. concludes her study of women who love psychopaths by saying, "First and foremost, all of the women reported that they were harmed by the relationship with the psychopath" (*Women Who Love Psychopaths*, 231). Fortunately, however, escape is possible. The philosopher Michel Foucault may have exaggerated when he claimed that knowledge is power. Yet my underlying assumption in writing this book is that knowledge is, indeed, very empowering if and when it leads to appropriate action. Learning about psychopathy and reading the testimonials of other victims helped free me from a toxic relationship and reclaim my life: at least once I started paying attention to my conscience and took seriously my intuitive warning signals.

Over the past few years, I've researched all the reliable sources I could find on the Internet and in printed books and articles that explained not only psychopathic individuals, but also the psychological profile of those who fall under their spell. I focus on women in particular both because that has been my personal experience and because, statistically speaking, psychopathic seducers tend to be men and their victims tend to be women. Of course, female psychopaths exist as well. They can be just as heartless, deceptive and destructive as their male counterparts. As I was working on this book, Melissa Huckaby, a Sunday school teacher, was arraigned on charges of rape and murder of an eight-year old girl, Sandra Cantu. As usual, experts expressed "bafflement" about her motives.

My book explains the *motivations* of psychopathic individuals, which are far more relevant to understanding their evil actions than their so-called *motives*. Motives are often rational and justifiable. By way of contrast, psychopaths' motivations are always pathological and unjustifiable. What I say here about male psychopaths applies to female psychopaths and male victims as well as to psychopaths and victims of the same gender. In my last book, *Velvet Totalitarianism*: *Post-Stalinist Romania*, I described the disordered mentality and policies of a psychopathic dictator, Nicolae Ceausescu, who wanted to control and destroy an entire nation. In *Dangerous Liaisons*, I'm sketching the psychological profile of the garden variety psychopath who wants to control and destroy individual women by seducing them, isolating them from their loved ones, undermining their moral compass and, if he gets the chance, eventually discarding them once he's sucked all the use value out of them.

Fortunately, I woke up in time to leave the psychopathic seducer and avoid this predictable conclusion. I was lucky to have a supportive family and a loving husband who cared about me enough to give our marriage a second chance. I would like to use this brush with evil to do some good. The first and most important way in which I can use this negative experience constructively is by treating my family, and particularly my husband, with the love and respect that they deserve. The second way is to try to help others in similar situations as well as to inform the general public about the hidden danger posed by psychopaths.

Of course, I'm not alone in this goal. My book draws upon previous studies of this subject. Hervey Cleckley's *The Mask of Sanity* (St. Louis: Mosby, 1976) paved the road for understanding psychopathy during the 1940's, with significant revisions of that work that continued into the 1970's. More recently, Robert D. Hare's *Without Conscience: The Disturbing World of the Psychopaths Among Us* (New York: Guilford Press, 1998), as well as the book he co-authored with Paul Babiak, *Snakes in Suits: When Psychopaths Go to Work* (New York: Harper Collins, 2006), gave us the contemporary criteria for recognizing its symptoms. Martha Stout's popular *The Sociopath Next Door* (New York: Broadway Books, 2005) increased public awareness of this phenomenon. In addition, the psychology research of Sandra L. Brown, M.A. in *Women Who Love Psychopaths* (Penrose: Mask Publishing, 2009) and in *How to Spot a Dangerous Man Before You Get Involved* (Alameda, CA: Hunter House, 2005) has helped attune readers to the psychological profile of those who fall prey to psychopaths. Last but not least, the work of Susan Forward, Steve Becker, Roger Melton and Joseph Carver also helps the general public understand better this dangerous personality disorder and its impact on victims.

As mentioned, when I was writing my own book on the subject, I also kept in mind the hundreds of anonymous testimonials I read on the website *love-fraud.com* by those who have been involved with and harmed by psychopaths. This book relies on all of these diverse sources—personal experience, testimonials of other victims and expert sources both printed and on the web—to synthesize the information I found in them into one convenient and accessible package for the general reader. I supplement them with my scholarly insight into how brainwashing works in totalitarian societies and illustrative examples from literature and art, which I've studied and taught at the university level for nearly fifteen years. I also cover notorious criminal psychopaths, such as Mark Hacking and Neil Entwistle, as well as well-known artists, such as Pablo Picasso, who was almost as infamous for his mistreatment of women as he was famous for his art. To inform readers about the widespread danger posed by social predators, *Dangerous liaisons* bridges the gap between personal experience and mainstream psychology and between popular culture (or true crime) and accessible scholarship in the arts and humanities.

Unfortunately, even many of the journalists who cover criminal psychopaths in the news appear to be uninformed about this personality disorder. Harrison Koehli, a writer who knows a thing or two about psychopathy, reprimands fellow journalists for not understanding that Neil Entwistle, a man who killed his wife and new baby for no apparent reason, was a psychopath. At the conclusion of his article, Koehli urges us to read carefully Hervey Cleckley's work and inform ourselves about psychopathy. He states, emphatically, "Widespread knowledge of the reality of psychopathy on this planet is the essential first step to securing our future and that of our children. Make it your priority to spread the word."

That's exactly what I do in *Dangerous Liaisons*. In the first part of the book, I revisit Cleckley's seminal work on psychopathy, *The Mask of Sanity*, to explain its most important elements clearly, for a general audience. I also rely upon high-profile media stories that readers are, most likely, already familiar with—such as the cases of Neil Entwistle, Mark Hacking and Drew Peterson—to sketch the psychological profile of psychopaths and their techniques of luring their targets. Identifying dangerous predators is our first line of defense against them. The second part of the book relies upon studies of the other side of the coin—the kind of targets psychopaths tend to select—in order to present a picture of who might be susceptible to psychopathic seduction, how it happens and why. Being aware of our vulnerabilities to social predators constitutes our second line of defense against them. In the third section, I draw upon studies of recovering victims—or survivors—to discuss strategies of escaping psychopathic seduction and reclaiming one's life. Freeing oneself and recovering from the psychopathic bond represents the third, and perhaps most powerful, defense against psychopaths. After all, as they say, living well is the best revenge.

Although I've put together here all the helpful psychological studies I could find on the subject, ultimately my book is written from the perspective of someone who has experienced the initially exhilarating, but ultimately painful and disorienting, process of psychopathic seduction. Just as nobody can understand addiction from the inside as well as a former addict does, so nobody can understand the psychopathic bond as well as someone who's been burned by it. I address other women who suspect that they may be involved with psychopathic partners in the hope of offering them a helping hand, so that they too will find the strength to escape their dangerous relationships. The clinical information I present here is as objective as psychology can offer. Yet my tone remains personal. My exhortations are emotional, not purely rational, appeals. I understand what victims have gone through. By all accounts, psychopathic seduction is unlike any other kind of human experience. It's more spellbinding and euphoric initially. For that reason, it's far more addictive and harmful than any other kind of human bond. It's also more fragile and illusory, likely to disintegrate, quite literally, overnight. Of course, even loving couples may grow apart over time. But previously warm relations with a psychopath can dissolve suddenly and for no apparent reason. When involved with a psychopath, your psychological and moral make-up undergo a radical transformation: always for the worse. When immersed in psychopathic relationships, strong, healthy and confident women can become anxious, insecure and depressed. Previously moral and compassionate women can behave unethically and uncaringly towards those they love.

It's very difficult for those who have not experienced this kind of mind-control to fully understand it or to relate to those who did. When people tell you, with the best of intentions, to just get over it, they don't quite grasp what they're advising you to get over. It's even harder for normal human beings to comprehend the mentality of the psychopaths themselves, since they're so abnormal and deficient, despite the mask of sanity that temporarily camouflages their malady. This is why, aside from addressing other victims of psychopathic partners, I also address the general public. I believe that information about this dangerous personality disorder can be potentially useful to everyone, not just to those who are or have been personally involved with psychopaths. Anyone can fall victim to these social predators, even if solid moral principles and clear-cut boundaries may help protect some individuals from (literal) psychopathic seduction. In addition, from a social and psychological perspective, there's nothing more dangerous, at least in terms of its potential to harm to others, than psychopathic individuals. The most inhumane and destructive leaders in history are psychopathic dictators. The most notorious serial killers, such as Ted Bundy and Jeffrey Dahmer, are psychopaths. The infamous individuals like Scott Peterson, Mark Hacking and Neil Entwistle, who, seemingly out of the blue and without any remorse, kill their wives or children, are psychopaths as well. Psychopathy is the malady of lovelessness and the psychological root of evil. To understand it better means to protect ourselves better from evil individuals.

Generally speaking, psychology isn't a precise science. Human behavior is highly complex and can't be reduced to scientific explanations. Psychopathy, however, may be the one exception to this rule. Like everyone else, psychopaths come from diverse backgrounds, cultures, upbringings and educations. They exhibit, as do other human beings, a wide range of characteristics and behaviors. They can be intelligent or not. They can be driven, cultured and successful or parasitic failures. They can be handsome or unattractive. They can be exceptionally charming or off-putting. Yet they all share one common denominator, which makes them different from the rest of humanity and very dangerous: a shallowness of emotion that renders *all* of them incapable of caring about other human beings. This has immense implications for society, which can touch any of us on a personal level. The social cost of psychopathy becomes obvious when we take into account that a high percentage of the criminals who commit violent crimes are psychopathic. In addition, research shows that 80 percent of the homicides of women are perpetrated by their husbands or boyfriends: which is to say, by the men they know and trust. The more psychopathic a criminal is, the more callous and remorseless he is, and therefore the more likely he is to repeat or even intensify his crime spree once he's freed from jail.

You may object that I'm exaggerating because most psychopaths don't commit violent crimes and therefore that those individuals aren't dangerous. If that's what you're thinking, then I wish to persuade you that, unfortunately, you're mistaken. What psychologists call "sub-criminal" psychopaths can be extremely harmful. They may be better camouflaged—better educated and come from wealthier backgrounds—than most criminal psychopaths. But that only makes sub-criminal psychopaths hide better in our midst to prey upon us more easily. They're the proverbial wolves in sheep's clothing. They're the conmen who pretend to be your friends and take away your life's savings. They're the lovers, spouses and boyfriends who seduce you, isolate you, abuse you, betray you and then dump you not only remorselessly, but with a sense of satisfaction that they were able to conquer and destroy another human being. They're the sons and daughters who spend their parents' financial and emotional resources to save them from their drug addictions, promiscuity, financial scams or whatever misdeeds they may engage in, yet nothing ever rehabilitates them. They're a curse upon anyone who has the misjudgment of becoming intimately involved with them or the misfortune of being part of their nuclear family.

Perhaps because they're so dangerous and destructive—the closest approximation to metaphysical evil that human beings can embody—the general public has a morbid fascination with psychopaths. We frequently see them featured on the news. The media seems to be intrigued by men like Scott Peterson and Neil Entwistle, who remorselessly murder their wives so that they can fool around more easily with other women. The public eats up this sordid information. True crime books about psychopathic killers tend to be best sellers. Similarly, biographical works about Hitler and Stalin continue to sell well. Yet, paradoxically, as fascinated as the general public may be with psychopaths and their evil deeds, they're far less interested in learning about what makes these people tick in order to recognize and avoid them in real life. As mentioned, there are a few highly informative studies of psychopathy, some of which—Stout's *The Sociopath Next Door*, Babiak and Hare's *Snakes in Suits* and Brown's *Women Who Love Psychopaths*—are written for a general audience. These books describe clearly and without unnecessary jargon the psychology of evil individuals. Unfortunately, however, such informative works tend to be less popular than the dramatic news coverage of psychopathic killers or the horror stories we read in true crime and thrillers. Why so?

The first answer I'll offer is in the form of an analogy. When I (and probably most other people too) shop for a car, I don't need someone to explain to me in great detail the mechanics behind how the car functions. I may read *Consumer Reports* online to see how the car's rated in various relevant categories, such as overall quality, safety and gas mileage. Then I look at it in person, to see if I like it and if it's the right size to suit my family's needs. In other words, a superficial knowledge of the car suffices for me. That's how most people feel about the psychopaths featured on the news, in history or true crime books and in the movies. They grasp the phenomenon superficially: that evil people exist and do horrible things to others. But they don't feel like they need to understand these people on a deeper psychological level. Which brings me to my second reason. We tend to view psychopaths as a form of titillating, if morbid, entertainment. We may disapprove of their horrific crimes, but their capacity for evil fascinates us. Third, and perhaps most importantly, we hold psychopaths at arm's length, so to speak, in our own minds. I can't even count how many times I've heard people interviewed on the news about a violent murder say that they can't believe it happened to their families or in their neighborhood. We believe that the great misfortune of being the victim of a psychopathic killer, rapist, conman, spouse or lover only befalls *others*. Somehow, we assume that our families and we are immune to such terrible things happening to us. Perhaps we believe that we're too wise, too well educated and live in too good of a neighborhood to fall into the hands of social predators.

If you think about it rationally, however, you come to realize that this belief rests upon an illusion. It may be true that you and your loved ones are not statistically likely to fall prey to a psychopathic serial killer. Experts estimate that there are only about 50 to 100 serial killers circulating in the country at any given moment. It's therefore rational not to live your life in the fear that you'll be attacked by one of them. But it's not statistically likely that you'll avoid any intimate involvement with a psychopath for the rest of your life. As mentioned, psychopaths constitute between 1 and 4 percent of the population. This is significant, given the number of lives they touch and the kind of damage they can inflict. Psychopaths are exceedingly sociable, highly promiscuous, have many children, move from location to location and, generally speaking, they get around. Their malady is technically called "*antisocial* personality disorder" not "*asocial* personality disorder." An asocial person avoids human contact. An antisocial person, on the contrary, continually seeks others in order to use, con, deceive, manipulate, betray and ultimately destroy them. That's what psychopaths do. They feed, like parasites, upon our lives. They live for the thrill of damaging healthier, more productive and more caring human beings.

Statistically speaking, there are decent chances that you have a psychopath in your extended family. There are even better odds that at some point you ran across one or will encounter one in your life. Perhaps it was a boyfriend who seemed perfect at first but turned out to be an abusive sex addict. It may be a difficult boss who makes work unbearable for his employees. Or maybe it was a manipulative professor who became a minor despot in the department. Perhaps it was a teacher who got too chummy with his students and even seduced some of them. Or perhaps it was a friend who appeared to be kind and loving, only to repeatedly backstab you. Maybe it was a con artist who took your elderly mother's life savings, or a portion of her hard-earned money, and vanished into thin air. Moreover, any psychopath can cause you physical harm and endanger your life. It doesn't have to be one predisposed to rape and murder. Keep in mind that Scott Peterson and Neil Entwistle were not sadistic serial killers. They were your garden variety charismatic psychopaths who found marriage a bit too inconvenient and incompatible with the new, wilder paths they wanted to pursue in life. Their incapacity to regard others as fellow human beings renders *all* psychopaths extremely dangerous. As psychotherapist Steve Becker explains:

> Commonly, the psychopath is upheld as the incarnation of the murderous bogeyman. While it's true than many cold-blooded killers are psychopaths, most psychopaths are not killers. The majority of psychopaths would find a messy murder too inconvenient and personally unpleasant a task to assume. This—the personal inconvenience and unpleasantness, not empathy for the slaughtered victim—explains why a great many more psychopaths than not, with chilling non-compunction, are more likely to target your life's savings than butcher you, and dispose of your remains in several industrial-strength Hefty bags. This doesn't make the non-murderous psychopath 'less psychopathic,' or 'more sensitive' than the murderous psychopath; it merely reflects the calculus psychopaths apply in their decision-making: how can I get, or take what I want, for maximum instant gain, at minimum personal inconvenience? (*powercommunicating.com*).

Since empathy, moral principles and the capacity to love don't play a role in any psychopath's decision-making process, the transition from sub-criminal to criminal psychopath can be fluid and unpredictable. Just about any psychopath could easily engage in violent behavior. My main point here is the following: learning about psychopathy is not a matter of technical psychology research or of abstract theories that are largely irrelevant to the general public. This information is highly pertinent to all of us. It's far more useful than learning all the technical details about how your car works, to return to the analogy I offered earlier. You will never need to rebuild your car from scratch. At most, you may need to learn how to change a spare tire. But it's likely that you'll need to defend yourself, at least emotionally and psychologically, from a psychopath who touches your life and aims to undermine your wellbeing. A basic knowledge of psychopathy can save you years of heartache at the hands of a spouse or lover whom you can never please, who never stops lying and cheating on you and who keeps you dangling on the hook. It can spare you a lifetime of struggles to save an incorrigibly bad child from his or her own misdeeds. It can help you avoid being scammed by con artists who are great at their game. It can give you the strength to move on from a job where your boss keeps everyone in terror by constantly oscillating between sugar-sweetness and abuse.

Obviously, such knowledge can't protect you from all harm caused by evil individuals. Even if you're informed about psychopathy, you may still have the misfortune of becoming the victim of a random crime or of being part of a society ruled by a psychopathic dictator. But at least a basic knowledge of psychopathy can help those of us who are fortunate enough to live in free societies determine that which lies largely within our control: whom we choose to associate with and whom we choose to avoid or leave. It can help us recognize the symptoms of this dangerous personality disorder so that we don't invite a bad person into our lives with open arms. It can give us the strength to end a toxic relationship with an emotional predator for good, once his disorder becomes obvious to us. In other words, knowledge about psychopathy constitutes the best defense that the general public, not just those who have been personally harmed, can have against evil human beings: to avoid them whenever possible and to escape them whenever we become ensnared into their webs. Needless to say, even those of us who become well informed about psychopathy won't be qualified to clinically diagnose them, unless we acquire professional training in this domain. But we can become capable of recognizing them well enough in real life to want to get away from them. For all practical purposes, that's what matters most.

The psychopathic bond resembles any other kind of powerful addiction. Nobody and nothing can save an addict unless she's willing to save herself. Others can only offer her emotional support, information and help. That's what I do here. Most books on romantic relationships tell readers what steps to take to get them or improve them. By way of contrast, I tell you bluntly and in detail why and how to disengage for good. If there's one kind of relationship that's not worth saving, it's one with a psychopath. You can't change a psychopath. Consequently, you also can't improve your relationship with him. Psychologists call psychopathy "pathological." They state that psychopaths suffer from a severe "personality disorder," not just normal human flaws that can be worked on and ameliorated. Sandra L. Brown, M.A. underscores in *How to Spot a Dangerous Man Before You Get Involved* that "Pathology is forever" (23). It's the result of a faulty brain wiring, sometimes coupled with emotional trauma that occurs during childhood development, which can't be altered in any significant way once the psychopath reaches adulthood. Brown doesn't mince words when she describes a psychopath as "an emotional predator" who represents "the pinnacle of poisonous and pathological dating choices" (179). When involved with such an individual, she cautions, "You will never change his physiology or his bad wiring. You will never love him into safety, sanity, or sanctity" (21).

Women involved with psychopaths have been conditioned by their partners to assume most of the blame for the problems that occur in the relationship. They're often deeply in love. They hope that the psychopath will magically improve and grow to love them more meaningfully. Often, they seek therapy, counseling or support groups. They grasp at any straw that can help them salvage the pathological relationship. As time goes on, they focus on the increasingly fewer positive aspects of the relationship. They cherish the memories of how well they were treated in the beginning. They go into denial so that they don't have to face the deliberate malice of the person they love, to whom they may have devoted their entire lives. When faced with the vast discrepancy between the psychopath's nice words and his malicious actions, they feel lost, disoriented and alone. They stubbornly cling to the psychopath and to the fantasy of romantic love he initially created.

After spending months or even years with a psychopathic partner, after building a family or dreaming of a bright future together, it's very hard to accept the fact that everything good about the relationship was an illusion. It's difficult to see that every one of his qualities, words and gestures were manipulative and fake, intended, as is everything a psychopath does, to get you under his spell and undermine your dignity and strength. It's painful to realize that the psychopathic partner has never cared about you, no matter how vehemently or how often he may have professed his devotion. It's infuriating to realize that you've been duped and used for his selfish and destructive purposes. It's frustrating to see that most other people, who aren't well informed about psychopathy, won't understand the degree of deception, brainwashing and betrayal you've gone through.

To give you an idea about how difficult it is for this highly abnormal experience to translate into a normal frame of reference, I'll offer an example. When I watch episodes of the *History Channel* on Adolf Hitler, he looks to me, as he probably does to many other viewers who didn't experience the mass indoctrination at the time, like a ridiculous looking madman, screaming and flailing his arms about. Quite honestly, I can't see anything appealing, much less mesmerizing, about this man. In watching Hitler's dramatic gestures and listening to his unappealing shouts, I find it hard to believe that he exercised such a powerful and destructive mind-control over an entire nation. But, clearly, he did: and not just over one nation, but over several. Those who have not fallen under a psychopath's spell are not likely to identify with the experience or to comprehend it viscerally. They will remain sufficiently objective to find attachment to a psychopath puzzling, perhaps even incomprehensible. But such unhealthy attachments aren't rational, to be examined from a distance, with hindsight and full information in one's hands. Psychopathic bonds are largely emotional in nature. They're also based upon a steady flow of misinformation and powerful mind control.

Consequently, if you've experienced the psychopathic bond, not many people will understand what you've been through and what kind of disordered human being you've had to deal with. It may be upsetting to witness that even (most of) the media coverage of criminal psychopaths doesn't grasp the nature of their personality disorder. Journalists often mistakenly attribute their crimes to more easily comprehensible and common motives (such as greed, sex, financial or emotional crises or substance abuse) rather than the psychological profile that makes these social predators so dangerous to others. It may be saddening to see that in therapy, if you fall upon someone unfamiliar with this personality disorder, you and your psychopathic partner are assumed to be equally at fault for the turmoil in your lives. Worst of all, it will be painful to face the truth that no amount of love or patience or therapy or medication can save a psychopath or your relationship with him. He will always remain what he is: an irredeemably selfish, shallow and heartless human being. If you've been involved with a psychopath, this truth will hurt. But ultimately, as one of the contributors to *lovefraud.com* wisely stated, it will also help heal your pain and set you free.

People tend to say that, as far as problems in romantic relationships are concerned, there are two sides to every story. This assumption doesn't apply at all to relationships with psychopaths. In those, one person deliberately damages the other. What remains true, however, is the related popular adage that it takes two to tango. A relationship with a psychopath represents a macabre dance that hurts only one partner, but that takes two partners to participate in and continue. If you've been involved with someone who exhibits psychopathic traits, you have the power to take back your life. You can choose to disengage from that disordered individual, learn from your mistakes and make far better choices in the future.

My hope in writing *Dangerous Liaisons: How to Recognize and Save Yourself from Psychopathic Seduction* is that facing the truth about psychopathy can help those who have been fortunate enough not to have had intimate contact with a psychopath recognize and stay away from anyone who exhibits the symptoms of antisocial personality disorder, to avoid future harm. Above all, this book aims to help those who have had the misfortune to be personally entangled with a psychopath find the inner strength and seek the external information and support to promptly end the relationship and move on, stronger and wiser, with the rest of their lives.

PART I. WHAT IS A PSYCHOPATH?

Chapter 1

Charismatic Psychopaths:
Mark Hacking and Neil Entwistle

The most dangerous social predators are, unfortunately, also the most common and the best camouflaged. *Charismatic psychopaths* rely upon their natural trademarks—glibness, magnetism and charm—to lure others into their lives. Romantic relationships with such individuals tend to have one thing in common: they initially appear to be absolutely perfect, the very picture of happiness and the envy of all your friends. Charismatic psychopaths give their partners flowers and say all the right things to win their trust and love. They often engage in ostentatious public displays of affection that leave other women drooling, wishing they too could have such romantic partners. But we must remember the age-old adage: what seems too good to be true usually is. If social predators weren't especially alluring and didn't behave exceptionally well at first, they wouldn't trap so many victims into their dangerous nets. They also wouldn't be able hold on to the partners they inevitably come to mistreat. Few women are so masochistic as to be enticed into a romantic relationship by overt and immediate signs of abuse. Yet many remain trapped in abusive relationships with psychopaths because of the lure of the initial honeymoon period and the vain hope that they can somehow recapture it. In her international study of 75 women who got romantically involved with psychopaths, entitled, appropriately enough, *Women Who Love Psychopaths*, Sandra L. Brown, M.A. observes:

> The early days of being wooed and lured by a psychopath are the most exciting times that women remember. The psychopath uses his personality as a drawing card and has been consistently described as: charming and engaging conversationalist, agreeable, seemingly insightful, sweet, twinkling eyes, a compelling talker, funny, a great storyteller, fun to be with, delightful, exciting, compan-

ionable, loyal and protective, enthusiastic and upbeat, sensitive. From this list of traits, it's easy to see why women are enamored with his personality. From this list of A+ qualities what's not to like? (188-9).

As it turns out, what's not to like is absolutely *everything* about this dangerous and sometimes deadly charmer. His image of perfection is only a mask, set up to ensnare his target into a vision of her dream come true, which eventually turns into a nightmare. This is precisely what happened to Lori Kay Soares and Rachel Entwistle, two young women who believed that they had married their dream lovers. In actuality, however, they fell into the clutches of psychopathic partners who killed them for the flimsiest of reasons. The most common question people ask when they hear or read about such cruel and senseless crimes is: why did he or she do it? Once again, psychopaths don't have rational or comprehensible motives. They don't steal primarily for money, which they could get through honest means. They don't rape primarily for sex, which they could get voluntarily. They don't kill their spouses primarily for freedom, which they could get through a legitimate divorce. They have malicious motivations. They harm others primarily for pleasure and fun: for the sport of it. Hurting others, sometimes even killing them, gives psychopaths the greatest rush of euphoria and power. This constitutes their only real purpose in life. Fooling their families, their partners, their colleagues, their buddies, the media and even the police into thinking that they're decent, caring human beings—or, when caught, that they feel genuine remorse or have been victimized themselves—offers the extra bonus. It's the icing on the cake, so to speak. It also enables psychopaths to sometimes get away with their evil deeds. In describing these infamous true crimes, which many readers may have already followed on the news, I will also introduce Hervey Cleckley's exposition of psychopathic traits, by revisiting his groundbreaking work, *The Mask of Sanity*.

Mark and Lori Hacking

Mark Douglas Hacking and Lori Kay Soares appeared to be the perfect couple. They were both in their late twenties and had been together for ten years. Their seemingly idyllic relationship was the envy of Lori's friends. From the moment they met on a trip in Lake Powell, Utah in 1994, Mark and Lori become practically inseparable. Mark seemed crazy about his wife. He was an outgoing, fun-loving young man who appeared to have a promising future ahead of him. The couple planned to move to Chapel Hill, where Mark was supposed to attend medical school. Lori was expecting their first child. According to family and friends, the couple was looking forward to the birth of their baby and to their promising life together in North Carolina. But tragedy struck on July 19, 2004, when Lori went out for a walk and didn't return. That morning, Mark called Lori's work to inquire about her whereabouts. Her colleague, Brandon Hodge, told him that she didn't come to work yet. This struck him as somewhat unusual, since Lori was punctual. Mark responded that his wife went jogging earlier that morning. He claimed it was the last time he saw her. Although Lori had been missing for only a few hours, Mark sounded very concerned. He told Hodge that he went jogging for three miles on the trail his wife took, but couldn't find her. About half an hour later, Mark called the police to report his wife as missing. They informed him that a person must be gone for at least 24 hours for them to start an official search.

Lori's family, friends and colleagues, however, were sufficiently alarmed to assist Mark in the search for his wife that very day. On the following day, Lori's parents held a press conference. They asked for the public's help in finding their missing daughter. Since Lori was extremely well liked in the community, 1,200 people volunteered to look for her. Mark claimed that he felt too distraught to join them. Police found him wandering around a local motel wearing nothing but a pair of sandals. He was admitted to the University of Utah psychiatric unit to recover from his apparent anxiety attack. The police, however, expressed skepticism. They wondered if Mark had faked his nervous breakdown to avoid a more thorough interrogation. Their initial inquiries led them to believe that he might have been involved in his wife's disappearance. Upon questioning Lori's family, colleagues and friends, they discovered that, in fact, the marriage wasn't going well lately. The couple had fought earlier that week after Lori found out that Mark had deceived her about whom he was and what he was planning to do in life.

Dr. Douglas Hacking, Mark's father, told the police that his son had lied to his wife about graduating with honors in psychology from the University of Utah. He had also deceived her about being accepted to the University of North Carolina Medical School. Lori discovered the lies by accident, when she called the medical school from work to ask about financial aid for her husband. Some of her colleagues stated that she was visibly upset during that conversation. She left work early that day, probably to confront Mark, they speculated. For a few days, however, the relations between the couple improved. As it turns out, Mark succeeded in persuading his wife of yet another lie. He told her that the reason he wasn't in the University of North Carolina's records was because of a computer malfunction. Apparently, however, Lori didn't buy that excuse for long. She proceeded to verify his claim. Afterwards, the situation went from bad to worse. A few days later, the couple had another altercation.

The extent of the deception led investigators to suspect that if Mark lied so easily and for so long to his wife and others about his education and life plans, he could just as easily be lying to them about his lack of involvement in Lori's disappearance. In addition, the evidence they found at the Hackings' residence led them to conclude that they were dealing with a homicide, not a missing person case. From that point on, they considered Mark to be "a person of interest." Inside the Hackings' apartment, they collected a receipt for a new mattress and bedding, a bloody knife found in the drawer of the couple's bedroom, clothing and a letter supposedly written by Lori warning her husband that she'd leave him "if things didn't change." Outside, they gathered a cut up mattress that matched the box spring found in the trash bin of University of Utah hospital, where Mark worked. They also removed a clump of dark hair matching Lori's from a dumpster outside a gas station near the hospital. In addition, the surveillance tapes taken from various locations—the hospital, a Mormon church near the park where Lori supposedly went on a walk and a convenience store—told a different story from the one Mark shared with the police.

The tapes revealed that on the morning when Mark told police he was searching for his wife in the park, he was actually buying a new mattress at a local store. In addition, the seat of Lori's car was adjusted for a tall person rather than for her petite frame. Mark was six feet tall, while Lori was only 5'4". More significantly, Mark's two brothers told investigators that he had confessed to murdering his wife. Mark told them that on the evening of July 18th, Lori confronted him about his newest lie, concerning the supposed computer malfunction. He finally admitted to her that he had deceived her for years about his education. This revelation resulted in a heated argument. Lori then went to bed and Mark began packing his belongings. During this process, he came across a .22-caliber rifle. Around 1:00 a.m., he shot his sleeping wife in the head. He then wrapped up her body in garbage bags and disposed of it in a local dumpster about an hour later. He also cut up the mattress (with the knife that the police removed from his bedroom drawer) and discarded it in the dumpster near the hospital, where it was later found.

Because the investigators couldn't find Lori's body for a few months, the prosecution team charged Mark with first-degree murder without seeking the death penalty. Two months later, on October 1, 2004, they found Lori's remains in the Salt Lake County Landfill. Her husband pleaded "not guilty" at the arraignment hearing. During the April trial, however, Mark confessed that he had murdered his wife. As he described how he killed Lori and disposed of her body, he showed no signs of emotion. Lori's family expressed not only grief, but also a sense of perplexity. They couldn't understand what might have led this seemingly adoring husband to kill the woman who was, by all accounts, the love of his life. They were also puzzled by the fact he disposed of her body in such an irreverent fashion, literally as one does of a pile of garbage.

Neil and Rachel Entwistle

The case of Neil and Rachel Entwistle resembles that of Scott and Laci Peterson, which has received enormous media attention and is the subject of several biographies and true crime books. According to his friends and family, Neil was a charming, handsome, polished and courteous British man. He fell in love with Rachel, a sunny, petite American woman. They met in the north of England on the Ouse River. Both attended the University of York and participated in the rowing team. Rachel was a coxswain, while Neil rowed. Their friends state that they took an instant liking to each other. Neil, they claimed, "adored" Rachel.

Their romantic relationship moved fast and got serious from the very start. The couple envisioned a bright future together. Rachel took a job as a teacher while Neil, described by some of his friends as a "computer wizard," took a programming job. Their wedding was so lavish and beautiful that it seemed right out of a fairy tale. They honeymooned in the Mediterranean. Pretty soon, Rachel gave birth to a little girl, Lillian Rose. Both Neil and Rachel appeared ecstatic about the birth of their baby. Neil set up a website, *rachelandneil.org*, to showcase their wedding pictures and their adorable newborn. Rachel described her husband to her friends as "her knight in shinning armor." She told her family that she was "blissfully happy" in her marriage. The young woman considered Neil to be her dream come true: handsome, charming, intelligent, humorous, a gentleman, a doting husband, a loving father and a stable provider. Shortly thereafter, the couple decided to move back to Boston, to be near Rachel's family. They bought an expensive 4-bedroom house in the suburbs and rented a BMW. On January 19, 2006, only a few days after they moved into their new house, Rachel talked on the phone with her good friend, Joanna Gately. They planned a visit that weekend, since Joanna wanted to see their new house and the baby. Rachel went to sleep that evening and never woke up. Neither did her nine-month-old daughter. Both had been murdered.

During the course of the investigation, what turned out to be most astonishing for Rachel's family was that the evidence pointed to the fact that the person responsible for killing them was none other than the doting husband and father who appeared to love them most. Moreover, the image of Neil Entwistle during the trial and his behavior after the murders sharply contradicted the impression of him that his family and friends used to have. Rather than being a faithful, adoring husband, the evidence revealed that he joined an Internet sex swinger site in England during the time that Rachel was in Boston with their newborn baby. As soon as he joined them in the United States, Neil advertised himself on *Adult Friend Finder*. He presented himself as a man looking for "American women of all ages," to see if they were "much better in bed than the women over the ocean." On January 4, 2006, he wrote to a woman saying that he was "currently in a relationship" but would like "a bit more fun in the bedroom."

His professional life also turned out to be largely a sham. Rather than being a successful computer programmer, as his wife and the rest of his family were led to believe, he was one of those annoying spammers who promise magical results in the bedroom and in the wallet. Unfortunately, his occupation didn't bring him such results. Neil was broke and in debt. In addition, the evidence found on his computer pointed quite clearly to premeditated murder. Weeks before his wife and daughter were shot, Neil looked up on the Internet methods of killing, including euthanasia, murder and suicide. Researching suicide doesn't imply he wanted to kill himself, as some speculated. Individuals who intend to murder others commonly look into how a homicide could be framed as a suicide, as Neil's trial later confirmed.

Nothing about Neil Entwistle's true identity fit with the outward impression he created for his family and friends. Immediately after murdering his family, Neil behaved even less like the loving husband and father he claimed to be. He bought a one-way ticket to England, to avoid police interrogation. He didn't return to the United States to attend his wife and daughter's funerals. During his murder trial, the prosecution presented evidence that Entwistle used a .22 caliber revolver to shoot his wife in the head and his daughter in the stomach, at close range. Perhaps to showcase his "sensitivity," he told police that he covered their bodies with bedding because he was "closing them off."

At the trial, Neil pleaded "not guilty." His defense team argued that Rachel killed the baby and then committed suicide. The only people who bought this implausible defense—even after Neil was found guilty and convicted of first-degree murder—were his parents. In spite of the overwhelming evidence that pointed to Neil's guilt, his mother cast him as the real victim and his murdered wife as the victimizer. She stated, "We know that our son Neil is innocent and we are devastated to learn that the evidence points to Rachel murdering our grandchild and then committing suicide." By way of contrast, after hearing and seeing the evidence against him, Lori's family had no doubts that their son-in-law had committed the crimes. But they, along with the prosecution and the press, couldn't understand what drove Neil to kill his own family. Joseph Flaherty, the spokesman for Priscilla Materazzo, Rachel's mother, and for her stepfather, Joseph, released the following statement on their behalf: "We may never know why this happened, but we do know Rachel and Lillian Rose loved and trusted Neil Entwistle."

Neil's mother denied her son's actions, while the media, which seemed convinced by the guilty verdict, mischaracterized his motives. Katherine Ramsland, from trutv.com and *thecrimelibrary.com*, describes accurately all the facts of the case. However, she characterizes Entwistle's pathological lying about pretty much every significant aspect of his life as symptoms of so-called "white lies," which got so far out of hand that he, himself, began to believe them. Psychopaths don't tell "white lies." They tell harmful lies to disguise their malicious actions and evil identities from others. The only journalist I've read who got the psychological profile of Neil Entwistle right on target was Harrison Koehli, who described him as a psychopath. Koehli expressed frustration that even the media, which routinely covers such crimes, doesn't grasp the phenomenon of psychopathy, given that psychopaths commit such a high proportion of these sensational murders. Koehli identifies several media misreadings of Neil Entwistle's behavior. He notes:

> The *Boston Globe* tells us that Entwistle 'breaks down' while watching video of his dead wife and daughter. In fact, the description deserves to be quoted in full: 'Neil Entwistle's face turned scarlet red and he covered his mouth with his hand, looking down to avert his eyes from the video played today in court that showed the bodies of his wife and infant daughter, found shot to death in bed

and frozen in an embrace. Entwistle trembled and for the first time since his 2006 arrest began to cry publicly, tears running down the cheeks of his quivering jaw. As the 20-minute video played for the Middlesex Superior Court jury, he turned his eyes back at the screen and watched, his hand covering his gaping mouth.'

Having watched this video, I agree with Koehli's interpretation of Neil Entwistle's reaction rather than that of the *Boston Globe* journalists, Franci R. Ellement and Andrew Ryan. I see no signs whatsoever of trauma or pain in Entwistle's expression. Sadistic buffoonery is more like it. I also see Entwistle trying to disguise the fact that he was laughing into his hand, as the evidence of his gruesome murder of his wife and child was presented before the jury. Apparently, he treated the trial as a joke and even as a personal triumph. As Koehli goes on to say:

> I have to say, to watch that video and to come away convinced that the scene 'appeared to have a profound impact' on Entwistle smacks of supreme credulity. A more honest description would appear as follows: 'Entwistle appeared to enjoy himself, using his hand to hide a large grin and occasional laughter. Every so often he appeared to attempt an unconvincing expression of emotion, forcing his eyes into a crude facsimile of sadness. His obvious smile and alert eye movements, however, betrayed his undisturbed composure and lack of guilt or despair.

While other media accounts automatically translate Entwistle's expression and gestures into more or less normal human responses, Koehli sees them for what they are: The decidedly *abnormal* and *inhuman* reactions of a psychopath. Koehli observes that "Entwistle cannot control the fact that his face appears to be smiling, but he can attempt to hide it by covering his face and attempting to fake crying, which is what he is obviously doing. He is smiling, but it is *not* because that is just how he looks when he cries. It is because he is thoroughly enjoying himself. He is sadistic and he is a psychopath." This description fits. Not only does Entwistle show no remorse about murdering his family, but also he obviously takes sadistic pleasure in the presentation of his crimes. If he tries to disguise his reaction, it's in a rather unsuccessful attempt to cover up his abnormality, which the prosecution is in the process of publicly unmasking. Deprived of his mask of sanity, a psychopath lacks the means by which he can fool and use others.

Koehli comments that even those who have written at length about psychopaths, such as Keith Ablow, a forensic psychiatrist and the author of *Inside the Mind of Scott Peterson*, mischaracterize Entwistle's reaction. Ablow states: "Men like Entwistle . . . feel like stripping their masks away is tantamount to killing them, because they believe those thin, synthetic disguises are all that keep them from dissolving into nothingness and feeling the full weight of unspeakable emotional turmoil, with roots that always reach deep into their pasts." This sounds existential and even poetic, but psychopaths lack the emotional depth to experience such angst. Their flashes of anger are as shallow and fleeting as their infatuations. I agree with Koehli, once again, when he advises the media and the general public to reread Hervey Cleckley's *The Mask of Sanity* in order to gain more insight into how the minds of psychopaths work:

> Sorry Keith, but you need to reread Cleckley. There's no fear of unspeakable emotional turmoil lying behind that mask of sanity. Psychopaths do not even know the meaning of those words. They hang on to their masks with such conviction because they are predators, and without them, they cannot survive... To let down that facade would reveal that they are little more than unfeeling intraspecies predators that feed off the pain and suffering of others and thus destroy their chances of feeding. Even a psychopath is aware of the consequences of such a revelation. His 'dreams' of a boot forever stomping on the face of humanity are crushed.

Without understanding the phenomenon of psychopathy, we're much more likely to fall into the traps set by these social predators. We're also more likely to give them second chances in life when they mistreat us or commit crimes, believing that they're capable of reform. They're not. All the evidence points to the fact that psychopaths don't learn from negative experiences. They're therefore not intimidated by punishment. When freed, they go out to commit the same kind of crimes again. Spreading information about this personality disorder constitutes the public's main line of defense against evil individuals. However, when even the police, that routinely runs across such criminals and the journalists that present their crimes in the news fail to understand psychopaths, what hope is there left that the general public will get the necessary tools to protect itself from them? Koehli advises all of us to inform ourselves—and others—about these perfect invisible predators in our midst. His appeal for spreading information about psychopathy is so well justified and eloquent that I'm citing it in full:

> When I read comments like Ablow's and the youtube commentator's, comments so steeped in ignorance and projection, I get in a bit of a funk. After all, if only people would first accept the existence of psychopathy, we would not be so likely to fall for their cheap 'emotional' manipulations. You see, psychopaths are wired differently than normal humans. They do not feel close to others, they do not feel remorse, they do not feel others' pain, they are completely egocentric, and they derive a pathological 'joy' from others' suffering. Neil Entwistle's sick display of joy at the sight of his dead wife and daughter, and his transparent attempt to feign sadness should be apparent to every normal, rational human being. Unfortunately it is not, and we all suffer as a result, and we will continue to suffer, and millions more will die, until we decide to grow up and accept the most pressing truth about our reality. What is that truth? That not only do psychopaths live among us, but also through our ignorance we have allowed them to rise to positions of almost absolute power over us. Widespread knowledge of the reality of psychopathy on this planet is the essential first step

to securing our future and that of our children. Make it your priority to spread the word.

That's exactly what I do in this book. In the next few chapters, I'll explain Hacking and Entwistle's seemingly puzzling behavior in light of the insights psychologists have gained about psychopathy. I'll focus in particular on *The Mask of Sanity* by Hervey Cleckley, the main twentieth-century expert on the subject and the one Koehli wisely advises us to reread. More specifically, I interweave a close analysis of Cleckley's text with a discussion of the criminal cases I've described above as well as, where relevant, with my own personal observations of psychopathic behavior.

Chapter 2

What is a Psychopath?
Close Readings of Hervey Cleckley's *The Mask of Sanity*

Unlike Alfred Hitchcock's Psycho, psychopaths don't usually come across as socially awkward, reclusive and bizarre. On the contrary, they often seem charming, outgoing and normal. That's a big part of their lure, or "mask of sanity." The main experts on psychopathy, Hervey Cleckley, Robert Hare and Martha Stout provide, essentially, the same list of personality traits to describe psychopaths. They state that such individuals exhibit superficial charm and intelligence. They use these qualities to attract people and to manipulate them. Contrary to other kinds of pathological individuals, psychopaths don't experience delusions or manifest any "other signs of irrational thinking." For that reason, they appear to be, and actually are, "sane." When they commit crimes, psychopaths know exactly what they're doing. They realize that it's wrong and know why society considers it wrong. They just happen to make exceptions for themselves and for their outrageous behavior, which, in their estimation, lies above the rules that govern the rest of humanity. Similarly, psychopaths lack nervousness or any "psychoneurotic manifestations." Not only are they unlike Woody Allen's comical antiheroes, but also they stay cool and collected even when a normal response would be to experience distress. Although they sometimes engage in histrionic displays of emotion to gain sympathy, psychopaths remain unflappable during a crisis, such as a break-up or divorce from their significant other (because no other is significant to them), a death in the family, when they're caught for committing a crime or even when they're being punished for their illegal activities. A psychopath's motto in life is: "Bad men do what good men dream." Psychopaths can't grasp the idea of conscience and feelings for others except as a form of weakness. They don't understand that their dreams are normal people's nightmares.

Although such individuals are very impulsive and can fly off the handle with little or no provocation, nothing rattles them for long. Analogously, although they can fulfill their obligations for a short period of time to win their targets' trust, they're unreliable in the long run. No matter what promises they make and how important their commitment to fulfill them may be to others, they'll eventually let people down. In fact, they go out of their way to hurt and betray those who trust them. Psychopaths pursue short-term goals. They say whatever they need to say in order to get what they want at the moment. Their minds function like a GPS system where they're constantly punching in a new destination. Whatever direction they take changes upon a whim, as soon as they spot anything or anyone they momentarily perceive as a better or more exciting opportunity. That's not only because psychopaths are shallow, but also because they're envious, greedy and power-hungry. They want whatever other people have that they find desirable. That may be a new partner, a good job, prestige, wealth or a family. They want successful relationships without offering love, honesty or fidelity. To bolster their sense of superiority—without having much to show in terms of personal qualities or accomplishments—they put their partners (and others) down and cultivate their weaknesses. To succeed in their jobs, without doing much work, they charm, intimidate, manipulate and bully their coworkers and staff. To acquire wealth, they commit fraud or engage in scams. But, generally speaking, psychopaths can't hold on to anything and anyone because their interests and needs change constantly. Sooner or later, they become dissatisfied with everything they have in life and want something more or simply something different.

Psychopaths are unpredictable even in their unpredictability. You can't tell in advance when they're going to sabotage your life and happiness, or even their own, for that matter. Psychopaths can be very believable pathological liars. Most people may lie sometimes. Psychopaths, however, tell harmful lies for the sport of it and with malice. To them, lying functions as a means of controlling others by manipulating their perception of reality. It also provides them with free entertainment. Because of their shallow emotions, psychopaths get easily bored. Their psychological hollowness propels them into a perpetual quest for new people to use, new sexual encounters, the newest business ventures as well as new and exciting ways to transgress social rules.

Psychopaths manifest poor judgment and fail to learn from experience. Epicurus defined pleasure as the absence of pain. By that standard, psychopaths aren't Epicurean. They seek positive pleasures: highs, thrills and the sensation of constant euphoria. But they aren't particularly bothered by pain or by negative consequences in general. They sabotage their own futures and harm others in momentary flashes of anger or for the sake of short-lived fun. A lot of their problems stem from their fundamental narcissism, or what Cleckley calls their "pathological egocentricity and incapacity for love." To psychopaths, people are objects whose needs and even lives don't matter except in so far as they can use them. After using people, they toss them away.

Psychopaths can't feel anything, not even joy or happiness, very deeply. They exhibit, Cleckley indicates, a "general poverty in all major affective reactions." Hare states that psychopaths experience "proto-emotions" rather than the full range of human feelings. They feel momentary pleasure, glee or delight when they do or get what they want. By way of contrast, they feel fleeting frustration or anger when their desires are thwarted. But they can't experience the deeper emotions, such as other-regarding love, empathy, remorse, sadness, regret or even anxiety and depression. Their main emotion is contempt for other human beings, which they often mask underneath a thin layer of sociability and charm. Upon meeting new people, psychopaths perform an intuitive cost-benefit analysis. They classify them as targets, accomplices or obstacles in the pursuit of whatever they want at the moment. Targets are used as accomplices, then discarded as obstacles once their usefulness has expired. Since psychopaths eventually alienate all those around them with their unscrupulous and callous behavior, the only people who continue to find their mask of sanity plausible over time are those who don't know them very well, those who suffer from a similar personality disorder, or those who have an unhealthy emotional investment in them. People who refuse to face the truth about the psychopath in their lives often become his alibis, sticking by him despite all rational evidence of his personality disorder and his wrongdoings.

Due to their shallowness, psychopaths suffer from what psychologists call "specific loss of insight." Not only are they incapable of understanding how others function on a deeper emotional level, but also they lack an understanding of their own motivations and behavior. They intuitively know *how* to deceive, hurt and manipulate others. But they can't grasp *why* they feel compelled to do it. Because they don't see anything wrong with themselves and their actions, they also fail miserably in therapy. Improving one's behavior requires having the insight to see your flaws and the desire to change for the better: especially for the sake of those you care about. Psychopaths lack such incentives. They live only for their own pleasure. To entertain themselves, they engage in what Cleckley calls "fantastic and uninviting behavior." This is made worse by various compulsions and addictions—to sex, drugs and/or alcohol—that are quite common for them, largely because of their low impulse control and need for constant excitement. Psychopaths thrive on depravity and transgression. After behaving more or less normally for a period of time, they can all of a sudden become boisterous and unruly, pull their pants down in public, hit their spouse or start a brawl without provocation. Cleckley also notes that for psychopaths, "suicide is rarely carried out." Just as they're incapable of experiencing a deeper form of happiness which for most people results from leading an orderly life and loving one's family and friends, they're also incapable of experiencing a deeper form of unhappiness, which drives some individuals to suicide.

Cleckley and Hare both observe that for psychopaths "sex life is impersonal, trivial, and poorly integrated." Psychopaths can, however, sometimes experience intense attachments without emotional bonding. Some of them have such obsessive infatuations that they may even stalk their targets for an extended period of time. This behavior, however, is not tied to any genuine feelings of love. Rather, it stems from a sense of entitlement and ownership. Psychopaths believe that it's their right to possess the women they momentarily desire and to discard them as soon as they no longer want them. Generally speaking, for psychopaths sexual relationships function as a release and as a form of exerting control over others.

They're not a means of connecting, which, over time, implies shared emotional ties and mutual moral obligations.

Finally, psychopaths are noted for their "failure to follow any life plan." A few psychopaths may be very ambitious. Yet fewer become powerful or famous. However, most lack the patience to pursue far-reaching goals that require dedication and hard work. Instead, they move from one temporary—and usually destructive—diversion to another, in search of something to alleviate their pervasive sense of boredom.

Having briefly reviewed the main symptoms of psychopathy, I'll go on to explain each of them in turn. I'll rely upon Cleckley's work and offer as illustration the behavior of Mark Hacking and Neil Entwistle. Like Koehli, I believe that it's crucial to look at psychopathy in greater detail by rereading closely Hervey Cleckley's *The Mask of Sanity*. To some of the symptoms he discusses, which require further elaboration, I'll devote a separate chapter. If I go into such detail, even at the risk of some repetition, it's because a brief overview isn't going to offer the deeper understanding of this personality disorder, which, I believe, the public needs to solve the apparent mystery of psychopathy and to protect itself better from the danger it poses.

Superficial Charm and Good "Intelligence"

Cleckley observes, "More often than not, the typical psychopath will seem particularly agreeable and make a distinctly positive impression when he is first encountered. Alert and friendly in his attitude, he is easy to talk with and seems to have a good many genuine interests. There is nothing at all odd or queer about him, and in every respect he tends to embody the concept of a well-adjusted, happy person. Nor does he, on the other hand, seem to be artificially exerting himself like one who is covering up or who wants to sell you a bill of goods. He would seldom be confused with the professional backslapper or someone who is trying to ingratiate himself for a concealed purpose. Signs of affectation or excessive affability are not characteristic. He looks like the real thing" (*The Mask of Sanity*, 339). Because they appear to be easy-going, friendly and genuine, psychopaths attract numerous partners. They tend to be great conversationalists, orienting the subjects of discussion around each of their targets' personal interests. Scott Peterson, Mark Hacking and Neil Entwistle seemed true gentlemen and fun-loving guys not only to their wives, but also to their in-laws and friends. Generally speaking, they behaved appropriately for the circumstances before committing their gruesome crimes. They knew how to open the car door for their partners, how to engage in polite conversation with their in-laws and how to joke around with their buddies.

Not only do psychopaths tend to be extraordinarily charismatic, but also they can appear to be rational, levelheaded individuals. They usually talk in a way that shows common sense and good judgment. "Very often indications of good sense and sound reasoning will emerge and one is likely to feel soon after meeting him that this normal and pleasant person is also one with high abilities," Cleckley continues (338). Psychopaths generally present themselves as responsible men. They seem to be in charge of their lives, their families and their careers. As we've seen, for several years Mark Hacking led his wife and her family to believe that he was a college graduate on his way to medical school. Only members of his own family knew (and hid) the truth. Similarly, Neil Entwistle convinced his entire family that he was a successful computer entrepreneur. In actuality, he was a bankrupt spammer. He also led Rachel to believe that he was a faithful, loving husband while actively seeking promiscuous liaisons on adult dating websites.

Although most psychopaths fail at their endeavors, it's usually not due to lack of natural intelligence. Cleckley notes, "Psychometric tests also very frequently show him of superior intelligence. More than the average person, he is likely to seem free from social or emotional impediments, from the minor distortions, peculiarities, and awkwardness so common even among the successful" (338). Psychopaths succeed in fooling others not just because of *what* they say, but also because of *how* they say it. Their demeanor tends to be self-assured, cool, smooth and collected. Even though, at core, they're more disturbed than individuals diagnosed with severe mental illnesses—such as psychotics or schizophrenics—their personality disorder doesn't show through. The fact that psychopathy tends to be well concealed beneath a veneer of normalcy makes it all the more dangerous to others: "Although the psychopath's inner emotional deviations and deficiencies may be comparable with the inner status of the masked schizophrenic," Cleckley goes on, "he outwardly shows nothing brittle or strange. Everything about him is likely to suggest desirable and superior human qualities, a robust mental health" (339).

Absence of Delusions and Other Signs of Irrational Thinking

Despite being capable of actions that we'd associate with insanity—such as killing their family members in cold-blood, then going out to party afterwards—psychopaths are in fact clinically sane. But what does it actually mean to be "sane," in light of such severely disturbed behavior? It simply means being in touch with reality and aware of the legal, social and moral rules that govern one's society. Sanity doesn't imply processing this information normally or behaving normally. Cleckley elaborates,

> The psychopath is ordinarily free from signs or symptoms traditionally regarded as evidence of a psychosis. He does not hear voices. Genuine delusions cannot be demonstrated. There is no valid depression, consistent pathologic elevation of mood, or irresistible pressure of activity. Outer perceptual reality is accurately recognized; social values and generally accredited personal standards are accepted verbally. Excellent logical reasoning is maintained and, in theory, the patient can foresee the consequences of injudicious or antisocial acts, outline acceptable or admirable plans of life, and ably criticize in words his former mistakes (339).

The psychopath constructs his mask of sanity by imitating the rest of us. He mimics our emotions. He pays lip service to our moral principles. He pretends to respect us and our goals in life. The only difference between him and normal human beings is that he doesn't actually feel or believe any of this on a deeper level. His simulation of normalcy functions as a disguise that enables him to fool others and satisfy his deviant drives. However, because of the psychopath's extraordinary charm and poise, those perverse needs aren't likely to be obvious to others. For as long as a psychopath can hide his true nature, his real desires as well as the seedier aspects of his behavior, he appears to be the very picture of sanity: an upstanding citizen, a loyal friend, a loving husband and father. "Not only is the psychopath rational and his thinking free of delusions," Cleckley pursues, "but he also appears to react with normal emotions. His ambitions are discussed with what appears to be healthy enthusiasm. His convictions impress even the skeptical observer as firm and binding. He seems to respond with adequate feelings to another's interest in him and, as he discusses his wife, his children, or his parents, he is likely to be judged a man of warm human responses, capable of full devotion and loyalty" (339).

Absence of Nervousness or Psychoneurotic Manifestations

Psychopaths display an almost reptilian tranquility. Their paradoxical combination of calmness and thrill-seeking behavior may render them, at least initially, more intriguing than normal individuals. A psychopath can appear to be the rock of your life, promising a solid foundation for a lasting relationship. Cleckley observes, "It is highly typical for him not only to escape the abnormal anxiety and tension fundamentally characteristic of this whole diagnostic group but also to show a relative immunity from such anxiety and worry as might be judged normal or appropriate in disturbing situations" (340). While their general aura of coolness and calmness can be reassuring, psychopaths tend to be too calm in the wrong circumstances. Upon closer observation, their mask of sanity includes fissures, or attitudes and elements of behavior that don't conform to their normal external image.

For instance, they may laugh when (and even because) others cry. They may remain too serene in traumatic circumstances. Or they may appear theatrical and disingenuous in their displays of emotion, as Neil Entwistle did in court. In those moments when they behave inappropriately, psychopaths reveal their underlying abnormality. This shows through not only before they commit some crime but also afterwards, in their lack of genuine remorse, regret or sadness. Neurotics feel excessive anxiety. By way of contrast, psychopaths feel too little anxiety. When they experience regret or pain, it's for getting caught or for being momentarily inconvenienced, not for having hurt others. When they get frustrated, it's for not getting their way or out of boredom, not because they're troubled by what they did wrong. As Cleckley puts it, "Even under concrete circumstances that would for the ordinary person cause embarrassment, confusion, acute insecurity, or visible agitation, his relative serenity is likely to be noteworthy... What tension or uneasiness of this sort he may show seems provoked entirely by external circumstances, never by feelings of guilt, remorse, or intrapersonal insecurity. Within himself he appears almost as incapable of anxiety as of profound remorse" (340). Empathy, fear of punishment, anxiety and remorse represent the main forces that prevent normal people from engaging in dangerous and harmful behavior. Psychopaths lack such restraints. No matter how good their disguise, dangerous and harmful behavior is all they enjoy and desire to pursue in life.

Unreliability

Obviously, if psychopaths were unreliable from the start, they wouldn't ensnare so many victims. Few women, for instance, would continue to date a man who stood them up on the first five dates. Unfortunately for their targets, however, at the beginning of a relationship psychopaths work very hard to present themselves as trustworthy individuals. All of their energy flows into offering a false front. Mark Hacking acted like a devoted husband, who was, by all accounts, madly in love with his wife. Carolyn Eisen, a mutual friend, describes Neil Entwistle in equally glowing terms. She recounts, "I would see him, like, opening the door for her. And he was very polite. I think he always called when he said he would call her. You know, the things that you're hoping to find when you're meeting a new guy. And he adored her." It's very rare, however, for a psychopath to hide his real nature so well that he doesn't wave any red flags under anybody's nose. Cleckley notes, "Though the psychopath is likely to give an early impression of being a thoroughly reliable person, it will soon be found that on many occasions he shows no sense of responsibility whatsoever. No matter how binding the obligation, how urgent the circumstances, or how important the matter, this holds true" (340). Neil Entwistle's behavior offers a perfect case in point. Neil may have opened the door for Rachel and called her when he said he would, at least in the beginning of their relationship. But when it really counted, once they married and started a family together, he wasn't there for his wife in any meaningful sense. When she moved to the United States, he hooked up with other women in England on adult websites. When they were supposed to establish a happy family life together with their newborn daughter in Boston, he killed them both. Unfortunately, it's very difficult to predict in advance when a psychopath's mask of sanity will crack open: which is to say, when he'll explode in a spectacular display of malice and unreliability that can cost you your happiness and perhaps even your life.

Psychopaths function like ticking time bombs. It's likely that they'll eventually explode to show their true, deviant nature. But it's impossible to predict when, why and how. In fact, even psychopaths' violent displays of anger are largely unmotivated. They're only loosely related (if at all) to objective negative circumstances or to the actions of others. Just as crises or distress that would make a normal person feel depressed or anxious don't rattle a psychopath, neither do periods of prosperity and well-being lead him to feel more stable and fulfilled. A psychopath's outbursts, Cleckley notes, "seem to have little or no relation to objective stress, to cyclic periods, or to major alterations of mood or outlook. What is at stake for the patient, for his family, or for anybody else is not a regularly determining factor. At the crest of success in his work he may forge a small check, indulge in petty thievery, or simply not come to the office. After a period of gracious and apparently happy relations with his family he may pick a quarrel with his wife, cuff her up a bit, drive her from the house, and then throw a glass of iced tea in the face of his 3-year-old son" (342). Cleckley characterizes the psychopath's behavior as "not even a consistency in inconsistency but an inconsistency in inconsistency" (342). You can't predict or react to a psychopath's behavior as you would to that of a normal human being. He'll remain motivated by his underlying desires and seek their gratification when, where, how and with whomever he pleases. And, if you're close to him, you can bet that it will be at your expense.

Chapter 3

Psychopaths and Pathological Lying

Untruthfulness and Insincerity

We've gotten to Cleckley's most significant symptoms of psychopathy: untruthfulness and insincerity. This is so central to the psychopath's character and way of life that it deserves its own chapter, if not its own book. Psychopaths are pathological liars. They not only lie profusely, but also their whole identity is an elaborate ruse. They use both truth and lies to manipulate others. Cleckley observes, "The psychopath shows a remarkable disregard for truth and is to be trusted no more in his accounts of the past than in his promises for the future or his statement of present intentions" (341). We've all told lies in our lives. Some lies, especially those we call "white lies," are relatively innocuous. They enable us to avoid hurting other people's feelings. If we tell a friend that she looks good in a pair of jeans that's a little too tight on her, it won't destroy her life. Other lies, however, deeply damage the lives of others. When we cheat on our spouse, it hurts him or her. It doesn't matter if he or she knows about the affair or not. It doesn't even matter if we lie, and say we were with a friend when in actuality we were with a lover, or if we don't say anything at all. In both cases, we're distorting the truth or withholding crucial information that would hurt our spouse and that deeply affects his or her life decisions. Among harmful lies, Susan Forward, the author of the best-selling book *When Your Lover Is a Liar* distinguishes between lies by "omission" and lies by "commission."

Neil Entwistle lied mostly by omission. He failed to inform Rachel that he was seeking other women for sex. He didn't tell her that he got bored with their marriage and no longer wanted the responsibility of having a wife and child. He also failed to inform her that he lacked the funds to cover their growing expenses. Had he given her this information, she might have left him. Both she and their baby might have escaped alive. By way of contrast, Mark Hacking preferred to lie by commission. He gave Lori false information about what he did and about what he was planning to do in life. He told her that he had a certain kind of education when he didn't. He told her that he was going to medical school when he wasn't. These lies were fundamental not only to the future they were planning together, but also to who Lori thought Mark was. For these psychopaths, the lies furnished convenient fictions. They held up the false image they wanted to project to their families and friends. They camouflaged their real, predatory desires and controlling nature. They hid their underlying self-absorption, their excessive concern with their image and their obsession with the pursuit of perverse pleasures at other people's expense. They bought them love, loyalty and time to have the family they wanted until they no longer wanted it.

Not only do psychopaths believe that they have compelling reasons to lie to others in order to achieve their goals, but also they fail to see why lying is wrong. Cleckley observes that upon questioning, a psychopath "gives the impression that he is incapable of ever attaining realistic comprehension of an attitude in other people which causes them to value truth and cherish truthfulness in themselves" (341). When caught in a lie, if convenient, sometimes a psychopath may pay lip service to honesty. But he doesn't actually believe in it. He certainly doesn't live by it. The problem remains, as before, that it's difficult to determine when a psychopath's lying. He can look you straight in the eyes and give you false information. He can make promises he knows to be unrealistic or untrue. Furthermore, he's so glib and uninhibited that he lies with great eloquence and conviction. As Cleckley observes:

> Typically [the psychopath] is at ease and unpretentious in making a serious promise or in (falsely) exculpating himself from accusations, whether grave or trivial. His simplest statement in such matters carries special powers of conviction. Overemphasis, obvious glibness, and other traditional signs of the clever liar do not usually show in his words or in his manner... Candor and trustworthiness seem implicit in him at such times. During the most solemn perjuries he has no difficulty at all in looking anyone tranquilly in the eyes (341).

How can you tell when a psychopath is lying? I'm tempted to say, only partly in jest, that it's when he's moving his lips. But even that wouldn't cover all the lies by omission. When dealing with a psychopath, or with any person for that matter, you need to judge his actions, not just his words. Very often, a psychopath's insensitive attitude and despicable actions will contradict his nice words. He will say that he loves you but remain unmoved when you suffer and consistently act against your best interests. He will promise to be faithful while frequently cheating on you. Based on my observations, a psychopath lies in large part because he enjoys playing a game with you as his pawn. The match doesn't follow any particular rules since psychopaths don't play fair. Yet, like all games, it includes certain maneuvers. To help others identify psychopathic deception, I'll describe below some of the strategies I've observed. Let me begin by analyzing first why psychopaths lie, since that gets to the heart of their malice and reveals their inherent cruelty.

Why Psychopaths Lie

Psychopaths lie pathologically about pretty much everything: their past, their present and their future. Whatever lies you discover about the psychopath in your life are likely to be just the tip of the iceberg. Be prepared for the sinking of the Titanic. He could be telling you, or his family, that he has one kind of job while having another kind or being unemployed. He could be saying that he's rich while being dirt poor. He could be preaching trust and fidelity to you while pursuing dozens of other women. He could be telling you that his partner is cold, frigid and uninterested in working on their relationship when he's the one who neglects her, plays hot-cold games to manipulate her and does everything possible to violate her trust and undermine her self-confidence. He could be telling you that he's looking for a job in your area, to be together, while leaving his options open and seeking employment all over the country, to separate you from your family and friends. He could be saying that he had no affairs while playing semantic games, since in his mind, all those other women were only friends with benefits. He could be telling you his ex cheated on him or left him, when he's the one who cheated on every woman he's ever been with, not just once, but innumerable times, and broke up with them after having used them. More ominously, he could be presenting himself as a decent person while secretly committing fraud, rape or even murder. What you *don't know* about him, along with the false information he offers you, *can* and *will* hurt you. He's got no friends, just people he uses and alibis for his lies. Lying feeds his underlying narcissism. Distorting other people's perception of reality gives him the false sense of being smarter than them.

Since psychopaths wallow in seediness, cruelty and perversion, they enjoy waving their lies under the noses of the people they dupe. They leave little trophies of their infidelities lying around, like a shampoo bottle or trinkets from their girlfriends. When they're questioned about them by their partner, they get the additional thrill of offering a false explanation. You've no doubt heard of psychopathic killers who take objects from their victims, such as a bracelet, ring or a lock of hair, as "trophies," to remind them of their criminal exploits. Signs of betrayal represent the sex addict's little trophies. Such disordered individuals also enjoy living on the edge. Just as serial killers often play cat and mouse games with the media and the police, so philandering psychopaths play games of catch-me-if-you-can with their spouses and girlfriends. They may be sitting across from their wife on the computer and sending sexually explicit messages to a girlfriend, while claiming to be doing work or looking up some innocuous information. They may be in a hotel with a girlfriend while having a lengthy phone conversation with their wife. They may take a call from one girlfriend while being on a date with another and telling her that it's a business call.

Psychopaths enjoy lying both because of the power it gives them over others and because of the risk of getting caught. The problem remains, of course, that the risk is never quite thrilling enough. To take a real risk in life, one has to value something or someone, so that one fears losing that object or that person. Psychopaths can't value anything but their immediate appetites and anyone but themselves. If they lose their jobs, there's always another one just as good (even when there isn't). If they lose their money, they can always mooch off or scam someone else. If they alienate their partner, there's lots of other fish in the sea. Since the stakes are always so low for psychopaths, their thrills are also very fleeting.

Lying makes them feel more powerful and superior to others. Needless to say, in reality, engaging in deception and manipulation is not a sign of great intelligence, but a symptom of lack of character. Psychopathic dictators such as Hitler, Stalin, Mao and Ceausescu weren't particularly bright individuals. They were just exceptionally manipulative, opportunistic and ruthless. But it's no use trying to persuade a psychopath that he's much less, rather than more, than the people he dupes. Once you see through his lack of character, his reactions become transparent. When he gets away a lie, he feels a cheap thrill. When caught in a lie, he feels no shame. He simply covers it up with another lie or, when that's not an option, blames you for his wrongdoing or accuses you of behaving in the same manner. Often, even when psychopaths believe that they're telling the truth, they're in fact lying. A psychopath can "sincerely" state that he's being faithful to you right before his date with another woman. Psychopaths live in an Orwellian doublethink world. We might as well call it a "psychopath-think," since such individuals have their own language.

For example, to a psychopathic seducer, "I love you" means "You give me a rush at this moment." "You love me" translates as "you forgo your needs to bend to my will." "Trust me" means "What a sucker!" "You're the woman of my life," translates into "You're one of a long, indefinite sequence of women that's also simultaneous" (Psychopaths have their own version of math as well). "Mutual fidelity" means "you need to be faithful to me while I cheat on you." "Betrayal" means "You dared disapprove of something I did" or "You disobeyed me." "Mutual commitment" translates into "You need to revolve everything in your life only around me while I do exactly what I want." "Honesty" means "My truth," or "Saying whatever gets me what I want at the moment." "I miss you" means "I miss the function you played in my life because I'm a little bored right now." "What my Baby wants, my Baby gets" means "I'll give you attention, flattery and gifts only until I hook you emotionally and gain your trust. Afterwards, Mazeltov Baby! You're on your own." "I cheat because my wife/girlfriend doesn't satisfy me" means "...and neither do you." "We belong together" means "I own you completely while I remain free." "If anything happens between us, it won't be because of me" means "Nothing's ever my fault. If I do something harmful, it's because you (and others) deserved it." Unless you learn to decipher the psychopathic code, you're likely to be "lost in translation."

Every so-called "truth" psychopaths utter is transient and contingent upon their immediate gratification. If you add "for now" to their declarations of love, they may sometimes ring plausible. For instance, during the euphoric seduction phase, psychopaths may believe when they tell a girlfriend that they love her and want to spend the rest of their life with her. But their passion lacks empathy, love and commitment. Since the euphoric state of "being in love" comes and goes even during the course of a single day, so does the truth-value of their statement. One minute they might tell a girlfriend with genuine emotion that they love her and will always be faithful to her. The next hour they might be pursuing another woman, just for the heck of it. While psychopaths scheme and manipulate a lot, they're short-term, or tactical, schemers. They can't see more than two steps ahead of their noses, to chase the next temporary pleasure. Tactics, or short-term maneuvers, prove to be far less effective than strategy, or long-term planning, however. Over the long-term, the lives of psychopaths tend to unravel in a sequence of failed careers, sordid crimes and disastrous relationships. While this fact doesn't particularly bother the psychopaths themselves—who live by a Dionysian hedonism—it bothers quite a lot everyone who comes into close contact with them.

To explain further why and how psychopaths lie so glibly and compulsively, I'll rely upon Dr. Susan Forward's *When Your Lover Is a Liar*. Her book addresses all kinds of liars. However, she devotes one chapter in particular to psychopaths. She describes this group as the most dangerous and predatory kind of liars. She also confirms that they're the only ones who are completely unchangeable. We've already seen how and why Mark Hacking and Neil Entwistle lied to their spouses. They told harmful lies, not mere white lies. The lies that harm us, either by omission or commission, involve the intent to deceive. Forward defines a harmful lie as a "deliberate and conscious behavior that either misrepresents important facts or conceals and withholds them in order to keep you from knowing the truth about certain facets of your partner's past, present, and, often, future" (*When Your Lover Is a Liar*, 6). She goes on to explain that when a man lies about important matters related to his identity, actions and intentions, certain implications follow: 1) he becomes the sole proprietor of the truth; 2) he acquires control over events in his partner's life; 3) those he dupes lack important information that can drastically influence their lives; 4) consequently, those he dupes can't make major life decisions based on this information, including whether or not to stay with him and 5) most importantly, those he dupes don't know who he really is (16).

Psychopaths typically deny or minimize their deception once it's discovered. As we recall, when Lori Hacking questioned her husband concerning his lie about going to medical school, Mark wiggled his way out of that lie by telling her yet another lie. This strategy, Forward maintains, constitutes a power game which has several negative implications for the person being duped: 1) she didn't see what she saw; 2) she didn't hear what she heard; 3) she doesn't know what she found out; 4) she's exaggerating, imagining things or being paranoid; 5) in holding the liar accountable for his deception, she's the one creating problems in their relationship; 6) she's to blame for the deception or her partner's misbehavior; 7) other people, who are exposing the psychopath's lies, are creating trouble in their relationship (*When Your Lover Is a Liar,* 16). These techniques of denying and compounding the lies relate to "gaslighting." They lead the victim to feel like she's "going crazy" and imagining things that don't exist or aren't true. Gaslighting turns reality topsy-turvy. It replaces truth with falsehood. It also shifts the balance of power between the honest person and the liar. The liar takes charge of the relationship and of his honest partner's perception of reality.

Given that, as we've seen so far, harmful lies constitute a power game, it's not that surprising that psychopaths, who live to control others, end up being the most irredeemable pathological liars of the human species. As mentioned, Forward devotes an entire chapter to psychopathic liars. By way of contrast to the rest of her book, which focuses on how to improve relationships tainted by deception, in this case she advises people to leave their psychopathic partners for good. She states:

> This chapter is about scorpions in human form, and continuous, remorseless lying is what they do. They lie to the women they're with, and to just about everyone else. They cheat repeatedly on the women they're married to, they steal from the woman they profess their love for. Their greatest thrill, their greatest high, is pulling the wool over the eyes of the women who love and trust them, and they do it without a moment of concern for their targets. This chapter is about the one kind of liar you must leave immediately. It is about sociopaths (*When Your Lover Is a Liar,* 66).

Forward goes on to explain that since psychopaths regard life as a power game, they suffer from an incurable addiction to deception as a way of life. All the experts on psychopathy and sociopathy state that such individuals lie even when the truth would make them look better or would sound more plausible. It's likely that if Mark Hacking had told Lori the truth from the very beginning— namely, that he lacked a college education and had no intention of going to medical school—she'd have still stayed with him and loved him anyways. According to her colleagues and friends, Lori was particularly hurt by the ease with which her husband had lied to her and others for so many years. The fact that Mark deceived her so convincingly for so long told her a lot more about his character than the content of the lie itself.

In addition, unlike normal human beings, psychopaths don't change their deceitful ways. The simple and short explanation for why not is that they don't want to change and aren't even capable of changing. As we've seen, psychopaths lack the emotional and moral incentives that motivate normal people to improve themselves. No matter how much suffering they cause others and no matter how much they, themselves, get into trouble as a result of their lies, psychopaths remain pathological liars and frauds throughout their lives.

Forward breaks down the main reasons why psychopaths don't change their ways: 1) they don't experience the pain and shame that motivates people to become honest; 2) they don't play by the rules and thus they never feel that they've done something wrong; 3) they lack the emotional depth to want to improve their character; 4) in their relentless search for excitement, they live to break, not follow, moral and social rules; 5) they believe that they're superior to those they dupe (*When Your Lover Is a Liar,* 71). I would add one more related point to this list: 6) they believe that the rest of humanity is just like them, i.e., manipulative and deceitful, only less intelligent or less adept at it than they are. Forward concludes that if anybody tells you a psychopath can become an honest, loyal and faithful individual, they're lying to you. Which is also why the person most likely to tell someone such a lie is the psychopath himself: especially if he still has something to gain from his target.

The Psychopath's Rhetorical Games

Having analyzed why psychopaths lie and why their lies are harmful to those they dupe, I'll now examine the psychopath's strategies of lying. The more informed we are about their pathology, the better we can protect themselves against them. We've seen that a psychopath gets you within his power largely through deception. As Cleckley noted, the main reason why people are easily taken in by their lies is not because the lies themselves are that convincing, but because of the psychopaths' effective rhetorical strategies. What are those?

1. *Glibness and Charm.* We've already seen that these are two of the main personality traits of psychopaths. They know how to use them to their advantage. Psychopaths lie very easily and in a smooth manner. They often pass lie detector tests as well because such tests register emotion, not deception. Psychopaths tend to remain cool under pressure. They can tell you the most implausible stories— such as when they get a call from their girlfriend but tell you that it's a random call from a jailbird—but do it so matter-of-factly that it makes you want to believe them. Sometimes they distract you from the content of their words with their charm. They look at you lovingly, stroke your hair or your arm and punctuate their speech with kisses, caresses and tender words, so that you're mesmerized by them instead of focusing on what they're actually saying.

2. *Analogies and Metaphors.* Because their facts are so often fabrications, psychopaths commonly rely upon analogies and metaphors to support their false or misleading claims. For instance, if they wish to persuade you to cheat on your husband or significant other, they may present their case in the form of an analogy. They may ask you to think of the cheating (or breaking up with your current partner) as a parent who is sparing his drafted child greater harm by breaking his leg to save him from going to war. This analogy doesn't work at all, of course, if you stop and think about it. Your significant other isn't drafted to be dumped for

a psychopath. You're not sparing him any pain by breaking his leg or, in this case, his heart. You're only giving credit to the psychopath's sophistry and misuse of analogy to play right into his hands, thus hurting both yourself and your spouse.

3. *Slander.* A psychopath often slanders others, to discredit them and invalidate their truth claims. He projects his faults and misdeeds upon those he hurts. To establish credibility, he often maligns his wife or girlfriend, attributing the failure of his relationship to her faults or misdeeds rather than his own.

4. *Circumlocution.* When you ask a psychopath a straightforward question that requires a straightforward answer, he usually goes round and round in circles or talks about something else altogether. For instance, when you ask him where he was on the previous night, sometimes he lies. At other times, he tries to divert you by bringing up another subject. He may also use flattery, such as saying how sexy your voice sounds and how much you turn him on. Such distractions are intended to cloud your reasoning and lead you to forget your original question.

5. *Evasion.* Relatedly, psychopaths can be very evasive. When you ask a psychopath a specific question, he will sometimes answer in general terms, talking about humanity, or men, or women, or whatever: anything but his own self and actions, which is what you were inquiring about in the first place.

6. *Pointing Fingers at Others.* When you accuse a psychopath of wrongdoing, he's likely to tell you that another person is just as bad as him or that humanity in general is. The first point may or may not be true. At any rate, it's irrelevant. So what if person x, y or z—say, some of the psychopath's friends or girlfriends—has done similarly harmful things or manifests some of his bad qualities? The most relevant point to you, if you're the psychopath's partner, should be how *he* behaves and what his actions say about *him*. The second point is patently false. All human beings have flaws, of course. But we don't all suffer from an incurable personality disorder. If you have any doubts about that, then you should research the matter. Of course, even normal individuals can sometimes be manipulative, can sometimes lie and can sometimes cheat. But that doesn't make our actions comparable to the magnitude of remorseless deceit, manipulation and destruction that psychopaths are capable of. Furthermore, most of us, whatever our flaws, care about others.

7. *Fabrication of Details.* In *The Postmodern Condition*, Jean-François Lyotard shows how offering a lot of details makes a lie sound much more plausible. When you give a vague answer, your interlocutor is more likely to sense evasion and pursue her inquiries. But when you present fabricated details—such as when you are with your girlfriend in a hotel room but tell your wife that you were with your male buddy named X, at a Chinese restaurant named Y and ate General Gao

chicken and rice which cost a mere $ 5 at a restaurant and discussed your buddy's troubles with his girlfriend, who has left him because he cheated on her—your wife's more likely to believe your elaborate fiction. Because they excel at improvisation, psychopaths are excellent fabricators of details. Even novelists have reason to envy their ability to make up false but believable "facts" on the spot.

8. *Playing upon your Emotions.* Often, when confronted with alternative accounts of what happened, psychopaths play upon your emotions. For example, if his girlfriend compares notes with the wife, a psychopath is likely to ask his wife: "Who are you going to believe? Me or her?" This reestablishes complicity with the wife against the girlfriend, testing the wife's love and loyalty to him. It also functions as a form of subterfuge. That way he doesn't have to address the information offered by the other source. To anybody whose judgment remains unclouded by the manipulations of a psychopath, the answer should be quite obvious. Just about any person, even your garden-variety cheater and liar, is far more credible than a psychopath. But to a woman whose life and emotions are wrapped around the psychopath, the answer is likely to be that she prefers to believe him over his girlfriend or anybody else, for that matter. Even in such a hopeless situation—if a psychopath's partner doesn't want to face the truth about him—it's still important to share information with her. Psychopaths form addictive ties with their so-called "loved" ones. They're as dangerous to their partners as any hard drug is likely to be. If their partners know about their harmful actions and about their personality disorder, then they're willingly assuming the risk. Everyone has the right to make choices in life, including the very bad one of staying with a psychopath. But at least they should make informed decisions, so they know whom they're choosing and are prepared for the negative consequences of their decision.

Deception constitutes a very entertaining game for psychopaths. They use one victim to lie to another. They use both victims to lie to a third. They spin their web of mind-control upon all those around them. They encourage antagonisms or place distance among the people they deceive, so that they won't compare notes and discover the lies. Often they blend in aspects of the truth with the lies, to focus on that small grain of truth if they're caught. The bottom line is that psychopaths are malicious sophists. It really doesn't matter how often they lie and how often they tell the truth. Psychopaths use both truth and lies instrumentally, to persuade others to accept their false and self-serving version of reality and to get them under their control. For this reason, it's pointless to try to sort out the truth from the lies. As a participant to the website *lovefraud.com* has eloquently remarked, psychopaths themselves are the lie. From hello to goodbye, from you're beautiful to you're ugly, from you're the woman of my life to you mean nothing to me, from beginning to end, the whole relationship with a psychopath is one BIG LIE.

Chapter 4

The Psychopath's Antisocial Behavior

Inadequately Motivated Antisocial Behavior

If lying about who they are and what they plan to do with their lives were their only crime, psychopaths wouldn't be quite so dangerous. Unfortunately, their lies often serve far worse objectives. In this section, I'll rely upon Cleckley's work to discuss the psychopath's antisocial behavior. One of the main symptoms of psychopathy is a lack of remorse and shame for immoral and harmful behavior: "The psychopath apparently cannot accept substantial blame for the various misfortunes which befall him and which he brings down upon others, usually he denies emphatically all responsibility and directly accuses others as responsible, but often he will go through an idle ritual of saying that much of his trouble is his own fault" (344). For instance, if you catch a psychopath cheating, he may say that he knows he's in the wrong, claim that he didn't love the other woman and promise you that he'll never do it again. You can bet that the only true part of his statements is that he didn't love the other woman. Every other excuse the psychopath offers and every promise he makes, you can safely delete since they're false. As Neil Entwistle's behavior in court revealed, psychopaths believe that if they duped, cheated on, scammed, raped or even killed other individuals, it's because the victims somehow provoked it or got in their way. Cleckley concludes, "Whether judged in the light of his conduct, of his attitude, or of material elicited in psychiatric examination, he shows almost no sense of shame. His career is always full of exploits, any one of which would wither even the more callous representatives of the ordinary man. Yet he does not, despite his able protestations, show the slightest evidence of major humiliation or regret" (344).

In his own mind, nothing the psychopath does is ever wrong. "Not only is the psychopath undependable, but also in more active ways he cheats, deserts, annoys, brawls, fails, and lies without any apparent compunction. He will commit theft, forgery, adultery, fraud, and other deeds for astonishingly small stakes and under much greater risks of being discovered than will the ordinary scoundrel" (343). Often, there seems to be no underlying logic to a psychopath's actions except for causing harm for its own sake. Scott Peterson could have divorced Laci. He didn't have to kill her and their unborn child. Mark Hacking could have explained to Lori that he wanted to appear more educated and accomplished than he actually was. He didn't have to kill her just because she no longer mirrored the idealized image of himself he wanted to see reflected in her eyes. Neil Entwistle could have told Rachel that he wanted a more exciting sex life with other women. He didn't have to kill her and their newborn baby in order to regain his bachelor freedom. In geometry they say that the shortest route between two points is a straight line. Psychopaths don't toe a straight line in life. They choose instead deviant routes even when those paths lead them straight to jail. Which is precisely the point Cleckley addresses next.

Poor Judgment and Failure to Learn by Experience

Just because psychopaths are theoretically capable of moral reasoning doesn't mean that they actually exercise it when it comes to their own lives. Like practically everything else about the psychopath's seemingly "normal" behavior, offering rational arguments is only a rhetorical strategy to them. They use it to impress others with their wisdom and common sense. Cleckley indicates, "Despite his excellent rational powers, the psychopath continues to show the most execrable judgment about attaining what one might presume to be his ends. He throws away excellent opportunities to make money, to achieve a rapprochement with his wife, to be dismissed from the hospital, or to gain other ends that he has sometimes spent considerable effort toward gaining" (345). The pursuit of a given goal excites a psychopath far more than its actual attainment. A psychopath wants to seduce a woman, not be her partner. He wants to get a job, not succeed in it. He wants to mark his women by having babies with them, not raise happy and well-adjusted children together. Unfortunately, even negative consequences, such as losing their partners or ending up in jail for his crimes, don't change a psychopath's pattern of destructive behavior. "This exercise of execrable judgment is not particularly modified by experience, however chastening his experiences may be," Cleckley observes (345). A psychopath regards as abstract and theoretical anything that's not closely related to his short-term pursuits, whims and pleasures. For him, immediate rewards far outweigh potential future costs. Moreover, in his own mind, the rules apply only to others, not to him. As Cleckley frames the problem, "He can offer wise decisions not only for others in life situations but also for himself so long as he is asked what he would do (or should do, or is going to do). When the test of action comes to him we soon find ample evidence of his deficiency" (346).

Pathological Egocentricity and Incapacity for Love

Clinically speaking, narcissism constitutes what Cleckley calls a "pathological egocentricity and incapacity for love." Narcissists are so self-absorbed that they can't envision the needs and reactions of others. They lack empathy and regard others as mirrors whose main role is to reflect—and magnify—the image of their own greatness. Although psychopaths are narcissistic to an extreme, in many respects they're far worse than most narcissists. At least most narcissists—excluding perhaps "malignant narcissists"—can experience self-doubt. They also need love and validation from other individuals. Psychopaths embody narcissism with a grotesque twist. They lack the depth to experience or need a personal, individuated kind of love. As Cleckley observes, "The psychopath is always distinguished by egocentricity. This is usually of a degree not seen in ordinary people and often is little short of astonishing" (347). Furthermore, unlike narcissists, who often show themselves to be vain to the point of self-caricature, psychopaths don't usually appear to be arrogant, self-absorbed or boastful. They can mask much better their grossly inflated egos, as they camouflage everything else that's deviant and dangerous in their personalities. They compellingly present themselves as loving, affectionate and other-regarding individuals. However, as Cleckley notes, "Deeper probing will always reveal a self-centeredness that is apparently unmodifiable and all but complete. This can perhaps be best expressed by stating that it is an incapacity for object love and that this incapacity (in my experience with well-marked psychopaths) appears to be absolute" (347). Cleckley correlates object-love, or caring about another person, with the capacity to feel empathy. Without empathy, you can't understand what others feel. You therefore don't have a disincentive to cause them harm or pain. Conversely, you lack the incentive to make them happier. Love, or even kindness, don't exist without empathy.

That's not to say that psychopaths can't experience any sort of fondness whatsoever. But their affection tends to be self-serving, fleeting and superficial. In some cases, it manifests itself as an intense, obsessive drive to possess another person. Cleckley grants that, "[The psychopath] is plainly capable of casual fondness, of likes and dislikes, and of reactions that, one might say, cause others to matter to him" (348). He qualifies, "These affective reactions are, however, always strictly limited in degree. In durability they also vary greatly from what is normal in mankind. The term absolute is, I believe, appropriate if we apply it to any affective attitude strong and meaningful enough to be called love, that is, anything that prevails in sufficient degree and over sufficient periods to exert a major influence on behavior" (347). Whenever they seem to be passionately in love or to experience genuine parental or filial devotion, psychopaths are faking it.

Let's return again to the case of Neil Entwistle. Opening the door for his wife, giving her romantic gifts, posting the pictures of her and their newborn baby on a joint website, doesn't mean anything if he's prepared to literally sacrifice his family to his whims. To this effect, Cleckley observes, "The psychopath seldom shows anything that, if the chief facts were known, would pass even in the eyes of lay observers as object love. His absolute indifference to the financial, social, emotional, physical, and other hardships that he brings upon those for whom he professes love confirms the appraisal during psychiatric studies of his true attitude. We must, let it never be forgotten, judge a man by his actions rather than by his words" (348). Because they can't love others, psychopaths also lack the motivation to improve their character and behavior. Cleckley concludes, "This lack in the psychopath makes it all but impossible for an adequate emotional rapport to arise in his treatment and may be an important factor in the therapeutic failure that, in my experience, has been universal" (348).

General Poverty in Major Affective Reactions

A psychopath lacks much more than empathy for others in his emotional repertoire. He also lacks the capacity to experience any kind of emotion that requires deeper insight and psychological awareness. He experiences only proto-emotions, which are as short-lived as they're intense. That doesn't make them any less dangerous, however. The evidence points to the fact that Scott Peterson and Neil Entwistle preplanned their murders weeks in advance. But Mark Hacking seems to have acted more or less on impulse, after having fought with his wife. If we believe his confession to his brothers, Mark was in the process of packing up his things, ran across a revolver and shot Lori while she was asleep. When angry or frustrated, a psychopath is capable of anything, even if his anger will dissipate a few minutes later. As Cleckley observes, "In addition to his incapacity for object love, the psychopath always shows general poverty of affect. Although it is true that be sometimes becomes excited and shouts as if in rage or seems to exult in enthusiasm and again weeps in what appear to be bitter tears or speaks eloquent and mournful words about his misfortunes or his follies, the conviction dawns on those who observe him carefully that here we deal with a readiness of expression rather than a strength of feeling" (349).

The proto-emotions experienced by a psychopath tie in, once again, to the satisfaction or frustration of his immediate desires: "Vexation, spite, quick and labile flashes of quasi-affection, peevish resentment, shallow moods of self-pity, puerile attitudes of vanity, and absurd and showy poses of indignation are all within his emotional scale and are freely sounded as the circumstances of life play upon him. But mature, wholehearted anger, true or consistent indignation, honest, solid grief, sustaining pride, deep joy, and genuine despair are reactions not likely to be found within this scale" (349). For this reason, psychopaths don't feel distress even when they land in jail. Even there they take pleasure in manipulating their fellow inmates and the prison staff. Even from there they write letters to people outside to use them for money, amusement and possibly even sex. Nothing ruffles a psychopath's feathers for long. The same emotional shallowness that leads him to be unresponsive to the needs of others and to experience no remorse when he hurts them also enables him to feel little or no distress when he, himself gets hurt. So far, I've covered the emotions psychopaths can't feel. I've also had the opportunity to witness up-close and personal the emotions a psychopath can feel, however. That's what I'll describe next.

The Psychopath's Emotions: What Does He Feel?

1. *Glee.* A psychopath feels elation or glee whenever he gets his way or pulls a fast one on somebody.

2. *Anger.* Hare notes in *Without Conscience* that since psychopaths have low impulse control, they're much more easily angered than normal people. A psychopath's displays of anger tend to be cold, sudden, short-lived and arbitrary. Generally you can't predict what exactly will trigger his anger since this emotion, like his charm, is used to control those around him. It's not necessarily motivated by something you've done or by his circumstances. A psychopath may blow up over something minor, but remain completely cool and collected about a more serious matter. Displays of anger represent yet another way for a psychopath to demonstrate that he's in charge. When psychopaths scream, insult, hit, or even wound and kill other individuals, they're aware of their behavior even if they act opportunistically, in the heat of the moment. They know that they're harming others and, what's more, they enjoy it.

3. *Frustration.* This emotion is tied to their displays of anger but isn't necessarily channeled against a particular person, but against an obstacle or situation. A psychopath may feel frustrated, for example, when his girlfriend doesn't want to leave her current partner for him. Yet he may be too infatuated with her at the moment to channel his negative emotions against her. He may also believe that his anger would alienate her before he's gotten a chance to hook her emotionally. In such circumstances, he may become frustrated with the situation itself: with the obstacles that her partner or her family or society in general pose between them. Psychopaths generally experience frustration when they face impersonal barriers between themselves and their current goals or targets. But that's also what often engages them even more obstinately in a given pursuit. After all, for them, overcoming minor challenges in life is part of the fun.

4. *Consternation.* As we've seen so far, psychopaths don't create love bonds with others. They establish dominance bonds instead. When those controlled by a psychopath disapprove of his actions or sever the relationship, sometimes he'll experience anger. But his immediate reaction is more likely to be surprise or consternation. Psychopaths can't believe that their bad actions, which they always consider justifiable and appropriate, could ever cause another human being who was previously under their spell to disapprove of their behavior and reject them. Even if they cheat, lie, use, manipulate or isolate others, they don't feel like they deserve any repercussions as a result of that behavior. In addition, psychopaths rationalize their bad actions as being in the best interest of their victims. For instance, if a psychopath isolates his partner from her family and persuades her to quit her job and then, once she's all alone with him, abandons her to pursue other women, he feels fully justified in his conduct. In his mind, she de-

served to be left since she didn't satisfy all of his needs or was somehow inadequate as a mate. In fact, given his sense of entitlement, the psychopath might even feel like he did her a favor to remove her from her family and friends and to leave her alone in the middle of nowhere, like a wreck displaced by a tornado. Thanks to him, she can start her life anew and become more independent. To put it bluntly, a psychopath will kick you in the teeth and expect you to say "Thank you." Being shameless and self-absorbed, he assumes that all those close to him will buy his false image of goodness and excuse his despicable actions just as he does. In fact, he expects that even the women he's used and discarded continue to idealize him as a perfect partner and eagerly await his return. That way he can continue to use them for sex, money, control, his image or any other services if, when and for however long he chooses to return into their lives. When those women don't feel particularly grateful—when, in fact, they feel only contempt for him—the psychopath will be initially stunned that they have such a low opinion of him. He will also feel betrayed by these women, or by family members and friends who disapprove of his reprehensible behavior. Although he, himself, feels no love and loyalty to anyone, a psychopath expects unconditional love and loyalty from all those over whom he's established a dominance bond. This mindset also explains psychopaths' behavior in court. Both Scott Peterson and Neil Entwistle seemed outraged that the jury found them guilty of murder. Psychopaths believe that those whom they have hurt, and society in general, should not hold them accountable for their misdeeds. After all, in their own minds, they're superior to other human beings and therefore above the law. How dare anybody hold them accountable and punish them for their crimes!

5.   *Boredom.* This is probably the only feeling that gives psychopaths a nagging sense of discomfort. They try to alleviate it, as we've seen, by pursuing cheap thrills, harming others and engaging in transgressive behavior. Nothing, however, can relieve for long the psychopath's fundamental ennui. He gets quickly used to, and thus also bored with, each new person and activity.

6.   *Histrionic flashes.* I'm not sure if this is an emotion, but I know for sure that the psychopath's dramatic displays of love, remorse and empathy lack any meaning and depth. If you watch the murder trials on the news or on *Court TV*, you'll notice that some psychopaths convicted of murder often put on shows of grief, sadness or remorse in front of the jury. The next moment, however, they're joking around and laughing with their attorneys or instructing them in a calm and deliberate manner about what to do and say on their behalf. The displays of emotion psychopaths commonly engage in are, of course, fake. They're tools of manipulation—to provoke sympathy or gain trust—as well as yet another way of "winning" by fooling those around them. I've already mentioned that Neil Entwistle engaged in such histrionic behavior. If you've followed crime features on the news, you may have noticed that Casey Anthony, the young woman accused of killing her toddler, behaves similarly. She was observed going out to dance

and party at clubs with friends the day after her daughter, Caylee, disappeared. Casey's lack of concern for her missing child doesn't necessarily prove that she murdered her. But it reveals highly suspicious and callous behavior. It also casts doubt upon the brief and dramatic displays of grief or concern that she sometimes puts on in front of the media and for her parents.

7. *Infatuation.* When they identify someone as a good potential target, psychopaths can become obsessed with that particular person. In *Without Conscience,* Hare compares the psychopath's focused attention upon his chosen target to a powerful beam of light that illuminates only one spot at a time. He also likens it to a predator stalking its prey. Because psychopaths tend to ignore other responsibilities (such as their jobs and their families) and have no conscience whatsoever, they can focus on pursuing a given target more intensely than multidimensional, loving men could. This is especially the case if their target presents an exciting challenge, such as if she's rich or famous, or if she's married to another man, which triggers their competitive drive. This single-minded infatuation, however, like all of their proto-emotions, is superficial and short-lived. Because for psychopaths such obsessions don't lead to any genuine friendship, caring or love, they dissipate as soon as they get whatever they wanted from that person, which may be only the conquest itself.

8. *Self-love (sort of).* Since psychopaths only care about themselves, one would think that self-love would be the one emotion they could experience more deeply. In a sense that's true, since their whole lives revolve around the single-minded pursuit of selfish goals. But this is also what makes psychopaths' self-love as shallow as the rest of their emotions. Just as they're incapable of considering anyone else's long-term interest, they're incapable of considering their own. By pursuing fleeting pleasures and momentary whims, psychopaths sabotage their own lives as well. Rarely do they end up happy or successful. They spend their whole lives hurting and betraying those who loved and trusted them, using and discarding their partners, disappointing the expectations of their families, friends, bosses and colleagues and moving from one meaningless diversion to another. At the end of the road, most of them end up empty-handed and alone.

9. *Contempt.* No matter how charming, other-regarding and friendly they may appear to be on the outside, all psychopaths are misanthropes on the inside. A psychopath's core emotion is contempt for the individuals he fools, uses and abuses and for humanity in general. You can identify the psychopath's underlying contempt much more easily once he no longer needs you or once his mask of sanity shatters. As we've seen, psychopaths hold themselves in high regard and others in low regard. To describe the hierarchies they construct, I'll use an analogy from my literary studies. I was trained in Comparative Literature during they heyday of Jacques Derrida's deconstruction as it was being applied to pretty

much everything: cultural studies, gender hierarchies, race relations, post-colonialism and the kitchen sink.

Although looking at life in general in terms of "indeterminate" binary hierarchies hasn't proved particularly useful, this polarized worldview describes rather well the mindset of psychopaths. For such disordered, narcissistic and unprincipled individuals, the world is divided into superiors (themselves) and inferiors (all others); predators (themselves) and prey (their targets); dupers (themselves) and duped (the suckers). Of course, only giving psychopaths a lobotomy would turn these binary hierarchies upside down in their minds. This is where the applicability of Derrida's deconstructive model stops. Although psychopaths consider themselves superior to others, they distinguish among levels of inferiority in the people they use, manipulate and dupe.

The biggest dupes in their eyes are those individuals who believe whole-heartedly that the psychopaths are the kind, honest, other-regarding individuals they appear to be. As the saying goes, if you buy that, I have some oceanfront property in Kansas to sell you. Such individuals don't present much of a challenge for psychopaths. They're usually quickly used up and discarded by them. The second tier of dupes consists of individuals who are lucid only when it comes to the psychopath's mistreatment of others, not themselves. Wives and girlfriends who are clever enough to see how the psychopath cheats on, lies to, uses and manipulates other people in his life, but vain or blind enough to believe that they're the only exception to this rule form the bulk of this group. This brings to mind an episode of a popular court show I watched recently. A woman testified on behalf of the integrity and honesty of her boyfriend. As it turns out, he had cheated on his wife with her (and other women as well). But his girlfriend nonetheless staunchly defended his character. She maintained that even though she knew that her lover was a cheater and a liar, because she herself was such a great catch and because they had such a special and unique relationship, he was completely faithful and honest to her. The judge laughed out loud and added, ". . .that you know of!" Women who are cynical enough to see the psychopath's mistreatment of others yet gullible enough not to see that's exactly what he's doing to them constitute his preferred targets. Such women are not so naive as to present no challenge whatsoever for the psychopath. But they're definitely blind enough to fall for his manipulation and lies. A psychopath will wrap several such women around his little finger. Those who finally see the psychopath's mistreatment as a sign of his malicious and corrupt nature occupy the third rung of the hierarchy. They're usually women who have been burned so badly by the psychopath that they don't wish to put their hands into the fire again.

Specific Loss of Insight

If psychopaths appear to be cardboard figures compared to normal human beings, it's because they not only lack the full range of human emotions, but also the awareness that they're in any way deficient. Cleckley observes, "In a special sense the psychopath lacks insight to a degree seldom, if ever, found in any but the most seriously disturbed psychotic patients" (351). They fail to see anything wrong with what they do to harm others: unless of course someone else is doing it to them. Cleckley adds that a psychopath "has absolutely no capacity to see himself as others see him. It is perhaps more accurate to say that he has no ability to know how others feel when they see him or to experience subjectively anything comparable about the situation. All of the values, all of the major affect concerning his status, are unappreciated by him" (351). Although he's incapable of deeper reflection and genuine emotion, simulated feelings come very naturally to a psychopath. In fact, he expresses fake emotions much more readily than normal people express genuine feelings.

Although a psychopath can mimic emotions, he's inconsistent in that capacity since the feelings themselves aren't real. If you pay closer attention, red flags appear in any relationship with a psychopath. For instance, he'll sometimes laugh when you're in pain. Or he'll dismiss your distress. Or, as Neil Entwistle in court, his attempts to simulate deeper human emotions, such as sorrow, will look phony. Cleckley explains that such glitches occur because the psychopath can't really grasp the emotions he acts out. "Perhaps it was less a voluntary deception than a simulation in which the simulator himself fails to realize his lack of emotional grasp or that he is simulating or what he is simulating... His clever statements have been hardly more than verbal reflexes; even his facial expressions are without the underlying content they imply. This is not insight but an excellent mimicry of insight. No sincere intention can spring from his conclusions because no affective conviction is there to move him" (352).

Unresponsiveness in General Interpersonal Relations

What seems very puzzling to most people about charismatic psychopaths is that they generally target the persons closest to them. That's whom they choose to hurt, betray and sometimes even murder. As we've seen in the cases of Mark Hacking and Neil Entwistle, they prey upon the women who trust and love them and on the children who depend upon them. Psychopaths lack any sense of reciprocity. The notion that if someone treats you well you should also treat them well is completely lost on them. On the contrary, they view decent behavior as a symptom of gullibility, weakness or stupidity, the qualities of an optimal target for their ruses. Cleckley elaborates:

> The psychopath cannot be depended upon to show the ordinary responsiveness to special consideration or kindness or trust. No matter how well he is treated, no matter how long-suffering his family, his friends, the police, hospital attendants, and others may be, he shows no consistent reaction of appreciation except superficial and transparent protestations. Such gestures are exhibited most frequently when he feels they will facilitate some personal aim. The ordinary

axiom of human existence that one good turn deserves another, a principle sometimes honored by cannibals and uncommonly callous assassins, has only superficial validity for him although he can cite it with eloquent casuistry when trying to obtain parole, discharge from the hospital, or some other end (355).

Yet at the same time, a psychopath can appear to be very generous. For instance, he may volunteer his time and money to worthwhile causes. He may help out a neighbor in need. He may attend church regularly. Such actions, however, don't reveal any genuine kindness. They only help bolster the psychopath's façade, to give others the illusion that he's a good person. Moreover, even in the rare instances when these generous impulses are genuine and without ulterior motive, they're too shallow and fleeting to add up to anything worth counting on. In other words, a psychopath can be generous when his investment remains low. But he can't put his partner or anybody else first when it comes to anything that really matters, such as trust, fidelity, mutual respect, raising children or leading a stable and fulfilling life together. If a psychopath has to choose between the welfare of his marriage and his impulse to screw his wife's best friend, needless to say, he'll chose the latter. Worse yet, he'll draw extra pleasure from the fact that the affair was with his wife's good friend, not a total stranger. As Cleckley observes:

> In relatively small matters psychopaths sometimes behave so as to appear very considerate, responsive, and obliging. Acquaintances who meet them on grounds where minor issues prevail may find it difficult to believe that they are not highly endowed with gratitude and eager to serve others. Such reactions and intentions, although sometimes ready or even spectacularly facile, do not ever accumulate sufficient force to play a determining part in really important issues" (355).

If keeping up his mask of niceness takes minimal effort, a psychopath may do it. But he won't be able to be other-regarding in any respect that truly matters to those closest to him and improves the quality of their lives. Which is why Cleckley concludes that even when a psychopath appears to be a decent and loving human being, it's always an act that will be consistently belied by his selfish attitude and harmful actions.

Sex Life Impersonal, Trivial, and Poorly Integrated

Cleckley observes that "In contrast with others, the psychopath requires impulses of scarcely more than whim like intensity to bring about unacceptable behavior in the sexual field or in any other" (361). Psychopaths engage in promiscuous sex to gain power over others, feel pleasure, transgress social boundaries and divert themselves. Sometimes, however, they also seek longer-term entertainment with individuals whom they can seduce. While psychopaths tend to be exceptionally good at faking and provoking romantic love, they're incapable of actually feeling it. Cleckley elaborates:

> The male psychopath, despite his usual ability to complete the physical act successfully with a woman, never seems to find anything meaningful or personal in his relations or to enjoy significant pleasure beyond the localized and temporary sensations... What is felt for prostitute, sweetheart, casual pickup, girlfriend, or wife is not anything that can bring out loyalty or influence activities into a remedial or constructive plan. The familiar record of sexual promiscuity found in both male and female psychopaths seems much more closely related to their almost total lack of self-imposed restraint than to any particularly strong passions or drives (364).

If psychopaths are particularly dangerous sexual partners, it's not just because they're so promiscuous that they're likely to transmit venereal diseases. More ominously, their quest for power and lack of empathy makes them very likely candidates for rape, pedophilia, incest, sadism and sometimes even murder. Generally speaking, the more transgressive and perverted an act is, the more it excites them. Cleckley explains:

> Entanglements which go out of their way to mock ordinary human sensibility or what might be called basic decency are prevalent in their sexual careers. To casually 'make' or 'lay' the best friend's wife and to involve a husband's uncle or one of his business associates in a particularly messy triangular or quadrilateral situation are typical acts. Such opportunities, when available, seem not to repel but specifically to attract the psychopath (364).

Since sex is so central to a psychopath's life, as well as a key weapon he uses to hurt others, I'll devote the next chapter to the subject of psychopaths as lovers.

Chapter 5

Psychopaths as Lovers

Some of the women who comment on *lovefraud.com*, as well as many of those interviewed by Sandra L. Brown, M.A. in *Women Who Love Psychopaths* state that psychopaths make good lovers. When you read their comments, however, you see that while superficially that may be true, fundamentally it is false. Psychopaths have low impulse control and are generally very promiscuous. Since they need transgression, risk and variety in their lives, they're likely to have tried a lot of sexual positions in many locations with numerous partners. Initially, their ample sexual experience can appear exciting even to a normal person. In the honeymoon phase of the relationship, a psychopath is generally hypersexual with you. He's excited by the chase and the "conquest," by the novelty, by the fact that he's (most likely) cheating on other women and on you, as well as by the increasing control he's exercising over you.

Analogously, from your perspective, the aura of romance, excitement and spontaneity can be very seductive. Initially, it may seem flattering, even if a bit disconcerting, to have a man who seems unable to keep his hands off you anywhere and everywhere, including in public. As social predators, psychopaths tend to stalk their victims, overwhelming them with attention at first. The movie *9 1/2 weeks*, staring Kim Basinger and Mickey Roarke, has been interpreted as a superficial erotic movie. But it's actually a psychologically insightful film about the process of psychopathic seduction. What starts out as a romantic relationship progressively turns into a menacing dominance bond. The man in the movie stalks the heroine and makes her feel desirable and special. He showers her with attention and gifts. But those don't come free. For instance, he gives her an expensive watch and tells her to look at it and think of him every day at a certain time. He ends up controlling her thoughts, her feelings and her sexuality. He begins by being very sensual and affectionate, but eventually induces her to engage in perverse sexual acts that she feels uncomfortable with. He pushes the envelope further and further to the point where she becomes just a puppet in his hands. Fortunately, she realizes this and escapes his control before she's seriously damaged. In real life, however, many women aren't so lucky.

It may seem exciting to play erotic games or to talk in a raunchy manner. But, over time, this behavior begins to feel strange and uncomfortable. What's worse, it also becomes normative, since psychopaths enjoy controlling you. They tell you how to dress and what to do or say to please them. They tell you what make-up to wear or to wear no make-up at all. Some psychopaths instruct women to dress very modestly, to cover themselves practically from head to toe, so that they won't tempt other men. Others, on the contrary, prefer that their women dress provocatively even in public, to demean them and satisfy their penchant for transgression. Many psychopaths engage in rape and other forms of domestic violence. Even giving you pleasure gives them a sense of power.

Eventually, psychopaths need more transgression, more depraved and sadistic acts, harder pornographic material, more sleazy places, more sexual partners and configurations, more everything, to derive the same degree of enjoyment from sex. You begin to feel like a sex toy, nothing more than an object, rather than the cherished, attractive human being you thought you were in your partner's eyes. It's no news that most women prefer to be both. We want to be desired as sex objects but also loved and appreciated as individuals. Unfortunately, psychopaths can't deliver both. Of course, they often convincingly fake feelings of love in the beginning. But, fundamentally, they can only view and treat you as a sex object that increasingly loses its appeal over time. After the honeymoon phase ends, there's no real sense of individuality with psychopaths. Sexual partners are interchangeable to them. You're placed in constant competition with other women. As we know, psychopaths constantly seek new "opportunities" to fulfill their insatiable desires. They're always ready to "upgrade." To compensate for the fact that you may be exchanged for a newer, younger, hotter, richer or simply different model at any point in the relationship, you need to do more and more things to satisfy the psychopath. Which is exactly what he wants from you in the first place: a total capitulation to his will.

Psychopathic lovers project upon their partners the fantasy of what psychologists call the "omniavailable woman." They envision a partner who's always turned on, always at their beck and call, always sexually available to them anytime and everywhere. They want a woman who makes love to them as easily in the privacy of their bedroom as in the public space of a movie theater or a parking lot. Men's magazines play upon this fantasy as well. But in real, loving, relationships your moral and sexual boundaries are respected without the fear (or the implicit threat) that you'll be punished for having such restraints. That doesn't happen in psychopathic bonds. In those, it's guaranteed that you'll be punished—with infidelity, emotional withdrawal, abandonment, divorce, psychological and sometimes even physical abuse—if you don't comply with the psychopath's requests. Of course, this emotional blackmail is itself only a sordid joke. The psychopath betrays you whether or not you meet his demands. The only question is: does he do it openly, to torment you, or behind your back, to deceive you?

Although being a plaything may seem initially exciting, a woman who becomes a psychopath's sexual partner loses her autonomy in a relationship where she's supposed to be, like some wound-up inflatable doll with holes, always available to that man for his sexual gratification (or else. . .). In time, she realizes that she isn't loved in any meaningful sense of the term. That, in fact, her needs and desires don't really matter to him. That just about any other woman could have been used in the same manner and for the same purposes. That many others already are. She's neither unique nor irreplaceable in her lover's eyes, as he initially made her feel. She's generic and disposable to him. She then sees that the multidimensional man she thought cared about her is nothing but an empty shell. His charming exterior masks a completely hollow interior. He can't love her. He can only own her. Not even exclusively, but as part of his collection.

With a possession, one can do anything at all. An object has no independent will, no separate needs, no sensibilities. Over time, sex with a psychopath begins to feel contrived, cold and mechanical. It becomes an exercise in obedience rather than a bond based on mutual pleasure and affection. Because psychopaths grow easily bored of the same acts, places, positions and persons, the sexual experience becomes tainted by perverse acts at her expense. The bottom line is that psychopaths are lovers who don't care about their partners. If they give them pleasure, it's only to make themselves feel more powerful and potent, not because they consider another person's needs. In addition, since psychopaths get a rise out of harming the people they're intimately involved with, they're sadistic lovers: always emotionally, often physically as well. Once they've "conquered" you, they start asking you to do things that are degrading or that hurt. What you may do as a fun experiment once or a few times becomes a "non-negotiable" element of your sexual repertoire. You're asked to do it over and over again, whether or not you enjoy it.

For psychopaths, the games normal people play to spice up their sex lives constitute their whole existence. There's no other reality, a world of empathy, compassion and caring outside of or even within the context of the sexual relationship. Psychopaths live and breathe in the realm of fantasy. They have no concept of standing by you during difficult times or of coping with your bad moods, illnesses, sadness or disappointments. You'll often feel alone and abandoned with a psychopath whenever you aren't satisfying his immediate needs. Moreover, when psychopaths listen to your troubles, it's usually to draw them out and make you feel weaker and more dependent on them. It's never because they genuinely care; never because they want you to overcome hardships and become a stronger person. On the contrary, psychopaths cultivate your weaknesses (they make them feel superior by comparison) and prey upon your vulnerabilities. The games they play, both sexual and emotional, are the only reality that counts for them; the only reality they know.

Psychopathic lovers may initially appear to be oceans of raging passion. However, once the honeymoon phase is over, you come to realize that they're only dirty little puddles. The chemistry between you is as shallow as their so-called love. Compare how the psychopath treated you in the beginning of the relationship to how he's treating you later on. You'll notice a drastic reduction in excitement, in interest, in affection, in pleasure and in romance. You'll sense a mechanization of the sex acts. You'll observe an escalation in control, demands, humiliation, domination and perhaps even violence. You'll see that for a psychopath affection, communication and tenderness become transparently instrumental as the relationship unfolds. At first, he was "nice" to you almost all the time. Later in the relationship, however, he's attentive and affectionate mostly when he wants something from you. Affection becomes his tool of conditioning you like an animal. He gives out little pellets of nice words and tenderness to get you to do what he wants. Conversely, he doesn't give you any positive reinforcement when you don't comply with his wishes. The rest of the time—which is to say, in regular day-to-day life—you feel neglected, ignored and unwanted. You struggle like a fish on land to recapture the magical attraction you experienced together in the beginning.

As lovers, psychopaths represent a contradiction in terms. They're lovers who can't love. This contradiction may not be obvious at first, when the psychopath is smitten with you and pursuing you intensely. But it becomes painfully apparent over time. If you don't grow numb to the mistreatment or take refuge in denial, you come to realize that everything that counts is missing from the relationship that seemed to have it all.

Psychopathy and Passion

In the previous section, I explained that psychopaths can't love in the normal sense of having genuine empathy for others. But they can, and do, fall in love. Now I'd like to delve more deeply into the subject of how they fall in love and with whom. As we've seen so far, because of their ability to charm people, their seductive skills, their penchant for pleasure and their intense focus on their most desired targets, psychopaths can be (for a short while) extraordinarily passionate lovers. Their passion, however, finds itself in a constant race against time. The time usually runs out when the balance of power in the romantic relationship shifts dramatically in the psychopath's favor. Picasso describes this process quite poetically when he tells his mistress, Francoise Gilot:

> We mustn't see each other too often. If the wings of the butterfly are to keep their sheen, you mustn't touch them. We mustn't abuse something which is to bring light into both of our lives. Everything else in my life only weighs me down and shuts out the light. This thing with you seems to me like a window that is opening up. I want it to remain open. We must see each other but not too often. When you want to see me, you call me and tell me so (*My Life with Picasso*, 53-4).

Basically, in a relationship with a psychopath, the sheen wears off when you're dominated by him. When you accept to engage in demeaning sexual (or any other kind of) acts or behavior. When you readily buy into his lies because they preserve the rosier, yet false, version of reality you want to believe. When you accept unfair double standards, where he enjoys important privileges you do not. When you need or want him far more than he needs or wants you. Psychopaths may begin romantic relationships on an equal footing with their partners. But, ultimately, they aim to end up on top. For themselves, they tend to adopt a pseudo-Nietzschean attitude towards conventional morality. They violate, with an air of entitlement and superiority, all moral principles. At the same time, they generally expect an almost fundamentalist prurience from their main partners.

Even those psychopaths who enjoy demeaning their partners by asking them to violate moral and sexual values—such as by dressing or acting like a "slut"—do so only on their terms. If a psychopath's partner cheats on him out of her own volition with someone she cares about or desires, he's likely to explode in self-righteous indignation and defile her public image. At the same time, however, he will proudly proclaim his right to fall in love with and date whomever he wants. He will lack the self-awareness to see the inconsistency of his attitude towards conventional morality and the emotional depth to care about its unfairness to others. You can't be above the moral norms of good and evil yourself while demanding that those you interact with abide by them. That's called hypocrisy, not transcending conventional values or being independent. Also keep in mind that even if a psychopath appears to respect his partner while regarding and treating other women as "hoes," his attitude reflects a deep underlying misogyny that touches every woman he encounters.

As mentioned, sometimes a psychopath may prefer to humiliate his own partner by "sharing" her with others: but, once again, only at his bidding and on his terms. By way of contrast to the scenario where she cheats on him by choosing her romantic partners, this kind of violation of conventional values is likely to be acceptable (and even highly desirable) to a psychopath. He enjoys her degradation. Of course, abiding by such grossly unfair double standards can only lead to humiliation and disaster for the victim. "Pimping" one's wife or girlfriend, as it's crudely but accurately called, represents the very *opposite* of granting a woman sexual freedom. Moreover, such self-abasement can never achieve the desired effect of winning the psychopath's interest and affection. For, as we've seen, although psychopaths enjoy dominance, easily dominated individuals don't attract them for long.

So then what kind of person can keep the sheen on the wings of the butterfly for a longer period of time (to borrow Picasso's metaphor)? Only a person who does not agree to demeaning or unfair conditions in the relationship and only for as long as she does not accept them. As the study conducted by Sandra L. Brown, M.A. in *Women Who Love Psychopaths* reveals, like most people, psychopaths tend to fall in love with individuals who manifest self-respect not only in their professional conduct and with acquaintances, but also—and most importantly—in the context of the romantic relationship itself. That is where one invests most time and emotional energy. Consequently, that is also where one's true character is tested and revealed. This applies to romantic relationships in general, not just to psychopathic bonds. It stands to reason that if you don't see yourself as equal to your partner, he won't regard you as an equal or give you the respect you deserve.

To be more specific, I'll offer two examples. As we know, psychopaths derive great pleasure from brief sexual liaisons. But those are not likely to spark their passion for two main reasons. The first one is that an unending series of sexual encounters make the psychopath himself jaded to physical and psychological pleasure. Sexual addiction resembles other addictions. Any kind of addiction, which necessarily implies excess and sheer volume (of a substance or number of partners), dulls one's sensibilities, including the sensory and aesthetic ones to which sensual individuals are so highly attuned. Sex addicts become increasingly jaded to both sexual activities and partners. Contrary to the modern connotations of the term "hedonism," the ancient hedonists practiced moderation, to better savor their pleasures. Recall how poignant even a simple kiss can be with a person you desire and respect. I'm not making a moral argument here, but an aesthetic and psychological observation, which is quite obvious. Thousands of sexually explicit images and acts can't replace the stimulation offered by real chemistry with a single person, which you cultivate, focus upon and appreciate. When you disperse your sexual energy and attention on numerous partners, you also reduce the chances of experiencing a more lasting and exciting pleasure in any of those so-called "romantic" relationships. Since sexual addiction is so central to psychopathic behavior, I will explore this subject further in the next section.

The second reason has to do with the partners psychopaths are likely to encounter in promiscuous settings. Because our culture remains "sexist" in the sense that promiscuous women are looked down upon more so than promiscuous men, the kind of women one casually hooks up with on adult websites, clubs and bars are unlikely to establish the balance of power that even psychopathic passion depends upon. Some truisms are true. If you don't treat yourself and your body with respect, chances are, neither will anyone else.

As one would expect, the issue of a balance of power is even more pertinent in long-term relationships. Any wife, girlfriend or lover who accepts glaring double standards in the relationship—relating to important issues such as fidelity, honesty and trust—is not going to hold a psychopath's interest for long. The relationship will turn into a toxic attachment that combines a strong psychological enmeshment, mutual utility and convenience. The dominated partner will oscillate between false hope, intense neediness, despair and resentment at the unfair conditions. The dominant partner will fall back upon a sense of entitlement that quickly turns into boredom. He's also likely to play catch and release games with his partner—essentially, engage in a series of break-ups and reconciliations—depending on whether he's more bored with her and their family life or with his other girlfriends at any given moment.

Ideally, in a loving relationship, passion entails an deeper bond that comes from being both physically and emotionally excited by each other's personalities and having an enduring mutual respect. In a psychopathic bond, however, passion translates into an intense physical attraction, an equally strong attraction to each other's personalities and—in lieu of any genuine empathy and mutual respect—a balance of power. Without these components, even physical pleasures become bland for the psychopath. In turn, life for his partner turns into a series of humiliating concessions that can't bring her happiness or reignite his interest. When you give up your pride and self-esteem for somebody else, you also lose your power and sense of identity. And, needless to say, any man who expects you to violate your self-respect and values for him doesn't really love you and never will.

I suppose this is one way of saying that even psychopathic passion requires more than just physical attraction to last more than a few days. It also depends upon chemistry, balance and equality in the relationship, for as long as these can be sustained. In a psychopathic bond, however, they can't last long. A psychopath needs to dominate, dupe and demean even the women he initially desires and admires. Once these elements are gone, as Picasso eloquently states, the window that used to allow light into the relationship closes for good.

Psychopathy and Sex Addiction

Neil Entwistle pretended to be a perfect husband. After marrying Rachel, he posted their wedding and honeymoon pictures on a website dedicated to their relationship. During the same period of time, however, he pursued other women on adult dating websites. Phil Markoff, the "Craigslist killer," hunted for victims on the Internet. If he is indeed a murderer, his intention wasn't simply to cheat on his unsuspecting and loving fiancée. It was also to kidnap, sexually assault and kill other women. Dating and personals websites are, quite notoriously, the playground for psychopathic sex addicts. The games they play there are limited only by their perverse desires and imaginations. If you fall into their hands, you risk anything from being merely used to being killed.

Such venues make it very easy to dupe several women at the same time, often behind the wife's or girlfriend's back. Psychopathic sex addicts can also broaden the spectrum of their experiences on these websites. They use chat rooms for entertainment. However, those aren't likely to satisfy them. Psychopaths get most aroused by controlling real, live individuals rather than images and words on a screen. They use adult/sex websites for more casual encounters and dating websites to find partners seeking real relationships. On the adult websites, they can be as explicit and perverted as they wish. After all, that's the whole point.

By way of contrast, on the dating websites, they can present themselves as normal, decent men. Sometimes a psychopath will post different kinds of ads on the dating websites themselves to get involved with different types of women. In one ad he might state that he's trapped in a loveless, lackluster marriage and wishes to have a fling with a married woman in similar circumstances. In another, he might imply that he's a principled, single individual seeking a serious relationship. In those cases, obviously, the psychopath won't advertise that his real intention is to use women emotionally and sexually for as long as they give them a rush, deceive them, damage their self-respect and then dump them. And that's only if his victims are lucky: if he's not into acts of physical violence.

As we've seen, psychopaths are masters of manipulation and disguise. They usually write in a very casual, neutral and non-threatening manner. They might say, for instance, that they're looking for someone to click with, or to share life experiences with. They tend to cast their net wide, leaving the description of what they want and of whom they seek open. This enables them to play it by ear and see what prey they can catch and for what purposes they can use each person. Likewise, they usually give out very little information about themselves at first, to leave themselves enough room to maneuver. They mirror each victim's tastes and personality traits during the seduction/idealization phase. They also hook several women at a time, leading each one to believe that she's the only one, or at the very least, the only one that counts. Since they have such a low emotional investment in their partner(s), when they get caught cheating, it's no big deal. Losing their long-term wife or girlfriend offers them yet another good excuse to hunt for new targets. Not that they need any excuses...

When looking for a partner on dating websites, women in particular have to be extra careful. The chances of ending up with a player or, worse yet, caught in the web of a psychopathic predator are high enough to pose a serious risk. The main difference between a regular player and a psychopath is that the psychopath wants to destroy, not simply enjoy, the women he hooks. His true identity remains disguised and his real intentions covert until he's ready to leave his victim after having misled, harmed and used her. Moreover, if any romantic relationship with a psychopath is bound to be shallow and short-lived, it's because so are the emotions behind it (at least on the psychopath's side) and because the circumstances that make it possible quickly change. A psychopath is excited by conquest, control, novelty, unrealistic mutual idealization, deception and constant sexual stimulation, largely based on variety and transgression. These factors can't last long and aren't conducive to a monogamous relationship.

In a popular article, Dr. Gail Saltz responded to a letter from a married man who bragged about his duplicity and manipulation of countless women. He writes:

Dear Dr. Saltz, I can't get enough of women. I have to look at every woman who walks by. I watch porn, I flirt, I keep in touch with past girlfriends, I make new ones, I browse for women online. I get up to 30 e-mails a day from women. Once I have seduced them online, they are dying to meet me and usually sleep with me on the first date. Then I find the simplest flaw and use that against them to break it off. They are devastated. They feel I have used them sexually, and they are right. The kicker is that I am married. My wife is great, beautiful, intelligent and we have a good sex life. I am 41. We have been together for 25 years. I, however, still have a constant rotation of new women. I just can't stop seducing other women and having sex with them. Nor do I want to, because I am having the time of my life.

The only thing that bothers this man turns out to be the inconvenience it poses for his job. He claims that he takes three hours a day to write women. He also calls those "higher on the rotation." He emails women again for three hours at night, after his wife goes to bed. Then he hunts on the Internet for new targets. Needless to say, he doesn't feel guilty towards his wife or any of the other women he misleads. Nor does he believe that he has a problem or sex addiction. His reasoning is quite impressive: consuming what you enjoy can't possibly be an addiction. He boasts:

> I have slept with an untold number of women. I would not call it an addiction because I like it so much and it makes me happy to meet them, seduce them, sleep with them and, yes, even break up with them. This week I will hit my all-time record of sleeping with 13 different women. They are all beautiful, intelligent and successful, and they all think we will live happily ever after. They have no idea that I am sleeping with so many other women, let alone married. I know hurting them emotionally is bad. I just can't stop. To me it is all fair game as long as it is consensual.

This man's definition of addiction is only outdone by his impressive moral reasoning. According to him, lying to, misleading and cheating on women can't possibly be wrong as long as it's "consensual." One wonders how many of those women "consented" to being used and deceived by him. Imagine your boyfriend kissing you, then looking into your eyes and telling you how much he loves you and that you're the only woman for him. It sounds very nice and fills you with feelings of love and devotion. Then imagine him doing exactly the same thing with another woman an hour before meeting with you and with a third woman an hour afterwards. Somehow, his kisses and vows of love no longer seem quite as meaningful. In fact, once you see the whole picture of the psychopath's behavior, all the so-called "positive" aspects of the relationship lose meaning.

Unfortunately, women involved with psychopaths don't usually get to see the whole picture. Like the man in this scenario, their husbands or boyfriends carry on behind their backs and routinely deceive them. Yet, to return to my previous point, wouldn't "consent" imply knowing all the relevant facts to reach an informed decision? Apparently, not according to this self-professed Don Juan. The only thing that matters him is the fact that he enjoys seducing, deceiving and dumping women. He elaborates:

> For me, it is not simply the sex, it is the seduction, and the mental games and pleasure I receive from this. To seduce a women to the point where she really wants to have sex with me is very stimulating to me. It is like I have scored a touchdown in the last few seconds of the Superbowl. I have gotten so good at the aftergame as well that I make only one call or e-mail. You are not what I

was looking for, please don't write me anymore. I never hear from them again. I find myself so manipulative it scares me sometimes. Can you please give me some insight into what is going on?

Dr. Saltz hits the nail on the head when she responds:

I think you are a sex addict and a sociopath. What you describe is sexual addiction. Like any addict, you have a feedback loop that provides you with positive reinforcement every time you make a conquest—hence your comparison to a winning touchdown in the big game... What is so very disturbing is your complete lack of guilt, remorse or empathy for the other parties involved. You know intellectually that this is bad behavior, because you are aware you are betraying your spouse and hurting all the other woman you deal with. Yet it seems that you understand this only on a purely observational level. It sounds as though you have no capacity for emotion. You lack any ability to hold yourself morally accountable for your dishonest and harmful actions. You are easily able to rationalize hurting and mistreating others, whether they are strangers or relatives. In fact, you take pleasure in it. Hence, I also think you are a sociopath, with an utter lack of concern and regard for others.

I'm not sure what or if the psychopath answered her back. I suspect, however, that he couldn't care less about her diagnosis or anyone else's assessment of him, at least in so far as it's negative. Compulsive seducers tend to be extremely narcissistic. They use their conquests as mirrors to reflect back to them an aggrandized image of their own desirability. Steve Becker distinguishes, however, between the motives of narcissists and psychopaths. Of the two, he suggests that psychopaths present a greater danger to others. He explains that all psychopaths are narcissists. But the converse isn't true. Not all narcissists are psychopathic, in the sense of living for the thrill of duping and harming others. In his essay, "Sociopath versus Narcissist," Becker argues that both narcissistic and psychopathic seducers share a tendency to treat others as objects. He states, "Welcome to the world of the narcissist and psychopath. Theirs is a mindset of immediate, demanded gratification, with a view of others as expected—indeed existing—to serve their agendas. Frustrate their agendas, and you can expect repercussions, ranging from the disruptive to ruinous." (*powercommunicating.com*)

Psychopaths and narcissists, however, have different motivations for why they seduce. Narcissists need an endless supply of validation. The more women they seduce, the more they feel reassured in their sex appeal. By way of contrast, a psychopath does it primarily for the pleasure of playing a game. The women he seduces, whether he's involved with them for one evening or several years, represent nothing more than pawns, to be used for his personal pleasure and amusement. Becker elaborates:

The psychopath is less obsessed than the narcissist with validation. Indeed, his inner world seems to lack much of anything to validate: it is barren, with nothing in it that would even be responsive to validation. An emotional cipher, the psychopath's exploitation of others is more predatory than the narcissist's. For the psychopath, who may be paranoid, the world is something like a gigantic hunt, populated by personified-objects to be mined to his advantage (*power-communicating.com*).

Just as they eventually tire of each game piece—be it a long-term girlfriend, casual lover or spouse—psychopaths also tire of each kind of game. Even promiscuous sex gets boring for them. Which is why they often feel the need to engage in acts of physical violence for additional thrills. However, their boredom is only temporarily relieved by each new addiction, transgression and act of depravity. This discussion brings us right back to Cleckley's *The Mask of Sanity*, where the author addresses the psychopath's mind-numbing sense of ennui.

Chapter 6

Psychopaths and Failure

Psychopaths and Boredom/Failure to Follow any Life Plan

Given that psychopaths tend to be bright individuals who have the ability to focus intensely on their goals, one wonders why they're not more successful. Because, as Martha Stout explains in *The Sociopath Next Door*, psychopaths rarely achieve anything in life. They tend to be short-distance runners. They sprint really fast at first, but lose steam rather quickly. They also change direction frequently, which leads them nowhere. Many start out showing a lot of promise as children. However, once they reach adulthood, most have little or nothing to show for it. They pass through life leaving behind a trail of failure: broken relationships, dysfunctional marriages, children they don't care about or take care of (if they have any), an education they don't bother to complete, jobs they don't pursue long enough to thrive in them. Basically, psychopaths end up disappointing the expectations of all those who care about them. If they had any sense of shame, they'd be disappointed in themselves as well. The principal reason for their failure is not their devious and manipulative nature—since, after all, many bad people succeed—but their boredom.

I'm grouping together two of Cleckley's (penultimate) symptoms of psychopathy—boredom and the failure to follow any life plan—since they're closely related. If psychopaths generally fail to bring to fruition their life objectives, it's because they're so easily bored that they give up on them or move on to something new. Cleckley observes, "The psychopath shows a striking inability to follow any sort of life plan consistently, whether it be one regarded as good or evil. He does not maintain an effort toward any far goal at all. This is entirely applicable to the full psychopath. On the contrary, he seems to go out of his way to make a failure of life" (365). Sometimes a psychopath will put on a mask of success. Neil Entwistle appeared to be a successful computer programmer, but in fact he wasn't. Mark Hacking appeared to be a future doctor, but in fact he wasn't. They both appeared to be loving husbands involved in happy marriages, but in fact they weren't. For a psychopath, false image replaces real identity just as lies replace truth. Going to medical school, maintaining a good job, nourishing a relationship, all take hard work, which may not always be exciting. Psychopaths prefer instant gratification and effortless results.

As we've seen, they also crave novelty and transgression. Which is why even when they do succeed in their work, they usually sabotage it. For instance, they may embezzle money from their company or engage in sexual harassment or some other kind of shady behavior at the peak of their careers. "By some incomprehensible and untempting piece of folly or buffoonery," Cleckley explains, the psychopath "eventually cuts short any activity in which he is succeeding, no matter whether it is crime or honest endeavor. At the behest of trivial impulses he repeatedly addresses himself directly to folly. In the more seriously affected examples, it is impossible for wealthy, influential, and devoted relatives to place the psychopath in any position, however ingeniously it may be chosen, where he will no succeed eventually in failing with spectacular and bizarre splendor" (365). This logic also applies to a psychopath's personal relationships. Just when he was about to start a happy new family life in a lovely home with a doting wife and their beautiful baby, Neil Entwistle murdered his family and got himself life in prison. Love, duty and empathy motivate most people to be caring and loyal to their families. Psychopaths, as we know, lack such feelings. A sense of satisfaction for a job well done—as well as financial responsibilities—motivate most people to be honest and dependable in their jobs. Psychopaths don't care about that either. Therefore, Cleckley reasons,

> If, as we maintain, the big rewards of love, of the hard job well done, of faith kept despite sacrifices, do not enter significantly in the equation, it is not difficult to see that the psychopath is likely to be bored. Being bored, he will seek to cut up more than the ordinary person to relieve the tedium of his unrewarding existence... Apparently blocked from fulfillment at deep levels, the psychopath is unnaturally pushed toward some sort of divertissement... What he believes he needs to protest against turns out to be no small group, no particular institution or set of ideologies, but human life itself. In it he seems to find nothing deeply meaningful or persistently stimulating, but only some transient and relatively petty pleasant caprices, a terribly repetitious series of minor frustrations, and ennui (392).

As we've seen, psychopaths attempt to alleviate their boredom by relentlessly pursuing a series of short-lived thrills. They move from one affair to another, one place to another, one job to another, one endeavor to another, one hobby to another and one vacation to another. Life, to them, represents a series of what any normal person would consider senseless activities, most of which are geared to dupe, con and harm others. Martha Stout notes that in viewing life as a game, psychopaths often sabotage themselves as well. They leave behind, like hurricanes, a trail of devastation. In college, psychopaths are much more likely to pursue a lot of women rather than focus on their education. Their marriages are usually short-lived or one-sided because they get bored with their partners. When they last, it's usually due to the gargantuan and self-defeating efforts of their spouses. As we noted, psychopaths aren't willing to work on improving their relationships and are incapable of any genuine self-sacrifice. They prefer to deal with problems in their relationships by assigning blame to their partners and by diverting themselves through manipulating, lying and cheating on them. In addition, psychopaths don't succeed in any positive sense of the term because their goals themselves are destructive.

For instance, a psychopath may "work" for years to persuade his wife to move far away from her family and leave her job and home, all under the pretext that he's going to offer her a better and happier life elsewhere. Then, as soon as she agrees to do so or actually moves to that location with him, he leaves her for another woman or, at any rate, loses interest in her. That's because his goal never was to build a better life together, as it would be for any normal person who wants a solid marriage. Instead, the psychopath wanted to isolate his wife from her family and job in order to get her under his thumb. Once he achieved this goal, he felt like he had "won" the match and moved on to a new challenge. To offer a second example, let's say a psychopath who engages in an extramarital affair asks his girlfriend to divorce her husband for his sake so that they can live happily together. Once she gives in to his pressure and asks her husband for divorce, however, the psychopath suddenly loses interest in her. His mask of "love" falls off and their relationship quickly disintegrates. To a normal person, he's failed because the relationship itself has failed. In the psychopath's mind, however, he "won" because he succeeded in isolating his girlfriend, bending her to his will, conquering her from her husband and perhaps even destroying her marriage. These were his real goals all along.

Whatever constitutes "success" for any normal person—a good, stable and lasting romantic relationship, love for one's children and grandchildren, close friendships and professional achievements—isn't likely to entertain a psychopath for long. Anytime the going gets tough in any aspect of their lives, psychopaths get going. They usually choose the path of least resistance and, above all, of most pleasure at other people's expense.

Psychopaths Wear a Mask of Sanity

We've now reached Cleckley's last symptom of psychopathy. So far we've seen that a psychopath's qualities are fake. A psychopath appears to be rational, other-regarding, generous and decent when he's just the opposite of that. He simulates love, fidelity and devotion when he fundamentally lacks such feelings. He also uses his real qualities—such as his education, looks, wealth, intelligence or whatever other attributes he may have—to lure others so that he can use them for his malicious purposes. In short, Cleckley concludes, the psychopath puts on a mask of sanity to pretend being fully human:

However quick and rational a person may be and however subtle and articulate his teacher, he cannot be taught awareness of significance which he fails to feel. He can learn to use the ordinary words and, if he is very clever, even extraordinarily vivid and eloquent words which signify these matters to other people. He will also learn to reproduce appropriately all the pantomime of feeling; but, as Sherrington said of the decerebrated animal, the feeling itself does not come to pass (375).

When reality is missing all you're left with is illusion. If we can wrap our minds around the fact that, psychologically, psychopaths are as two-dimensional as cardboard cutouts of real human beings, we also come to understand better their outrageous behavior. We see how opening the door and being courteous to his wife didn't preclude Neil Entwistle from cheating on Rachel and killing both her and their baby, when they became inconvenient for him. Unfortunately, as Koehli remarked, people only come to see the real psychopath unmasked only after he's committed a violent crime. Even then, as in the case of Entwistle's behavior in court, they may still misread his reactions as human. In reality, however, almost everything positive a psychopath reveals about himself is a mirage.

This is precisely the message of *Coraline*, the movie with which I'll conclude my exposition of Cleckley's psychological analysis of psychopathy. You may have read the book, which, given its deeper message, is as entertaining for adults as it is for kids. Coraline is a little girl who has an average family life. Like most tweens, she finds many things wrong with her parents. Her mom can't cook and her dad's cooking leaves much to be desired. Both parents are too busy with their jobs to give her the undivided attention she craves, even though they love her. One day, as she's exploring around her new house, Coraline discovers a little secret door in the wall. Once she opens it and steps inside, she inhabits an alternate universe, with seemingly perfect versions of her parents. In this parallel household, everything revolves only around Coraline's needs and appeals to her tastes. Her new mom prepares only the dishes that the little girl prefers. Her new dad plays the piano just for her and plants a beautiful garden that, from above, resembles Coraline's face. The neighbors entertain her with a spectacular circus performance.

Yet, as it turns out, this magical world is completely fake, the opposite of what it initially appears to be. It's the creation of an evil witch who lures people in by preying upon their dissatisfactions with reality and promising them an ideal life. In actuality, she wants to suck the living soul out of them. Why? Because she loves controlling others and playing mind games. Does this sound familiar? Since everything generally ends on a happy note in children's movies, however, Coraline escapes just in time to save herself and her parents. She realizes that the imperfections of a real life with loving individuals are far preferable to any illusory ideals created by those who want to control and destroy you.

As *Coraline* also illustrates, psychopaths don't just lie through omission and commission, to use Susan Forward's terms. More fundamentally, they lie about who they are and what they intend to do with you once you become emotionally attached to them and invested in whatever they originally promised you. Their whole identity is a lie and so are their good intentions. They attract you with the illusion of love and compatibility only to repeatedly stab you in the back. They act as if they support your goals in life, while covertly undermining them or openly discouraging you from their pursuit. They act as if they care about your family and friends, only to isolate you from them. They fake interest in your interests, only to narrow the range of your activities to a complete, and servile, focus on them. When you deal with human nature, just remember the age-old adage so thoroughly elucidated by Cleckley in *The Mask of Sanity* and so entertainingly expressed by *Coraline*: what seems too good to be true usually is.

When the Psychopath's Mask Shatters: The Picture of Dorian Gray

What happens when a psychopath's mask of sanity shatters? The result is rarely as spectacular as it was in the cases of Mark Hacking and Neil Entwistle. Fortunately, most psychopaths don't commit gruesome murders. Even when they do, their crimes are rarely featured so prominently on the national news. But once you unmask a psychopath, the picture you come to see is very ugly and deeply disturbing.

As we've observed, on the outside, a charismatic, garden-variety psychopath appears to be charming, nice, helpful, loving, calm and collected: sometimes uncannily so, and in inappropriate circumstances, but even that may seem, at first, like a blessing. But on the inside, a psychopath is always a repulsive individual: completely self-absorbed, unreliable, unethical and unloving. A psychopath's social and moral boundaries are almost entirely based on his ability to create a positive impression on those around him. Those moral boundaries, which he violates behind people's backs, and his phony yet often compelling displays of emotion function as his disguise. Through them, he gains other people's trust, respect, admiration and sometimes even love. He then uses them for his selfish and destructive purposes.

A psychopath is unmasked in life over and over again. Because his disorder is so deeply engrained in his character, he uses, dupes and manipulates people everywhere he goes. When he gets bored with one location, job or set of acquaintances—or when he's unmasked in that environment—he moves on to the next. There he has the opportunity to make a fresh start: to dupe and use new people; to charm and destroy a new set of unsuspecting victims.

Quite often, psychopaths also depend upon a few individuals with whom they've established their main dominance bonds: their life partners, their parents, their children or their closest friends. After periods of open transgression, they return to them acting repentant, declaring their love or promising to reform. Such individuals often forgive them and accept them back into their lives. This is not just out of love, but also out of denial: accepting reality would be too painful to bear. They're too emotionally invested in the psychopath and in the central role he plays in their lives.

Often, the women who love psychopaths justify staying with their disordered partners because they have a child or children with them. But this can only be a rationalization, given the fact that having no conscience, psychopaths frequently abuse their own children. It's *never* in the best interest of any child to be in close proximity to a psychopathic father. In fact, the psychopath can only be a very bad influence on his child or children and even put their lives in peril. Therefore, when a woman stays with a known psychopath "for the sake of the children," it's usually because he has gutted out her identity to such an extent that she feels empty and lost without him.

This logic applies to all family members who can't let go of the psychopath even after they come to see him for what he is. Cutting ties with him and, by extension, coming to terms with his inherent and unchangeable evil would mean, to them, living the rest of their lives with an open wound. Keep in mind, however, that at least wounds have the chance to heal. Living with a psychopath, on the other hand, is like living with a growing gangrene that exposes the entire family—especially young and impressionable children—to his infectious evil.

Because he finds such receptive and forgiving targets, after bouts of promiscuity, stealing, drug use and other depravities, a psychopath periodically returns to the people closest to him. They're the ones who protect him from the consequences of his wrongdoings and uphold his mask of sanity. But over time, this mask becomes less and less solid. Its fissures begin to show even in the eyes of those who love him most and have his best interest at heart.

The goal of maintaining a false image of human decency to his wife, girlfriends, parents and colleagues (in order to better manipulate them) motivates a psychopath to lead a more or less orderly existence: to come home at regular hours, have a job and behave sociably. When a crisis occurs and this fictional identity unravels, so does the psychopath's life. Having lost his incentive to appear a decent human being because others finally see through his façade, he becomes consumed by his own penchant for meaningless diversion and limitless perversion. Once a psychopath is unmasked, what he always was on the inside begins to manifest itself on the outside as well, in his overt behavior and in the eyes of others. Like the picture of Dorian Gray in Oscar Wilde's famous novella, a psychopath unmasked presents a pathetic spectacle. It reveals a deteriorating individual whose depravity, ugliness and shamelessness take over his life and contaminate the lives of all those who remain close to him.

PART II. THE PROCESS OF PSYCHOPATHIC SEDUCTION

Chapter 1

The Case of Drew Peterson

It may seem strange that I'm choosing to open my discussion of psychopaths as lovers and, more generally, of the process of psychopathic seduction itself, by revisiting the case of Drew Peterson. By now we've seen and heard enough about—and from—Drew Peterson to strongly suspect that he murdered two of his wives. Despite his reputation as a contemporary Bluebeard—or perhaps because of it—he's engaged to be married to yet another much younger woman. Drew Peterson offers a case in point in how psychopaths manage to seduce numerous desirable women in spite of their dubious reputations. Although the evidence suggests that he mistreated his partners, Peterson obviously has great ease in reeling them in to begin with. Psychopaths tend to be very seductive—and extraordinarily dangerous—lovers. I'll rely upon Hoda Kotb's interview with Drew Peterson to use his case as a point of departure for describing how psychopaths use charm, deceit, money, gifts, emotional blackmail and eventually intimidation and abuse to ensnare women into their sometimes fatal nets. I'll also make use of Robert Hare and Paul Babiak's insights elaborated in *Snakes in Suits* to outline the process of psychopathic seduction, from the initial idealization, to the inevitable devaluation, to the (sometimes literal) discarding of the women they target.

Many of us followed on the news the story of Stacy Peterson's disappearance on October 28, 2007. Stacy was Drew's fourth wife. His third wife had died under mysterious circumstances a few years earlier. The more investigators probed into the details of Drew Peterson's personal life—particularly his turbulent relationships with women—the more they suspected that Stacy met with foul play at the hands of her husband. In fact, Drew was recently arrested and charged with the murder of his third wife, Kathy Savio. During the past few years, he welcomed the news coverage. He basked in the public attention, even though it was negative. He also enjoyed playing cat and mouse games with the police. In his interview with Kotb, Drew stated that he believed that Stacy, who was starting to express dissatisfaction with their marriage, had run off with another man. He placed his hand to his chest and declared, "I'm still in love with Stacy and I miss her so."

Yet his subsequent actions belied this statement. His so-called grieving period for the disappearance of his fourth wife was rather brief. Only a short while later, he became involved with and eventually got engaged to another young woman. Although Stacy's family, the police and the media believed that Drew Peterson murdered his wife, he vehemently denied any wrongdoing. In fact, Drew described himself as a victim of the media. "I'm really being portrayed as a monster here. Nobody's defending me. Nobody's stepping up to say, 'No, he's a decent guy. He helps people. He does this. He does that.' So somebody's got to say something." That somebody was none other than Peterson himself, who tooted his own horn. During the interview with Kotb, he not only proclaimed his innocence but also waxed poetic about the honeymoon period with his fourth wife. He claimed that the seduction was mutual: in fact, that Stacy pursued him. "But I— she was beautiful. And it was exciting having a young, beautiful woman interested in me. And I pursued the relationship... Every time I tried to get out of the relationship, she would pursue me. Leaving little roses and notes on my car and stuff. So it was like it was exciting." According to Drew, they met while he was still married to his third wife. In his own words, their affair moved "Pretty quick. Pretty quick."

Tellingly, Drew focused on his wife's difficult upbringing. He told the journalist that Stacy was one of five children, two of whom had died young. Stacy's mother was, as he puts it, "in and out of trouble with the law." He emphasized that as an older, seasoned man with a good career and decent income, he appeared to the young woman like a knight in shinning armor. Stacy hoped that he would rescue her from a troubled life and poverty. Drew also stated that he was attracted not only to Stacy's youthful vulnerability, but also to her kind, trusting and loving nature. Stacy's friend, Pam Bosco, also describes her as "a darling. Bubbly, warm caretaker, you know. Just very, very, very sweet. Very much a family girl. Someone who wanted a family and wanted to be part of a family."

Drew Peterson's buddy, Steve Carcerano, offers an equally glowing description of Peterson himself. "Drew's a nice guy. He's a happy guy. Happy go lucky. A jokester type of guy." Drew's charm, sense of humor and superficially happy disposition impressed not only his buddies, but also Stacy herself. Initially, they also inspired her trust. Members of her family stated that the nice policeman who showered her with attention and promised her security seemed like a dream come true to her. Drew had a good job and a house in the suburbs. By Stacy's standards, he was wealthy. In the beginning of their affair, he didn't hesitate to share some of that wealth with her. Kerry Simmons, Stacy's stepsister, stated in an interview that Drew bought Stacy a car, furnished her apartment and bought her jewelry and other gifts that a young woman would appreciate. "And she's 17 years old so—it looked good to her. It looked good. It felt good. It was good. She was head over heels over him. She really did like him," Simmons added. By all accounts, Drew seemed to reciprocate Stacy's feelings. Steve Carcerano stated, "When he met Stacy, it seemed like he had a glow in his eye. You know, she's young. She's attractive. He seemed very happy with her."

Yet in the eyes of many, this May-December romance fell short of the ideal. First of all, Drew was already married, which, to Stacy's family, wasn't exactly a detail. Not only did he already have a wife, but also she was his third wife. They didn't find this pattern particularly reassuring. He also had four children, including two young sons who lived with him. Stacy's family believed that she was much too young to marry Drew Peterson. Yet Stacy felt too much in love, or too attracted to what she perceived as a golden opportunity, to heed her family's warnings. She stayed with Drew. In 2003, he divorced his third wife—who, incidentally, had also been his mistress—to marry her. Drew admitted during his interview with Kotb that he was very persistent with Stacy. He stated, "I proposed to her on several occasions. Just asked her to marry me. First couple times she said no. Third time she said yes." When they married in a Bolingbrook Field on October 2003, Stacy was only nineteen. She had already given birth to their first child. The second child, a girl, followed shortly thereafter. The couple also lived with Drew's younger sons from his previous marriage.

According to her family and friends, Stacy enjoyed motherhood. Kerry Simmons stated that she "Never saw her upset with those kids. I mean she loved those kids so much. Those were like—they were her life. And I think she really wanted to give those kids the life that she felt she didn't have, or the opportunities that she didn't have growing up. She did birthday parties, marshmallow roasts, and backyard barbeques." Before her disappearance, Stacy told her friend that she was looking forward to her daughter's first trick-or-treating outing. She never got that opportunity, however. Three days before Halloween, Drew reported his wife missing. Stacy's family, friends and volunteer groups formed search parties to look for her. Drew, however, refused to participate. He speculated that his young wife had run away with another man.

But Stacy's family didn't buy his story. They knew enough about their marriage and about Drew's behavior from what Stacy herself had told them to suspect that her husband had murdered her. Stacy had confided in her stepsister, Kerry Simmons, in particular. During her interview, Simmons stated that initially the couple "seemed to be doing well. They looked happy, they acted happy and they looked, you know they looked fine." But after awhile, slowly but surely, their marriage started to deteriorate. Family and friends told investigators that the couple was fighting frequently. Furthermore, whereas in the beginning of their relationship Drew had been very polite and flattering towards Stacy, after they got married he began to criticize her. As a result, they claimed, Stacy became insecure about her appearance. She had several plastic surgeries. Kerry Simmons also alleges that Drew's abusive behavior escalated to physical violence. "He threw her down the stairs. There was an instance where he had knocked her into the TV. I think one time he actually picked her up and threw her across the room. I mean she's small. She's 100 pounds." At that point, Stacy's family and friends urged her to leave her husband. She confessed that she was too afraid of him. She feared that he'd kill her.

Given Drew's behavior, Stacy had sound basis for her fears. During the course of their four-year marriage, he became increasingly controlling, to the point of stalking her. Their neighbor, Sharon Bychowskyi, stated during her interview that Drew "would check in at home like clockwork throughout his shift. So he would go in at five, he would do his roll call, he'd come back. He would eat here in uniform, then he'd go back out on the beat. He'd stay an hour or so. Come back." Stacy's family told investigators that Drew followed his wife around in his car even when she went out to meet her sisters. He grew increasingly jealous and wanted to make sure that Stacy wasn't seeing another man. Not that he had been above that kind of behavior himself. In fact, each time he divorced it was because of infidelity. Each time he married his newest girlfriend. Moreover, in each marriage, Drew had numerous affairs. But this time he had married a much younger and attractive woman. The tables were turned. He was the one worried about Stacy's infidelity rather than the other way around.

In his interview, Peterson put an entirely different spin on the facts presented by Stacy's family, friends and neighbors. He denied that their marriage was going as badly as they maintained. He also denied engaging in any kind of domestic abuse, be it verbal or physical. As for the claim that he fostered Stacy's insecurity through criticism, thus leading her to get several plastic surgeries, he turned that statement around. He maintained that if his wife sought to improve her appearance, it's because he indulged her vanity and catered to her every whim: "Stacy was spoiled. I pampered her. It's—a lot of that's my fault. Stacy wanted it, she got it. High-end jewelry. Name it. She got it." Peterson asserted that it's because he pampered his wife, giving her everything she asked for, that she had so many cosmetic surgeries. "Stacy wanted it she got it. I mean she wanted a boob job, I got her a boob job. She wanted a tummy tuck, she got that. She wanted braces, Lasik surgery, hair removal, anything. Stacy loved male attention."

Stacy's family, neighbors and friends, however, offer a different interpretation of Drew's so-called generosity. They believe his gifts to Stacy functioned as bribes, to persuade her to stay with him despite the abuse. They see Drew as alternating between the carrot and the stick. The physical violence, intimidation, stalking and threats were obviously the stick. The gifts represented the carrot. Sharon Bychowski observed: "Most recently he bought her a motorcycle to ask her if it would buy him three more months with her." Apparently, however, neither the carrot nor the stick worked anymore. Stacy's family and friends told investigators that by the time she disappeared, the young woman was determined to leave her husband. Stacy had told them that she didn't want to end up like Kathy Savio, the previous Mrs. Peterson.

Drew had also wooed Kathy very romantically at first, when she had also been his mistress. Initially, their marriage also appeared to be the very picture of happiness. Steve Carcerano stated, "My first impression of Drew and Kathy was a happy couple when they first moved there. Drew says he met Kathy Savio on a blind date in 1992." Moreover, Kathy was also significantly younger than Drew, in her late twenties, when they became involved. He swept her off her feet, seducing her with his charm, sense of humor, flattery, gifts and promises of a happy future together. Even Kathy's sister, Sue Doman, felt initially impressed with the jovial policeman. In an interview she stated, "He was funny. He talked—you know, he would joke around, got along with everybody. Went out of his way to meet people." Not only was Drew outgoing, but also he came on strong. He acted extremely affectionate with his girlfriend, even in public. Doman recalled that he told her, "'Hey, you know, I love your sister.' Would hug her and kiss her in front of us. Just a very happy person, joking around." Shortly thereafter, Peterson proposed to her. Unlike Stacy, Kathy said "yes" on the first try. The couple married in 1992 and had two sons together. The pattern that would emerge in Drew's fourth marriage was already present in his third. Although he had been highly flattering at first, once they married Drew began criticizing Kathy's looks. The constant put-downs led her to feel increasingly insecure about her physical appearance. He started cheating on her as well, as he had on his previous two wives. As a result, the couple fought. Characteristically, Peterson blamed their altercations solely on his wife's hot temper. He told Koeb, "Our relationship started deteriorating. She was more—she was easy—easily agitated and more demanding. She would snap quickly."

Sue Doman, however, remembers it differently. She asserted in her interview that Peterson was the one abusing his wife, not the other way around. "He would call her names... Horrible, swearing names. 'Bitch,' 'whore.' 'You look like a dog.' She needed to go to Jenny Craig. She needed to do anything to make herself look better because she was looking horrible." She also stated that Peterson beat his wife. Hospital records confirm that Kathy went to the emergency room, following one of their fights. Sue Doman elaborated on this incident: "He took her head and took her hair, she had long hair, and he beat her against a wooden table. He was angry with her... She had a laceration on her head. She became dazed. She had black and blue marks all over her." But even physical violence didn't persuade Kathy to divorce her husband. An anonymous letter that informed her about his affair with Stacy did, however. Although Drew denied the romantic relationship, and even attacked his wife for voicing such suspicions, there was overwhelming evidence that he was being unfaithful to her.

Kathy finally filed for divorce. At the same time, however, she felt apprehensive. She feared that her husband would kill her. She expressed her anxiety to family members and friends. As their relationship deteriorated further while his relationship with Stacy progressed, Drew launched a smear campaign against his ex-wife. Sue Doman described it as follows: "He convinced everyone and anyone that she was absolutely crazy, mentally ill." Shortly after their 2004 divorce, Drew found Kathy dead in the bathtub. Her death was officially declared an "accidental drowning." But following Stacy's disappearance, investigators reopened

Kathy Savio's case. Certain facts didn't fit this description. For one thing, the bathtub had been empty. Also, Kathy had bruises and a gash on her body, which suggested physical assault. In addition, Stacy's own mysterious disappearance established an unsettling pattern.

How does Drew Peterson explain the fact that out of four wives one ended up dead and another missing without a trace? "I guess this is bad luck," he told Hoda Koeb. Not bad enough, apparently, since shortly thereafter he ended up courting another attractive young woman. She agreed to marry him despite the fact that her family, along with the general public, saw a disturbing pattern in Drew Peterson's pursuit and treatment of women.

This pattern, I believe, follows the process of psychopathic seduction, which I'll describe in greater detail next. Fortunately for the rest of society, not all psychopathic seducers end up disposing of their partners quite as literally as Drew Peterson probably did. But they all end up damaging their lives. In the next few chapters, I'll rely upon psychology research by experts to explain how the process of psychopathic seduction tends to unfold as well as how to identify its early warning signs.

Chapter 2

Red Flags: How to Identify a Psychopathic Bond

The most important self-defense against psychopathic seducers consists of recognizing the initial warning signals so that you can escape the relationship early on, hopefully before you're seriously harmed. Dr. Joseph Carver has put together a helpful and instructive list outlining the early symptoms of a dangerous relationship with a psychopath, or as he puts it quite aptly, with "a Loser." As we've already seen in the previous account of Drew Peterson's behavior, not all the signs of psychopathic seduction are obviously negative. But, as we'll see, even the symptoms that seem positive (such as the instant attachment and over-the-top attention, flattery and gifts) are in fact negative. Similarly, Carver notes that the Loser doesn't have to exhibit all of the symptoms listed below to be dangerous. The presence of even three of these symptoms indicates a potentially harmful relationship. Anything above this number points to not just probable, but certain harm. Carver begins by defining "the Loser": "'The Loser' is a type of partner that creates much social, emotional and psychological damage in a relationship... The following list is an attempt to outline the characteristics of 'The Loser' and provide a manner in which women and men can identify potentially damaging relationships before they are themselves severely damaged emotionally or even physically" (*drjoecarver.com*).

1. *The Loser Will Hurt You on Purpose.* "If he or she hits you, twists your arm, pulls your hair, kicks you, shoves you, or breaks your personal property even once, drop them," Carver advises. As we've seen, Drew Peterson escalated the abuse of his partners. He began with criticism, went on to name-calling and moved on to physical violence and (probably) murder. It's very important to get away from a Loser at the slightest hint of violence, including verbal aggression, since abuse usually increases in frequency and severity over time.

2. *Quick Attachment and Expression.* "The Loser," Carver notes, "has very shallow emotions and connections with others. One of the things that might attract you to the Loser is how quickly he or she says 'I Love You' or wants to marry or commit to you. Typically, in less than a few weeks of dating you'll hear that you're the love of their life, they want to be with you forever, and they want to marry you. You'll receive gifts, a variety of promises, and be showered with their attention and nice gestures." Drew Peterson and other dangerous seducers wouldn't get any partners, much less attractive young women, if they showed their true colors from the very beginning. Psychopaths generally pour on the romance. They deluge their targets with flattery, promises and gifts at the beginning of the relationship. No matter how promiscuous they actually are, they focus their energies on their most desirable targets. Yet, Carver cautions, this seemingly positive sign is, in fact, also negative. It signals shallowness of emotions rather than strength of love. He elaborates, "Normal, healthy individuals require a long process to develop a relationship because there is so much at stake... The rapid warm-up is always a sign of shallow emotions which later cause the Loser to detach from you as quickly as they committed." Which is exactly what Drew Peterson (and others like him) did after seducing each of his partners. As easily as he attached to them initially, he later detached from them to pursue his next conquest(s).

3. *Frightening Temper.* Sooner or later the Loser reveals his hot temper. Carver states that Losers often begin with indirect violence—such as demonstratively hitting the wall with their fist or throwing objects—before they start pushing, punching or hitting their partners. The physical outbursts towards inanimate objects function as a form of intimidation. Through such behavior, Losers show their targets that they're capable of doing the same thing to them. Such outbursts also train the partners to become gradually habituated to acts of violence.

4. *Killing Your Self-Confidence.* Losers generally prefer flings and short-term affairs, which provide constant new thrills. They also engage in long-term relationships, however, to gain more lasting control over certain more promising targets. It's nearly impossible to control strong human beings who have clear boundaries and a healthy self-esteem. This is why psychopaths eventually move from the initial over-the-top flattery to scathing criticism. Once they have secured their chosen partners in their grasp, they put them down to erode their self-esteem. Carver states that, for instance, Losers "constantly correct your slight mistakes, making you feel 'on guard', unintelligent, and leaving you with the feeling that you are always doing something wrong... This gradual chipping away at your confidence and self-esteem allows them to later treat you badly—as though you deserved it." According to Tracy's and Stacy's families and friends, after seducing them, Drew undermined both women's self-confidence. His assertion that he pampered Stacy by indulging her obsession with plastic surgery rings false. By way of contrast, her friends' and family's claim that he criticized her to

the point that she felt compelled to make constant "improvements" in her physical appearance sounds much more plausible. Stacy's growing insecurity also placed her under Drew's power to determine how she felt about herself.

5. *Cutting Off Your Support*. In the wild, predators isolate their prey from the rest of the herd to better attack and devour it. That's precisely what psychopaths do to their targets. Losers isolate their partners from their friends, colleagues and families. They may do so through overt criticism and by following them around when they meet with others, as Drew did to Stacy. Sometimes they opt for more subtle manipulation, such as by covertly turning the victim against her own family and friends (and vice versa). As Carver observes, "The Loser feels your friends and family might influence you or offer negative opinions about their behavior... Eventually, rather than face the verbal punishment, interrogation, and abuse, you'll develop the feeling that it's better not to talk to family and friends. You will withdraw from friends and family, prompting them to become upset with you."

6. *The Mean and Sweet Cycle*. As we recall, Drew Peterson bought his wife a motorcycle and expensive jewelry even during the period of time when he was criticizing her, throwing her up against the wall, isolating her from her loved ones, accusing her of infidelity and calling her pejorative names. If they were consistently mean or violent, psychopaths wouldn't be able to hold on to their partners. Which is why, as Dr. Carver observes, "The Loser cycles from mean to sweet and back again. The cycle starts when they are intentionally hurtful and mean. You may be verbally abused, cursed, and threatened over something minor. Suddenly, the next day they become sweet, doing all those little things they did when you started dating." The period of sweetness leads the partners of Losers to cling to the relationship in the misguided hope of finding what psychologist Susan Forward calls "the magic key" that will make the psychopath stay nice to them. That magic key, however, doesn't exist. The psychopath invariably cycles back to his real, nasty self. Over time, the meanness cycle escalates in severity and increases in duration. It's interspersed with increasingly fewer "nice" moments, which trap the victim in her own wishful thinking. As Carver observes, "You hang on, hoping each mean-then-sweet cycle is the last one. The other purpose of the mean cycle is to allow The Loser to say very nasty things about you or those you care about, again chipping away at your self-esteem and self-confidence."

7. *It's Always Your Fault*. As we've seen, psychopaths never accept blame for anything they do wrong. They deny obvious facts and accuse their victims of wrongdoing. Their spurious logic goes something like this: I didn't do it, but even if I did, you deserved it. When he didn't outright deny the domestic abuse, Drew Peterson blamed it on each of his wives for provoking it. According to him, they lied about being hit by him. They also lied about his verbal abuse. They were the

ones who were "on edge" and "disturbed," not him. He never hit them, even if Kathy had to go to the emergency room to recover from his blows. Carver notes, "The Loser never, repeat never, takes personal responsibility for their behavior— it's always the fault of someone else."

8. *Breakup Panic.* Psychopaths need to maintain control of everything in their lives, especially their romantic relationships. When they get bored with one partner or find a replacement, they can leave her on the spur of the moment, heartlessly, often without even bothering to offer an explanation. But they get very angry when the tables are turned and their partners leave them. Drew Peterson didn't mind cheating on his wives and abandoning them for other women. Yet when they wanted to leave him to escape the misery and abuse, he resorted to violence, threats, bribes and, when none of these strategies worked, (probably) murder. As Carver notes, "The Loser panics at the idea of breaking up—unless it's totally their idea—then you're dropped like a hot rock. Abusive boyfriends often break down and cry, they plead, they promise to change, and they offer marriage/trips/gifts when you threaten ending the relationship... Once back in the grasp of the Loser, escape will be three times as difficult the next time."

9. *No Outside Interests.* To further control their victims, psychopaths don't just isolate them from other people. They also narrow the range of their interests and activities, leading their partners to focus exclusively on them. Drew Peterson discouraged Stacy from working outside the home. He gave her money and gifts, not out of any real generosity but to keep her financially and emotionally dependent on him. He also followed his wife around everywhere. He wanted to monitor if she was seeing other men. But his stalking made her feel on edge about any kind of activity or pursuit that was external to their relationship. Carver goes on to state, "If you have an individual activity, they demand that they accompany you, making you feel miserable during the entire activity. The idea behind this is to prevent you from having fun or interests other than those which they totally control."

10. *Paranoid Control.* Notoriously, psychopaths stalk their principal targets. They suspect other people, including their partners, of being as manipulative, deceptive and unscrupulous as themselves. Although they routinely cheat on their spouses, often with countless sexual partners, they tend to be plagued by the fear that their spouses may be cheating on them as well. Which is why, as Carver observes, "The Loser will check up on you and keep track of where you are and who you are with. If you speak to a member of the opposite sex, you receive twenty questions about how you know them. If you don't answer their phone call, you are ask where you were, what were you doing, who you were talking to, etc." Drew Peterson worked as a detective not only in his job on the police force, but also in his dealings with his wife. He followed Stacy around to monitor her.

11. *Public Embarrassment.* Psychopaths tend to put down their partners not only in private, but also publicly, to embarrass and isolate them. They want to build a psychological, if not physical, prison around their primary targets. They do everything possible to undermine their confidence, reduce their sociability, narrow the range of their interests and eliminate all positive human contact from their lives. Consequently, as Carver observes, "In an effort to keep you under control while in public, 'The Loser' will lash out at you, call you names, or say cruel or embarrassing things about you in private or in front of people... If you stay with The Loser too long, you'll soon find yourself politely smiling, saying nothing, and holding on to their arm when in public." As we'll see in the chapter on Pablo Picasso, psychopaths aim to transform strong and proud individuals into their doormats.

12. *It's Never Enough.* Psychopaths don't want to have successful relationships. They want to assert dominance by destroying, at the very least psychologically and emotionally, their partners. In the long run, there's nothing anybody can do to please a psychopath. Apparently, Drew Peterson flattered both his third and his fourth wives when they were still his girlfriends, which is to say, during courtship. But the honeymoon period ended once they decided to marry him. Nothing they did or failed to do henceforth pleased him for long. According to their families and friends, Stacy and Tracy constantly jumped through more and more hoops, while Drew lifted the bar higher and higher. Through this insidious process, a psychopath wears down his partner's self-esteem. Eventually, she feels too insecure to leave the abusive relationship. As Carver puts it, "The Loser convinces you that you are never quite good enough. You don't say 'I love you' enough, you don't stand close enough, you don't do enough for them after all their sacrifices, and your behavior always falls short of what is expected. This is another method of destroying your self-esteem and confidence. After months of this technique, they begin telling you how lucky you are to have them— somebody who tolerates someone so inadequate and worthless as you."

13. *Entitlement.* As we've seen, psychopaths feel entitled to do and have everything and everyone they want. Laws, ethics and other people's feelings don't matter to them. "The Loser has a tremendous sense of entitlement, the attitude that they have a perfectly logical right to do whatever they desire," Carver continues. "If you disobey their desires or demands, or violate one of their rules, they feel they are entitled to punish you in any manner they see fit." In the case of Drew Peterson, even thought crime, or the intention to leave him, was punishable with (probably) murder. His interviews show that he felt entitled to mistreat each of his wives as he pleased. However, he believed that they didn't have the right to object to his mistreatment or to leave him as a result of it.

14. *Your Friends and Family Dislike Him.* Psychopaths tend to be pleasant and charming, at least superficially, at the beginning of a relationship. But once

they have their partner firmly in their clutches, they proceed to isolate her from her support system. In so doing, they alienate her family and friends. Carver notes, "As the relationship continues, your friends and family will see what the Loser is doing to you. They will notice a change in your personality or your withdrawal. They will protest. The Loser will tell you they are jealous of the 'special love' you have and then use their protest and opinion as further evidence that they are against you—not him." Drew Peterson stalked his wife even when she was visiting with her sisters. Initially, at least some of Stacy's family members and friends liked Drew and considered him a good match for her. But as he began to isolate and abuse her, they became unanimous in their dislike of him. In the end, they all saw the relationship as seriously damaging for Stacy.

15. *Bad Stories*. They say that the best indicator of future behavior is past behavior. There may be exceptions to this general principle. Fortunately, some people can improve their character and behavior with genuine and consistent effort. A psychopath can never be one of those exceptions, however. Generally speaking, if a man cheated on every wife he's ever been with, it's highly probable that he'll cheat on the next one as well. Most likely, the problem isn't the woman or women he was with, but his underlying lack of character. Similarly, if he abused his previous partners, he's very likely to abuse the next ones as well. Stacy knew enough about how Drew treated his previous wife to see that he was a philanderer and potentially dangerous. But the intensity and perseverance with which he pursued her blinded her from seeing the same warning signals in their relationship. In addition, since psychopaths don't find anything wrong with their harmful behavior, they're likely to boast about it. This also sends out some glaring warning signals. As Carver states, "The Loser tells stories of violence, aggression, being insensitive to others, rejecting others, etc... They brag about their temper and outbursts because they don't see anything wrong with violence and actually take pride in the 'I don't take nothing from nobody' attitude. . . Listen to these stories—they tell you how you will eventually be treated and what's coming your way."

16. *The Waitress Test*. Just as how people behaved in the past tells a lot about how they'll behave in the future, so how they treat others functions as a pretty good indicator of how you'll eventually be treated. A person who's uncaring and unethical towards others will most likely also be that way to you when you no longer serve his interests. Carver calls this "the waitress test." In his estimation, how a Loser treats people who aren't immediately useful to him reveals how he'll treat you once your use has expired. "It's been said that when dating, the way an individual treats a waitress or other neutral person of the opposite sex is the way they will treat you in six months. During the 'honeymoon phase' of a relationship, you will be treated like a king or queen. However, during that time the Loser has not forgotten how he or she basically feels about the opposite sex. Waitresses, clerks, or other neutral individuals will be treated badly. If they are

cheap—you'll never receive anything once the honeymoon is over. If they whine, complain, criticize, and torment—that's how they'll treat you in six months." Psychopaths lack consistency in their "good" behavior because for them "goodness" is only a façade. The manner in which they treat someone relates strictly to that person's perceived use value. When people are useful to them they treat them (superficially) well. When they aren't, they ignore or mistreat them. By way of contrast, genuinely nice people treat others well regardless of their perceived utility. Carver advises, "If you find yourself dating a man who treats you like a queen and other females like dirt—hit the road." Pretty soon, you'll be the dirt he walks on, on his way to conquering other temporary queens.

17. *The Reputation.* Psychopaths tend to have polarized reputations. Their victims often describe them, in retrospect, as Janus figures (since they're two-faced) or as Jekyll and Hyde personalities (since they switch from nice to mean). We've seen that for a psychopath the Jekyll side is a mask he constructs to attract, fool and use others. The Hyde side represents his true identity, which becomes increasingly dominant over time. To his buddies, Drew Peterson appeared to be an easy-going, nice guy. But that's because they only saw one side of him, the jovial facet he wanted them to see. To his wives and their families—which is to say, to anyone who had extensive intimate contact with him—Drew exposed another, much more menacing side of his personality. Any sign of independence from his partners meant escaping his control: something he couldn't tolerate and which he punished through abuse and (probably) murder. Carver states, "As mentioned, mentally healthy individuals are consistent in their personality and their behavior. The Loser may have two distinct reputations—a group of individuals who will give you glowing reports and a group that will warn you that they are serious trouble." In addition to paying attention to what others say, trust your own intuition and powers of observation. Pay close attention to how your partner treats you over time and in different circumstances. Be particularly attuned to how he responds when you express different needs or opinions. Psychopaths can't tolerate any real assertion of independence from others. They also can't treat those they're intimately involved with well for long. Although some psychopaths may consistently maintain the mask of charm in superficial interactions with their buddies, colleagues and acquaintances, their real controlling, selfish and aggressive natures tend to show through in extended intimate contact.

18. *Walking on Eggshells.* During the course of their marriages to Drew Peterson, at least two of his wives reported losing their self-confidence as a result of his emotional and physical abuse. While they both entered the relationship with Drew feeling desirable, in love and valued, by the end they were overpowered and intimidated by him. When involved with a psychopath, over time, his partner finds herself walking on eggshells. She fears that anything she does or says might trigger his emotional detachment, hostility or abuse. Carver observes that, "Instead of experiencing the warmth and comfort of love, you will be constantly on

edge, tense when talking to others (they might say something that you'll have to explain later), and fearful that you'll see someone you'll have to greet in public."

19. *Discounted Feelings/Opinions.* For psychopaths, their fundamental callousness and capacity for evil stems from their absolute selfishness and inability to respect other individuals, as fellow human beings with independent needs and desires. That's why those involved with a psychopath, following the initial stage when he praises everything they do and say, come to realize that their feelings, needs and opinions don't matter to him. The Loser's narcissism is, as Hervey Cleckley's study of psychopathy concluded, absolute. Carver elaborates, "The Loser is so self-involved and self-worshiping that the feelings and opinions of others are considered worthless... The Loser is extremely hostile toward criticism and often reacts with anger or rage when their behavior is questioned." Narcissists and psychopaths flatter others only to use and manipulate them. They lack genuine consideration for others.

20. *They Make You Crazy.* According to her friends, Kathy Savio felt overcome by rage, jealousy and anger when Drew cheated on her with Stacy. While her emotional response was perfectly understandable under the circumstances, Drew depicted Kathy to others as "insane" to justify his mistreatment of her. In some ways, however, this statement isn't far removed from the truth. Sometimes, psychopaths quite literally drive their partners crazy. They lie to them to the point where they start doubting their knowledge of reality. They discourage and belittle them to the point where they lose their self-confidence and become reclusive. They mistreat them to the point where they're overcome with rage. As Carver goes on to explain, "The Loser operates in such a damaging way that you find yourself doing 'crazy' things in self-defense... You become paranoid as well—being careful what you wear and say... While we think we are 'going crazy'—it's important to remember that there is no such thing as 'normal behavior' in a combat situation. Rest assured that your behavior will return to normal if you detach from the Loser before permanent psychological damage is done." When involved with a psychopath, you may, unlike Drew Peterson's misfortunate wives, escape alive. But unless you end the relationship in its earliest stages, you're not likely to escape unharmed.

What do these warning signs indicate? They show that psychopathic seducers can fake decency and love convincingly in the beginning of a relationship. That's how they manage to attract so many potential partners. But they can't sustain their mask of sanity over time in intimate contact, since it's fake and instrumental. If you remain vigilant, you'll be able to see red flags early on in the relationship with a psychopath despite his veneer of charm and extravagant romantic words and gestures. As psychotherapist Steve Becker indicates on his website, *powercommunicating.com*, most of his clients recognized the warning signals in their relationships with exploitative partners. They just minimized those red flags or downright ignored them. They preferred to focus on their romantic fantasies rather than face an unpleasant reality. According to Becker, the most difficult challenge isn't *noticing* the red flags, but actually *heeding* them. He states:

> I find that many of my clients were in fact cognizant of odd, disconcerting be-haviors/attitudes that their exploitative partners were reckless enough to reveal (or incapable of concealing). They may have even felt troubled by them. But in their intense need to want the relationship, and the partner, to be the elusive fit they so hungrily sought, they found ways to suppress their uneasiness: to ignore and/or minimize the significance of these signals; and rationalize the alarms their instincts triggered (*powercommunicating.com*).

If you encounter a man who is aroused primarily by the circumstances sur-rounding your relationship—especially the perverse and forbidden ones—rather than by you, yourself, run. If you encounter a man who does a bait and switch to gain your trust only to violate his promises or raise the bar higher and higher, run. If you encounter a man who behaves in a despicable manner towards any other woman, no matter what he says about her, examine his behavior carefully since that's how he'll eventually treat you and, needless to say, run.

Truth is not a convenient fiction. Similarly, love is not a power game for anyone capable of this emotion. It's the deepest and most significant bond human beings form with one another and the foundation of our lives. If you encounter a man who gives any signs that he regards love as a game and you as a "prize" to be won, fold your cards and quickly leave the table. Or, better yet, refuse to en-gage with him at all. Any intimate relationship with a psychopath is a gamble where you risk losing everything and from which you have nothing to gain.

Chapter 3

The Process of Psychopathic Seduction:
Idealize, Devalue and Discard

Having relied upon Joseph Carver's insights to describe the red flags in a relationship with a psychopath, now I'll rely upon Paul Babiak and Robert Hare's work, as well as upon *lovefraud.com* testimonials and my own personal experience, to describe in greater detail the process of psychopathic seduction itself: from its seemingly ideal beginning to its invariably bitter end. In their book on psychopaths in the workplace, entitled *Snakes in Suits*, Babiak and Hare state that the psychopathic bond follows certain predictable stages: idealize, devalue and discard. This process may take several years or only a few hours. It all depends on what the psychopath wants from you and whether or not you present a challenge to him. If the psychopath wants the semblance of respectability—a screen behind which he can hide his perverse nature and appear harmless and normal—he may establish a long-term partnership with you or even marry you. If all he wants is to have some fun, it will be over within a couple of hours. If he wants the stimulation and diversion of an affair, he may stay with you for as long as you excite him. Despite the differences in timeline, what remains constant is this: eventually, sooner or later, you'll be discarded (or be led by the psychopath's bad behavior to discard him) as soon as you no longer serve his needs.

Babiak and Hare explain that although psychopaths are highly manipulative, the process of idealize, devalue and discard is a natural outgrowth of their personalities. In other words, it's not necessarily calculated at every moment in the relationship. Whether consciously or not, psychopaths assess and drain the use-value out of their romantic partners (*Snakes in Suits*, 42). During the assessment phase, psychopaths interact closely with their targets to see what makes them tick. They ask probing questions, to discover their unfulfilled desires and weaknesses. They also commonly lure their targets with promises to offer them whatever's been missing from their lives. If you're recovering from a recent divorce, they offer you friendship and an exciting new romantic relationship. If you've suffered a death in the family, they act like sympathetic friends. If you're going through financial difficulties, they lend you money to appear generous. As we've seen, Drew Peterson honed in on the fact that Stacy had a difficult childhood and was looking for a stable, reassuring father figure. In the beginning, he conveniently fit that paternal role for her. He also lured her with lavish gifts, knowing that they'd tempt her.

During the manipulation phase, Babiak and Hare go on to explain, psychopaths construct the "psychopathic fiction." They pour on the charm to hook their victims emotionally and gain their trust. They present themselves as kind-hearted individuals. Of course, in order to do so, psychopaths resort to outrageous lies since, in reality, they're just the opposite. In romantic relationships in particular, they depict themselves as your soul mate. While seeming your complement, they also present themselves as your mirror image. They claim to share your interests and sensibilities. Babiak and Hare observe: "This psychological bond capitalizes on your inner personality, holding out the promise of greater depth and possibly intimacy, and offering a relationship that is special, unique, equal—forever" (*Snakes in Suits*, 78).

Because psychopaths are great manipulators and convincing liars, as we've seen, many of their victims don't heed the warning signals. During the early phases of a romantic relationship, people in general tend to be too blinded by the euphoria of falling in love to focus on noticing red flags. Also, during this period, the psychopaths themselves are on their best behavior. Yet, generally speaking, they get bored too easily to be able to maintain their mask of sanity consistently for very long. The honeymoon phase of the relationship usually lasts until the psychopath intuitively senses that he's got you on the hook or until he's gotten bored by the relationship and moved on to other targets. He shows his true colors when he's got no incentive left to pretend anymore. As Babiak and Hare note, "Once psychopaths have drained all the value from a victim—that is, when the victim is no longer useful—they abandon the victim and move on to someone else" (*Snakes in Suits*, 53).

This raises the question of why a psychopath idealizes his targets in the first place. Why do psychopaths invest so much effort, time and energy into giving the illusion of intimacy and meaning in a relationship, given that they never really bond with other human beings in the first place? One obvious answer would be that they do it for the sport of it. They enjoy both the chase and the kill; the seduction and the betrayal. They relish creating the illusion that they're something they're not. They also enjoy observing how they dupe others into believing this fiction. Moreover, whenever a psychopath expresses admiration, flattery or enthusiasm for someone, it's always because he wants something from that person. I think, however, that this explanation is somewhat reductive. Many psychopaths experience powerful obsessions that resemble intense passions. Besides, this explanation doesn't distinguish conmen, who fake their credentials and interest in a person, from psychopaths "in love," who are pursuing their targets for what initially seems even to them as "romantic" reasons.

A broader explanation, which would include both kinds of psychopaths, might look something like this: as research confirms, all psychopaths suffer from a shallowness of emotion that makes their bonding ephemeral and superficial, at best. When they want something—or someone—they pursue that goal with all their might. They concentrate all of their energies upon it. When that goal is your money or a job or something outside of yourself, their pursuit may appear somewhat fake. You're a means to an end. You were never idealized for yourself, but for something else. But when their goal is actually you—seducing you or even marrying you—then their pursuit feels like an idealization. Temporarily, you represent the object of their desire, the answer to their needs, the love of their life and the key to their happiness. But this feeling of euphoria doesn't last long because it's empty to the core. As we've observed, once psychopaths feel they have you in their grasp—once your identity, hopes and expectations are pinned on them—they get bored with you and move on to new targets. We've seen in Cleckley's study that the same logic applies to their other goals as well. Psychopaths tire rather quickly of their jobs, their geographic location, their hobbies and their educational endeavors. But it hurts so much more, and it feels so much more personal, when what they get tired of is you, yourself.

Their loss of interest appears as a devaluation. From the center of their life, you suddenly become just an obstacle to their next pursuit. Since psychopaths are skilled at "dosing," or giving you just enough validation and attention to keep you on the hook, you may not immediately notice the devaluation. It's as if the psychopath intuitively knows when to be charming again (in order not to lose you) and when to push your boundaries, further and lower. Your devaluation occurs gradually yet steadily. One day you finally notice it and wonder how you have allowed yourself to sink so low. Occasionally, he throws you a bone—takes you out, plans a romantic evening, says kind and loving things—to lead you to dismiss your healthy intuitions that you're being mistreated. If the psychopath allows himself to treat you worse and worse it's not only because you're much less exciting in his eyes. It's also because he's conditioned you to think less highly of yourself and to accept his bad behavior. Because you want to hold on to the fantasy of the ideal relationship he cultivated, you go into denial. You accept his implausible excuses. You put up with your growing fears and doubts. You rationalize his inexplicable absences, his increasingly frequent emotional withdrawals, his curt and icy replies, his petty and mean-spirited ways of "punishing" you for asserting your needs or for not bending to his will.

But at some point, when he sinks to a new low or when you catch him in yet another lie, you slip out of the willful denial which has been your way of adjusting to the toxic relationship. Because he has lowered your self-esteem, you ask yourself why this has happened and what you did wrong. If he cheated on you, you blame the other woman or women involved. The psychopath encourages you to pursue such false leads. In fact, he encourages anything that deflects attention from his responsibility in whatever goes wrong with your relationship. He leads you to blame yourself. He also inculpates the other women. He implies that you were not good enough for him. He claims that the other women tempted or pursued him. But that's only a diversionary tactic. You have flaws and you made mistakes, but at least you were honest and real. The other women involved may have been decent human beings, the scum of the Earth or anything in between. Think about it. Does it really matter who and what they were? You are not involved with the other women. They are not your life partners, your spouses, your lovers or your friends. What matters to you most is how your own partner behaves. He is primarily accountable for his actions.

Also, keep in mind that psychopaths twist the truth to fit their momentary goals and to play mind games. When you actually pay attention to what they say instead of being impressed by how sincere they may appear, their narratives often sound inconsistent and implausible.

What they say about other women, both past and present, is most likely a distortion too. Psychopaths commonly project their own flaws unto others. If they tell you they were seduced, it was most likely the other way around. If they tell you that their previous girlfriends mistreated them, cheated on them, got bored with them, abandoned them, listen carefully, since that's probably what they did to those women. Their lies serve a dual function. They help establish credibility with you as well as giving them the extra thrill of deceiving you yet again.

So why were you discarded? you may wonder. You were devalued and discarded because you were never really valued for yourself. As we've seen, for psychopaths relationships are temporary deals, or rather, scams. Analogously, for them, other human beings represent objects of diversion and control. The most flattering and pleasant phase of their control, the only one that feels euphoric and magical, is the seduction/idealization phase. That's when they pour on the charm and do everything they possibly can to convince you that you are the only one for them and that they're perfect for you. It's very easy to mistake this phase for true love or passion. However, as the case of Drew Peterson illustrated, what inevitably follows in any intimate relationship with a psychopath is neither pleasant nor flattering. Once they get bored with you because the spell of the initial conquest has worn off, the way they maintain control of you is through deception, isolation, abuse, gaslighting and undermining your self-confidence.

That's when you realize that the devaluation phase has set in. You do whatever you can to regain privileged status. You try to recapture the excitement and sweetness of the idealization phase. You want to reclaim your rightful throne as the queen you thought you were in his eyes. But that's an impossible goal, an ever-receding horizon. Every women's shelter tells victims of domestic violence that abuse usually gets worse, not better, over time. For abusers, power is addictive. It works like a drug. The dosage needs to be constantly increased to achieve the same effect. Control over others, especially sexual control, gives psychopaths pleasure and meaning in life. To get the same rush from controlling you, over time, they need to tighten the screws. Increase the domination. Increase the manipulation. Isolate you further from those who care about you. Undermine your confidence and boundaries more, so that you're left weaker and less prepared to stand up for yourself. The more you struggle to meet a psychopath's demands, the more he'll ask of you. Until you have nothing left to give. Because you have pushed your moral boundaries as low as they can go. You have alienated your family and friends, at the psychopath's subtle manipulation or overt urging. You have done everything you could to satisfy him. Yet, after the initial idealization phase, nothing you did was ever good enough for him.

It turns out that he's completely forgotten about the qualities he once saw in you. If and when he talks about you to others, it's as if he were ashamed of you. That's not only because he lost interest in you. It's also the instinctive yet strategic move of a predator. If your family, his family, your mutual friends have all lost respect for you—if you're alone with him in the world—he can control you so much easier than if you have external sources of validation and emotional support. Psychopaths construct an "us versus them" worldview. They initially depict your relationship as privileged and better than the ordinary love bonds normal people form. This is of course always a fiction.

In fact, the opposite holds true. An intimate relationship with a psychopath is far inferior to any normal human relationship, where both people care about each other. Such a relationship is necessarily one-sided and distorted. It's a sham on both sides. Being a consummate narcissist, he loves no one but himself and cares about nothing but his own selfish desires. If and when he does something nice, it's always instrumental: a means to his ends or to bolster his artificial good image. Dr. Jekyll is, in fact, always Mr. Hyde on the inside. And even though you may be capable of love, you're not in love with the real him—the cheater, the liar, the manipulator, the player, the hollow, heartless being that he is—but with the charming illusion he created, which you initially believed but which becomes increasingly implausible over time. From beginning to end, all this phony relationship can offer you is a toxic combination of fake love and real abuse. He constructs the psychopathic bond through deception and manipulation. You maintain it through self-sacrifice and denial.

But pretty soon, when you find yourself alone with the psychopath, you see it's not us versus them, your couple above or against everyone else. It's him versus you. And he will act like your worst enemy, which is what he really is, not as the best friend and adoring partner he claimed to be. If he criticizes you to others—or, more subtly, fosters antagonisms between you and family members and friends—it's to further wear you down and undermine your social bonds. Once he tires of you, he induces others to see you in the same way that he does: as someone not worthy of him; as someone to use, demean and discard. Before you were beautiful and no woman could compare to you. Now you're at best plain in his eyes. Before you were cultured and intelligent. Now you're the dupe who got played by him. Before you were dignified and confident. Now you're isolated and abject.

Right at the point when you feel that you should be rewarded for your sacrifice of your values, needs, desires and human bonds—all for him—the psychopath discards you. He's had enough. He's gotten everything he wanted out of you. Bent you out of shape. Taken away, demand by demand, concession by concession, your dignity and happiness. As it turns out, the reward you get for all your devotion and efforts is being nearly destroyed by him. Ignoring your own needs and fulfilling only his—or fulfilling yours to gain his approval—has transformed you into a mere shadow of the lively, confident human being you once were.

He uses your weaknesses against you. He also turns your qualities into faults. If you are faithful, he sees your fidelity as a weakness: a sign that you weren't desirable enough to cheat. Nobody else really wanted you. If you are virtuous, he exploits your honesty while he lies and cheats on you. If you are passionate, he uses your sensuality to seduce you, to entrap you through your own desires, emotions, hopes and dreams. If you are reserved and modest, he describes you as asocial and cold-blooded. If you are confident and outgoing, he views you as flirtatious and untrustworthy. If you are hard-working, unless he depends on your income, he depicts you as a workhorse exploited by your boss. If you are artistic and cultured, he undermines your merit. He makes you feel like everything you create is worthless and cannot possibly interest others. You're lucky that it ever interested him. After the idealization phase is over, there's no way to please a psychopath. Heads you lose, tails he wins. But remember that his criticisms are even less true than his initial exaggerated flattery. When all is said and done, the only truth that remains is that the whole relationship was a fraud.

The psychopathic bond is programmatic. It's astonishingly elegant and simple given the complexity of human behavior. It involves three steps: idealize, devalue and discard. Each step makes sense once you grasp the psychological profile of a psychopath, of an (in)human being who lives for the pleasure of controlling and harming others. 1) Idealize: not you, but whatever he wanted from you and only for however long he wanted it. 2) Devalue: once he has you in his clutches, the boredom sets in and he loses interest. 3) Discard: after he's gotten everything he wanted from you and has probably secured other targets.

For you, this process is excruciatingly personal. It may have cost you your time, your heart, your friends, your family, your self-esteem or your finances. You may have put everything you had and given everything you could to that relationship. It may have become your entire life. For the psychopath, however, the whole process isn't really personal. He could have done the same thing to just about anyone who allowed him into her intimate life. He will do it again and again to everyone he seduces. It's not about you. It's not about the other woman or women who were set against you to compete for him, to validate his ego, to give him pleasure, to meet his fickle needs. He wasn't with them because they're superior to you. He was with them for the same reason that he was with you. To use them, perhaps for different purposes than he used you, but with the same devastating effect. Idealize, devalue and discard. Rinse and repeat. This process was, is and will always be only about the psychopath for as long as you stay with him.

Chapter 4

Artistic Psychopaths: The Case of Picasso

For those who admire his art, Pablo Picasso exemplifies the greatest and most innovative artist of the twentieth century. But even those who don't still view him as one of the shrewdest businessman in the art world. He had the resourcefulness to reinvent himself in new styles and to market each and every one as "cutting-edge" to art dealers, critics and the public. From the beginning of his career to the end of his life, Picasso never became passé. His personal life, however, is an entirely different story. Whether or not you like his art, there's a general consensus that Picasso was a misogynist who mistreated his partners. Arianna Huffington published a popular book on this subject—*Picasso: Creator and Destroyer*—that was made into the movie *Surviving Picasso*, staring Anthony Hopkins. Dora Maar, Picasso's most creative and eccentric girlfriend, accused the artist of being incapable of loving anyone but himself. Although she said this out of jealousy once Picasso had already left her for his next girlfriend, the evidence suggests that her statement was correct.

There are dozens of biographies on Picasso, but his psychological profile comes to life with nuance, insight and sensibility in the autobiographical writings of his long-term partner, Françoise Gilot. In *Life with Picasso*, Gilot illustrates that there's no contradiction whatsoever between being a great and innovative artist, or an "artistic genius" if you prefer, and being an irredeemably bad and selfish human being, or a psychopath. Although Gilot doesn't use this clinical label, I believe that this is the psychological profile that emerges from her personal accounts of Picasso's personality traits and behavior. She also offers unique insight into the artist's immense creativity and resourcefulness, which doesn't in any way contradict the image she sketches of his emotional poverty.

My point here is not to clinically diagnose Picasso, since I'm not qualified to do so. Nevertheless, I'd like to offer from an informed lay perspective a vivid and high profile example of the manifestations of psychopathic traits in someone with extraordinary artistic sensibilities and intellectual acumen. I will rely upon Gilot's autobiography to dispel the popular misconception that being gifted, cultured and sensitive implies that you can't be evil. Of course you can. As Hannah Arendt illustrates in her work on the banality of evil, during the Holocaust tens of thousands of intelligent, educated and seemingly "normal" men and women participated in Nazi crimes against humanity. Most of them probably had a conscience and felt some remorse. Some, like Eichmann, did it of their own volition, for their benefit and completely remorselessly. That smaller subset of cruel men and women do not prove, pace Arendt, the banality of evil. They were *not* ordinary human beings who fell prey to extreme external pressures during extraordinary times. Instead, those shameless individuals prove the banality of psychopathy: namely, of being born with the psychological drive to use and destroy others.

The German people, like the Russian people, have no particular character traits that made them more likely to commit genocide. Unfortunately, psychopathic rulers rose to power in their midst. They encouraged other similarly disordered individuals, as well as the rest of society, to behave ruthlessly towards fellow human beings. Such evil individuals have existed throughout human history, everywhere around the world. They become particularly dangerous and influential in certain social circumstances, such as during war, civil war or in totalitarian societies, when crimes against humanity are condoned and even encouraged.

Analogously, I'm surprised to hear people interviewed on the news about a violent crime remark that "Such horrible things don't happen in our neighborhood." Why would they not? Disordered, conscienceless individuals exist in every kind of neighborhood. Until they're caught and sentenced for their crimes, they're free to live wherever they want. I also sometimes hear people express great surprise when the vicious murderers turn out to be educated men and women: teachers, professors, doctors, scientists, lawyers, musicians, writers or artists.

Psychologically speaking, there's no contradiction whatsoever between being naturally gifted in all sorts of ways and being a psychopath. Psychopathy constitutes an *emotional* deficiency that leads to lack of empathy for others. It's not an intellectual or artistic deficiency. If anything, as Robert Hare observes in *Without Conscience*, the opposite logic applies. The more charming, educated, refined and talented a psychopath is, the better his camouflage. Such an individual is more likely to get away with his misdeeds because others will give him the benefit of the doubt or excuse his bad behavior. If you look at evil people throughout history, you'll see that they cut through every culture, society, level of education, occupation and class. Most psychopaths, as we've seen, don't achieve great success because they tire quickly of their endeavors. But some of them become rich, powerful or famous. A few can even be "artistic geniuses" like Picasso.

In *Life with Picasso*, Gilot describes Picasso in terms of nearly every key symptom of psychopathy: his total absence of empathy and love; his lack of remorse and facile rationalizations for hurting others; a lust for seduction as a form of exercising power over women; duplicity and manipulation as a way of life; the pattern of idealize, devalue and discard in every romantic relationship he's had; the underlying desire for control; an unshakable narcissism and the drive to do evil by damaging the lives of the women who became his partners. I'll now describe Picasso's pathological behavior in greater detail by relying upon Gilot's autobiographical account, coupled with relevant psychological explanations of how psychopaths and narcissistic controllers behave.

1. *Seduction as a Power Game.* Gilot describes how from the very beginning of their relationship, Picasso wanted to be the one in charge. He regarded seduction as a power game, in which he reserved the right to make all the key moves. When she refused to be a passive pawn and didn't play the predictable role of a "respectable" woman who resists his advances, Picasso was taken aback. She states:

> When he dropped the last piece back unto the table he turned abruptly and kissed me, full on the mouth. He looked at me in surprise. "You don't mind?" I said no—should I? He seemed shocked. "That's disgusting," he said. "At least you could have pushed me away. Otherwise I might get the idea that I could do anything I wanted to." I smiled and told him to go ahead... He looked at me cautiously, then asked: "Are you in love with me?" I said I couldn't guarantee that, but at least I liked him and felt very much at ease with him and I saw no reason for setting up in advance any limit to our relationship. Again he said "That's disgusting. How do you expect me to seduce anyone under conditions like that? If you're not going to resist—well, then it's out of the question. I'll have to think it over" (*Life with Picasso*, 24).

It's not surprising that Picasso subscribes to traditional gender roles and expects a certain behavior from a "proper" middleclass woman. After all, many men of his generation did as well. More striking is the manner in which he views courtship as a game of conquest with no real adversary. He expects his partner to play into his hand as a passive pawn. Of course, since psychopaths also enjoy a challenge, Gilot's failure to conform to gender stereotypes also initially intrigued Picasso. In fact, it led him to pursue their relationship further.

2. *The Aesthetization of Erotic Experience as a Substitute for Emotional Bonding.* Instead of bonding with their partners, psychopaths conduct sensory experiments. They explore how each woman responds to their touch. They sense her taste and feel the shapes of her various body parts. Of course, erotic experience commonly includes a sensual component. For psychopaths, however, the aesthetic and sensory appeal of sexual pleasure completely replaces establishing an emotional connection with their partners rather than supplementing it. Sensual and sexual experimentation is part of a psychopath's general tendency to view others solely as objects to be used for his gratification. Gilot describes her first intimate experience with Picasso as follows: "He took his hands away. Not suddenly, but carefully, as though my breasts were two peaches whose form and color had attracted him; he had picked them up, satisfied himself that they were ripe but then realized that it wasn't yet time for lunch" (26). To Picasso, his new

girlfriend represents a beautiful, pleasurable aesthetic object meant to appeal to his senses and satisfy his desires when and where he wants her.

3. *The Assessment/Mirroring Phase.* Robert Hare and Paul Babiak describe in *Snakes in Suits* how during the "assessment phase" of the relationship a psychopath will convey to his target four main messages: 1) I like you; 2) I share your interests; 3) I'm like you, and 4) I'm the perfect partner or soul mate for you. This process constitutes the "mirroring phase" of the psychopathic bond. Granted, most romantic relationships entail some aspects of mirroring. After all, that's how couples discover their points in common. But with a psychopath the reflection tends to be instant and total. It's a simulated bonding that's way too fast, too soon and too good to be true.

This happens before any real emotional connection can take place. It occurs before the partners have gotten to know each other well, over time and in different circumstances. Instant bonding, as we've seen in Carver's analysis, is a symptom of shallowness of emotions rather than of miraculous compatibility. It means that the psychopath will detach from you and latch on to another target as easily as he initially attached to you. Yet through their conversational glibness and innate charm, as well as through their extraordinary capacity to identify and reflect your deepest desires, psychopaths can initially make you feel like they're your dream come true. They present themselves as the only partners who could possibly fulfill whatever's been missing from your life. This is exactly how Picasso makes Gilot feel after only a few brief encounters:

> It was in November before I had a chance to visit Picasso again. One thing stood out very clearly: the ease with which I could communicate with him. With my father there had been no communication for years. Even my relations with the one boy my own age I thought I loved were often difficult and complicated, almost negative. Now suddenly with someone who was three times as old as I was, there was from the start an ease of understanding that made it possible to talk of anything. It seemed miraculous. Seeing him after an absence of four or five months and across the filter of my summer's experiences, I had the impression I was rejoining a friend whose nature was not very far from my own (31).

If you read other biographies of Picasso, you'll notice that each of his partners felt this way initially, when he was in the process of courting her. Yet these women were radically different from each other. Picasso couldn't have possibly been identical to them all. He only pretended to be like them in order to hook them emotionally. Then, after he lost interest in each one, he no longer mirrored her particular personality traits and interests. With Olga, the Russian socialite and ballerina, the subversive and misanthropic artist transformed into a social butterfly. For several years, he joined her at the parties of prominent politicians and aristocrats.

Until, that is, he tired of her after having met Marie-Thérèse Walter. She was a seventeen year-old girl who made the middle-aged Picasso feel young again. With her, he acted like a rebellious, sex-starved and in some ways sadistic adolescent. That role fit, since Marie-Thérèse was not only very young, but also sensual and submissive. With Dora Maar, his eccentric, demanding, unstable and artistic girlfriend who was a Surrealist photographer herself, Picasso engaged in stormy fights, intellectual conversations, joint artistic projects and heated aesthetic debates.

Until he met Françoise Gilot. To her, he revealed a more reserved and cynical persona. In his eyes, she was a somewhat timid, awkward and androgynous misfit. Having no deeper sense of identity and being motivated by an insatiable hunger for conquest and control, a psychopath will become whatever you want him to be in order to seduce you. He just doesn't stay that way for long because this isn't who he really is. Once he conquers you, his interest in you naturally diminishes. Consequently, so does his incentive to be, do or say whatever pleases you. In fact, after the seduction phase, the roles reverse. The target is increasingly pressured to do everything possible to please the psychopath, not the other way around.

4. *The Custom-made Mask of the Psychopath.* As we've seen, psychopaths instinctively know what it takes to seduce a woman. They not only reflect your identity, but also anticipate your desires and conform to your needs. With a promiscuous woman, a psychopath may cut to the chase. He'll make the process short and sweet. By way of contrast, with a woman who presents a more "respectable" image, that same psychopath can be slow, gentle and disarmingly shy.

This is the role the usually impatient and assertive Picasso chooses to play with Gilot. "He stretched me out on the bed and lay down beside me. He looked at me minutely, more tenderly, moving his hand lightly over my body like a sculptor working over his sculpture to assure himself that the forms were as they should be. He was very gentle, and that is the impression that remains with me to this day—his extraordinary gentleness" (52). Picasso intuitively knows that he's dealing with a reserved and intelligent woman. Making steamy declarations of love might have worked with more naive and sentimental targets. But with Gilot, he takes a slower, more cerebral, approach to seduction. This strategy pays off. She recounts with nostalgia and lyricism the seemingly promising beginning of their romantic relationship:

> I lay there in his arms as he explained his point of view, completely happy without feeling the necessity of anything beyond just being together. . . We continued to lie there, without saying a word, and I felt it was the beginning of something marvelous—in the true sense of the word... If he had taken possession of me then by the power of his body or unleashed a torrent of sentiment in declaring his love, I would not have believed in either one. But as it was, I believed him completely... I had not thought before then that I could ever love him. Now I knew it could be no other way. He was obviously capable of side-

stepping all stereotyped formulas in his human relations just as completely as in his art. One recognizes stereotypes even if one has not experienced them all. . . When I left there that day, I knew that whatever came to pass—however wonderful or painful, or both mixed together—it would be tremendously important (53-4).

Certainly, Gilot's relationship with Picasso turned out to be very important to her. He became not only her lover, but also her life partner, her artistic mentor, her best friend and the father of her children, Claude and Paloma. But their relationship was not filled with mutual caring and respect, as she had hoped. By the end of their love affair, the pain Picasso caused her far outweighed the initial pleasure she experienced with him. In addition, her narrative shows that the relationship that she, herself, came to regard as the foundation of her life represented just another game of conquest to him. In clinical terms, she was his "narcissistic supply," like all the other women in his life. As Dr. Roger Melton explains in his illuminating article, "Romeo's Bleeding: When Mr. Right Turns out to be Mr. Wrong":

> Unlike men that can honestly struggle with their own uncertainties and confusions about a relationship, and recognize the part they play in creating problems and conflicts, there are other kinds of men that see love as a game and you as their pawn. In this cruelly covert contest, cunning is their watchword, deception is their fix, and control is their high. Just as addicts are unrelenting in pursuit of making the next score, these kinds of men are unyielding in their hunt for women that they can deceive and manipulate. Unlike emotionally sound men and women, who respect others as much as they do themselves, controlling men respect no one. To them, people are things. And things can be used (*ob-gyn.net*).

Gilot realizes early into their relationship that Picasso wouldn't be able to give her any real emotional warmth and support in life. But before their children are born, she implicitly consents to participating in an unequal relationship. She gives him all the love and support she can while he gives her nothing but his artistic talent in return. It's only after having kids together that Gilot realizes that she can no longer tolerate this fundamental asymmetry between them. It drains her strength and emotional energy. From that point on, the role of martyr no longer suits her. She explains, "At the time I went to live with Pablo, I had felt that he was a person to whom I could, and should, devote myself entirely, but from whom I should expect to receive nothing beyond what he had given the world by means of his art... During the next five or six years... I had had the children, and as a result of all that I was perhaps less capable of satisfying myself with such a Spartan attitude. I felt the need of more human warmth" (335).

5. *Cracks in the Psychopath's Mask.* As we've seen, psychologists who treat victims of psychopathic seduction state that it's very rare for a psychopath's mask

of charm to remain seamless over time. Early on in the relationship—in fact, usually as soon as the manipulation phase begins—psychopaths tend to give out signs of their real selves. Unfortunately, victims tend to ignore those red flags because by then they're already emotionally hooked on, or at the very least intrigued by, the psychopath. Picasso, for one, reveals the ugly aspects of his character. He tells Gilot that he regards other human beings as mere objects to be used and disposed of once their value has expired.

She recalls, "One day when I went to see him, we were looking at the dust dancing in a ray of sunlight that slanted in through one of the high windows. He said to me, 'Nobody has any real importance for me. As far as I'm concerned, other people are like those little grains of dust floating in the sunlight. It takes only a push of the broom and out they go'" (84). Obviously, this is not a very auspicious sign for Gilot herself. It signals not only Picasso's underlying narcissism, but also his utter contempt for humanity. Yet by this point, she's too smitten with her lover to leave him. She also mistakenly believes, as do many women who get involved with dangerous men, that she can improve his bad character through her good example and nurturing love. She'll eventually discover that love can't change everyone. Some people are irredeemably bad.

6. *Psychopathic Possessiveness.* When psychopaths want a woman, they become very possessive of her. Such men view their wives, lovers and children the same way that the rest of us view our cars or stereos: as objects they own, which nobody has the right to take away from them. When a psychopath is still in the idealization phase of the relationship, you're like a hot new Ferrari in his eyes. When he's tired of you and is ready to discard you, you become a beat-up Yugo to him. Either way, he regards you as his property, to do with as he wishes. Viewing Gilot as his possession, Picasso attempts to isolate her from others in order to control her more completely. She recounts: "'You should wear a black dress right down to the ground,' he had told me one afternoon, 'with a handkerchief over your head so that no one will see your face. In that way you'll belong even less to others. They won't even have you with their eyes.' He had this idea that if someone is precious to you, you must keep her for yourself alone, because all the accidental contacts she might have with the outside world would somehow tarnish her and, to a degree, spoil her for you" (81).

The need to keep the current object of their desire "pure" is not the only reason why psychopaths isolate their targets. More importantly, as we've seen in Carver's explanation, once a woman is removed from others, the psychopath can manipulate and control her far better than when she has external sources of support. Needless to say, the opposite doesn't hold true since psychopaths have double standards. You can't really "own" or limit a psychopath's contact with others as he does yours. At best, he will tell you what you want to hear and do whatever he wants behind your back anyway. Psychopaths strive to maximize their options in life—by being free to pursue anyone or anything at any time—while narrowing down the options of their targets, which they keep on a very tight leash. Picasso's quite explicit about his intention to lock up his new girlfriend in this little box of an existence—living solely for and through him—when he tells her: "'There's one thing I'd like very much,' he said, "and that is if you would stay there, beginning right now, up in the forest; just disappear completely so that no one would ever know you were there. I'd bring you food twice a day. You could work up there in tranquility, and I'd have my secret in my life that no one could take away from me... You'd be completely happy, because you wouldn't have to worry about the rest of the world, just about me'" (47).

Although Picasso couches his request in flattering and even romantic terms, he describes a gilded cage: the prison-like existence in which you might keep a household pet, not the woman you trust, respect and love. In addition, Picasso is quite explicit about the fact he doesn't intend to return the favor. He's not willing to limit his own freedom for her sake. In fact, he even voices the fear that having his girlfriend move in with him might restrict his movements, a downside which he's not prepared to accept. Gilot recounts, "But then he began to think it over and he said, 'I don't know whether it's such a good idea or not because it's binding on me, too. If you're agreeable to having no more liberty, that means I wouldn't have any more, either'" (47). Only once she refuses to move in with him, does Picasso become very adamant about this idea. Living together becomes, as it often does for psychopaths, more about taking possession of and exercising control over his latest prey than about embarking on a promising new life together.

7. Lack of Remorse for the Harm Inflicted on Others. As we've seen, research shows that the most dangerous quality of psychopaths is their ability to rationalize their misdeeds. When Picasso leaves his previous partner, Dora Maar, for Françoise Gilot, Maar suffers a nervous breakdown. Her close friends and even her casual acquaintances are genuinely worried about her. Some fear that she'll commit suicide. But Picasso, her long-term lover, couldn't care less. By now he's in the midst of his hot pursuit of Gilot. He's already done with Maar, ready to toss her away like an old sock. His callous attitude and actions show that he regards his former "soulmate," who had been his partner in both life and art for several years, only as a handicap or (at best) as a potential back-up, in case he might wish to use her again. When a mutual friend, the poet Paul Eluard, reproaches him for the heartless manner in which he left his girlfriend, Picasso blames the Surrealist movement (to which Maar belonged) and the psychoanalyst Jacques Lacan (whom Maar was seeing to cope with her anxiety and depression). Adding insult to injury, he also points fingers at the friends who try to help her. He sees everyone as a potential culprit except, of course, for himself. Picasso complains to Gilot:

"After Lacan had left with Dora, Eluard was so upset he accused me of being responsible for her state because I had made her so unhappy," Pablo said. "I told him that if I hadn't taken her up, she'd have reached that state long ago. If anyone is to blame, it's you and the surrealists, I told him, with all those wild ideas promoting antirationalism and the derangement of all the senses. Eluard said that any influence they had had on her was indirect, since it was all theoretical, but that I had made her unhappy in a very concrete way. What I do know," Pablo told me, "is that after she met me she had a more constructive life than before. Her life became more concentrated. I built her up" (89).

Psychopaths are so self-absorbed that they believe that even the women they've used, deceived, hurt and abandoned should feel grateful for the mistreatment. In their pathological minds, at least those women had the great privilege of being a part of the psychopath's life. Of course, the inverse is never the case. If any woman dares to cheat on or leaves a psychopath, he harbors a grudge against her for the rest of his life. This sums up Picasso's attitude towards Gilot, once she becomes the only woman to stand up for herself and eventually (after years of suffering and self-sacrifice) leave him. Normal people, however, can't comprehend the psychopath's callousness. When she hears her lover's excuses for mistreating his former girlfriend, Gilot takes her rival's side rather than Picasso's: "I felt very upset by this story. I suggested that we had talked about it, he might like to be alone. He said, 'No. The present always takes precedence over the past. That's a victory for you. . . Life must go on and life is us'" (89). Gilot, however, doesn't feel victorious. She refuses to participate in her rival's humiliation. She insists that Maar deserves more consideration from Picasso even if he's no longer in love with her.

Picasso dismisses her moral qualms as purely sentimental: "'That kind of charity is very unrealistic,' he said. 'It's sentimentality, a kind of pseudo-humanitarianism you've picked up from that whining, weeping phony, Rousseau. Furthermore, everyone's nature is determined in advance'" (90). As we've seen, psychopaths are skillful sophists. They commonly present human values as useless, dated norms followed by sheep-like individuals. Using pseudo-intellectual arguments, they persuade their current partner to hurt their former partner. As a result, the women end up turning against one another rather than uniting forces against the psychopath, who is the real culprit. Such machinations also fulfill the psychopath's sadistic tendency to inflict maximum emotional damage upon the woman he discards while turning into an accomplice the woman he currently pursues. Gilot recognizes this strategy. But she succumbs to Picasso's pressure anyway. "He told me he had already given Dora to understand that there was no longer anything between them. He insisted they understood each other perfectly on that point. When I seemed reluctant to believe him, he urged me to go to her apartment with him so I could see for myself. I was even more reluctant to do that. But he kept on urging" (103).

When Picasso takes his new girlfriend to Dora Maar's house to rub his newest affair in her face, Maar sees him more lucidly, as a person incapable of genuine love. Of course, since she's jealous of Gilot, who has just replaced her, she also insults his current victim in the process: "'You're very funny,' Dora said to him. 'You take so many precautions in embarking on something that isn't going to last around the corner.' She'd be surprised, she said, if I wasn't out on the ash heap before three months had passed, all the more so since he was the kind of person who couldn't attach himself to anyone. 'You've never loved anyone in your life,' she said to Pablo. 'You don't know how to love'" (106).

Seeing her new lover without his mask of charm momentarily triggers Gilot's self-preservation instinct. It makes her want to flee from Picasso's grasp and end their relationship. After all, reasons Gilot, if her lover is capable of mistreating his former girlfriend, why wouldn't he behave the same way with her once he tires of their relationship as well? But Picasso manages to turn this situation around. He makes Gilot feel "special," both through her association with a man as talented and famous as he is and in her own right. He convinces her that she's the woman he prefers to the one he's just discarded. If he wants her and not Dora Maar (or anyone else), Picasso reasons, it's because in his eyes Gilot is superior to Maar. Furthermore, if he mistreated his former girlfriend, he continues, it was only because he wanted to prove his love for Gilot. Yet even this declaration of love reveals his underlying sense of entitlement. It also hints, quite ominously, at physical violence. Gilot recalls:

> "I did that for you," he said, "just to make you realize there's nobody else as important as you are in my life. And this is the thanks I get! You have no grasp of what life is really like. I ought to throw you I into the Seine. That's what you deserve." He grabbed me and pushed me into one of the semicircular setbacks on the bridge. He held me against the parapet and twisted me around so that I was looking down into the water. "How would you like it?" he said. I told him to go ahead if he wanted to—it was spring now and I was a good swimmer. Finally he let go of me and I ran down into the subway, leaving him behind me on the bridge (107).

With hindsight, Gilot admits that if she had not been deeply in love with Picasso, she'd have seen her lover's behavior—not only towards Dora Maar, but also his bullying of her—as a terrible sign and run away from him. But by this point, she was too far-gone, under her lover's hypnotic control, to heed the blatant red flags and escape the relationship unharmed. "I suppose I should have cooled off towards Pablo. But I didn't. I was bothered by what had happened and its implications, but my feeling for him had deepened to the point where it was stronger than any of the warning signals" (107). Psychopaths bank on their victims' emotional attachment once they gradually abandon the pretense of goodness and begin to show, more and more, their true colors.

8. *Psychopathic Manipulation.* Many of the women who recount their life experiences with psychopaths on the website *lovefraud.com* state that the more they gave in to the psychopath's manipulation and the more they colluded with his unprincipled acts against others, the more he demanded from them and the weaker they became to resist his bullying in the future. Placating a psychopath

doesn't buy anyone peace for long. In the long run, it only feeds his insatiable hunger for control and penchant for evil deeds. Françoise Gilot learns this painful lesson as she struggles to appease her lover by repeatedly giving in to his demands. After getting her to contribute to hurting her rival, Picasso strikes next much closer to home.

He asks Gilot to leave her ailing grandmother, who needs her attention and care, so that she can move in with him. In so doing, he asserts his power over his girlfriend and tests her loyalty to him. As we recall, psychopaths view their partners' love and loyalty as a zero-sum game. If their partners care about their parents, grandparents, children or friends, to them that means less love and control for themselves. Only once their victims are both physically and emotionally isolated from everyone and everything else, do psychopaths feel like they're "in charge." At that point, however, they also become bored with their defeated targets and move on to new ones. Power isn't always bad, just as charisma isn't always dangerous. But psychopaths use the power of charisma for predatory purposes. As Roger Melton elaborates in his article on narcissistic controllers,

> Unhealthy control originates in a desire to dominate another, either through words or actions designed to both charm and harm—to captivate while simultaneously damaging the emotionally captured. It is this pairing of charm with harm that is the hallmark of Controller manipulations. Preaching sugar while practicing poison, they are experts at concealing their true natures. Hiding bad intentions beneath polished appearances, they have perfected the art of 'looking good.' It is this uncanny ability of Controllers to alternate looking good with manipulative behavior that perpetuates tormenting emotional snares for those they target as victims ("Romeo's Bleeding: When Mr. Right Turns out to be Mr. Wrong," *obgyn.net*).

Picasso tries to convince Gilot that abandoning her grandmother isn't really personal. After all, he generalizes, any action for yourself is bound to hurt someone else. There's no way to live in such a way that doesn't cause pain to others. Besides, he adds, Gilot's romantic love for him should trump her familial love for her grandmother:

> "Look at it this way," he said. "What you can bring to your grandmother, aside from the affection you have for her, is not something essentially constructive. When you're with me, on the other hand, you help me to realize something very constructive. It's more logical and more positive for you to be close to me, in view of the fact I need you. As far as your grandmother's feelings are concerned, there are things one can do and make them understood, and there are other things that can only be done by coup d'etat since they go beyond the limits of another person's understanding. It's almost better to strike the blow and after people have recovered from it, let them accept the fact" (100).

Such nonsense doesn't persuade Gilot. "I told him that sounded rather brutal to me," she recounts (100). She counters that hurting those you love is, indeed, very personal. Furthermore, you can easily prevent it by not doing whatever it is that would hurt them. In response to her reasonable objection, Picasso presents a more metaphysical argument. He depersonalizes the whole scenario again. "'But there are some things you can't spare other people,'" he said. "'It may cost a terrible price to act in this way but there are moments in life when we don't have a choice. If there is one necessity, which for you dominates all others, then necessarily you must act badly in some respect. There is no total, absolute purity other than the purity of refusal. In the acceptance of a passion one considers extremely important and in which one accepts for oneself a share of tragedy, one steps outside of the usual laws and has the right to act as one should not act in ordinary conditions'" (100-1).

This argument gets to the core of a psychopath's self-centered worldview. In the first part of his defense, Picasso stated in general terms that hurting others was unavoidable. But Gilot easily refuted this proposition by saying that she could, indeed, avoid it by staying with her grandmother. Picasso then flatters his girlfriend's self-love. He tells her that she, and their love for each other, is extraordinary. They're therefore above the pale of the moral codes that govern the rest of humanity. Some of the women who contribute to *lovefraud.com* have described in their testimonials how they have abandoned their partners, their friends and sometimes even their children for such an illusory cause as being considered "special" by their psychopathic lovers.

Picasso describes the supposedly unique bond between himself and Gilot in terms of a higher power, perhaps the hand of fate itself. "'It's a question of the recognition of one's destiny and not a matter of unkindness or insensitivity,'" he tells her (101). What Picasso's really saying here is that his needs are supremely important while those of others don't matter. But he's framing this egocentric assumption in seemingly ethical terms, which would sound more acceptable to his scrupulous girlfriend. Any savvy psychopath knows how to use the fact that most people have a conscience as leverage for his own selfish purposes. The appeal to moral standards, just like the histrionic simulation of love, constitutes yet another one of the psychopath's many ruses. It enables him to get what he wants from others while making it his life's goal to undermine both the moral and the emotional fabric that binds other human beings together. Above all, Picasso's argument reflects his absolute selfishness. As Melton elaborates,

> At his core, every Controller is monumentally self-centered. He is not just on an ego trip. He is on an expedition. In his mind, everyone orbits around him, as if people are his planets and he is their shining sun. What he wants he should have, simply because he wants it. He needs no other justification. Seeing himself as the center of everyone else's universe, he is blind to the fact that anyone else's wants or needs are more important than his own. Doggedly locked into this self-image of grand, "godlike" proportions, he may literally feel entitled to other's worship ("Romeo's Bleeding: When Mr. Right Turns out to be Mr. Wrong," *obgyn.net*).

Gilot recognizes her lover's argument as sheer nonsense covering up an act of immorality. "I told him that a primitive person could face up to that idea much more easily than someone who thought in terms of principles of good and evil and who tried to act on the basis of them" (101). When a psychopath can't win an argument using his charisma, eloquence and sophistry, he usually falls back upon the strategy of bullying others. In this case, Picasso tortures Gilot by branding her with his lit cigarette. Needless to say, she doesn't take it well. "I told him I often thought he was the devil and now I knew it. His eyes narrowed. 'And you, you're an angel,' he said, scornfully, 'but an angel from a hot place. Since I'm the devil, that makes you one of my subjects. I think I'll brand you'" (101).

Since even physical violence fails to intimidate her, Picasso relies upon a purely emotional—and highly manipulative—appeal: whom do you love more? he asks her to choose. Your grandmother or me? He then turns the tables on his girlfriend and makes her feel guilty for not caring enough about him to sacrifice her relationship with her grandmother for him. "'Don't I count in your life?'" he demands. "'Is this all a game for you? Are you so insensitive as that? ... You should be worrying about me. I need you... And since I can't get along without you, you have to come live with me'" (101). The repeated emotional blackmail eventually wears her down. Gilot moves out of her grandmother's house to live with her lover. It's a decision that she'll soon come to regret.

9. *The Psychopath's Mask Peels Off.* Some people say that the best way to kill passion is by moving in together. While this cynical view may be only partially true of normal, loving relationships, it's one hundred percent true of psychopathic bonds. In a Schopenhauerian perversion of love, once a psychopath establishes a dominance bond with a woman, he also starts to get bored with her. Not surprisingly, when looking back upon their life together, Gilot concludes that the only time she and Picasso seemed happy together was during the three years before she moved in with him and when she was carrying his children. She states, "As I began to think back on our life together, I realized that the only time I ever saw him in a sustained good mood—apart from the period between 1943 and 1946 before I went to live with him—was when I was carrying Claude. It was the only time he was cheerful, relaxed and happy, with no problems. That had been very nice, I reflected, and I hoped it would work again, for both our sakes. I knew I couldn't have ten children just to keep him that way, but I could try once more at least, and I did" (212). If psychopaths often ask their partners to have children with them, it's obviously not because they care about kids, since they can't love anyone meaningfully. Psychopaths enjoy marking their women, whom they consider their property. Impregnating women makes such men feel more potent and virile, especially as they age, as was the case with Picasso, who was much older than Gilot.

10. *Stringing Women Along: The Psychopath as Puppet Master.* Since, as we've seen in previous discussions, psychopaths enjoy sex and power—

especially when the two are combined—they're great jugglers of women. They especially relish creating rivalry and jealousy among their partners. They instigate feelings of mutual disrespect and even hatred. Watching several women fight over them validates their ego. It also offers priceless entertainment. Picasso unabashedly confesses to Gilot his delight in having women assault each other over him. He recounts how Marie-Thérèse and Dora Maar had an altercation over who was his real girlfriend. Instead of diffusing the tension, he encouraged them to escalate from a verbal to a physical fight. Picasso tells Gilot, "'I told them they'd have to fight it out themselves. So they began to wrestle. It's one of my choicest memories'" (211). Jealous fights, as well as mutual insults and devaluation, offer an amusing spectator sport for psychopaths. It makes them feel in charge: like they're the puppet masters manipulating all these women's emotions. This rivalry also has the additional advantage of creating artificial barriers among the victims. The women's aggression turns against one another rather than towards their real enemy, the psychopath who is using and mistreating them both, plus several others that they may not even know about.

Psychopaths tend to select trusting and trustworthy women whom they can manipulate and taint. They enjoy the thrill of getting them to collude in their lies and machinations against others, including family members and friends. They resort to emotional blackmail to get their victims, who are often decent human beings, to cooperate. This establishes a link of complicity in the psychopathic bond: something along the lines of, you lied to your family (or my family, or our friends, or your spouse) too, so therefore you're just as bad and deceitful as I am. Furthermore, psychopaths need to have their sense of power over you constantly reaffirmed. Since they're at core malicious human beings, the way you help confirm their power best is by colluding with their projects to deceive and hurt others.

By turning "their" women against one another, psychopaths make each of them simultaneously their co-conspirator and their dupe, the deceiver and the deceived. When she deflects her negative emotions towards other women, the psychopath's wife or girlfriend remains blind to the real threat posed by her own partner. Emotionally, this perspective may be easier to accept than the truth: namely, that your supposed soul mate wants to destroy you and is using you as a weapon to hurt others and vice versa. Only when you're strong enough to open your eyes and face reality do you begin to see the machinations of the psychopath as puppet master. Françoise Gilot describes this strategy with characteristic lucidity. She compares Picasso's habit of stringing several women along to a Bluebeard complex and to a bullfight. Although these analogies may seem radically different, they describe the same phenomenon. In this process, the real enemy—the one who gores you in the end—is the man generating all the drama and rivalries among women in the first place:

> Pablo's many stories and reminiscences about Olga and Marie-Thérèse and Dora Maar, as well as their continuing presence just off stage in our life to-

gether, gradually made me realize that he had a kind of Bluebeard complex that made him want to cut off the heads of all the women he had collected in his little private museum. But he didn't cut the heads entirely off. He preferred to have life go on and to have all those women who had shared his life at one moment or another still letting out little peeps and cries of joy or pain and making a few gestures like disjointed dolls, just to prove there was some life left in them, that it hung by a thread, and that he held the other end of the thread. Even though he no longer had any feeling for this one or that one, he could not bear the idea that any of his women should ever again have a life of her own. And so each had to be maintained, with the minimum gift of himself, inside his orbit and not outside. As I thought about it, I realized that in Pablo's life things went on just about the way they do in a bullfight. Pablo was the toreador and he waved the red flag, the muleta. For a picture dealer, the muleta was another picture dealer; for a woman, another woman. The result was, the person playing the bull stuck his horns into the red flag instead of goring the real adversary—Pablo. And that is why Pablo was always able, at the right moment, to have his sword free to stick you where it hurt. I came to be very suspicious of this tactic and any time I saw a big red flag waiving around me, I would look to one side of it. There, I always found Pablo (242-3).

Aside from the entertainment value and the sense of being in charge, the psychopath gets something else out of generating conflict among his targets. He also gets back-ups to his back-ups. Given that he's bound to mistreat every woman he's involved with, he certainly needs them. It seems as if psychopaths know, through both intuition and experience, that the honeymoon phase won't last long no matter how exciting and promising a given relationship may seem in the beginning. I'm reminded once again of a beautiful quote by Gilot, who herself paraphrases Picasso:

He said, "We mustn't see each other too often. If the wings of the butterfly are to keep their sheen, you mustn't touch them. We mustn't abuse something which is to bring light into both of our lives. Everything else in my life only weighs me down and shuts out the light. This thing with you seems to me like a window that is opening up. I want it to remain open. We must see each other but not too often. When you want to see me, you call me and tell me so" (53-4).

What a touching way to describe the whole process of psychopathic seduction, from the initial idealization to devalue and discard! It almost makes it sound appealing rather than appalling. If relationships with psychopaths are so fragile and delicate, like the sheen on the wings of a butterfly, it's because they have no foundation whatsoever in reality. Or rather, because everything positive about them is based on illusion, manipulation and deceit. The psychopath knows this at all times. Yet he may sometimes engage in double think: which is to say, believe at a given moment that his love for you will last even though he knows from experience that every feeling, interest and relationship he's ever had was ephemeral. Unfortunately, once you've fallen under his spell, you're much more convinced than he is that your relationship's solid and real, based on mutual caring and genuine respect.

As we've seen from Gilot's juxtaposition between her feelings for Picasso and his for her, the difference in your attitudes is not necessarily one of intensity, but one of depth and duration. There's a huge, unbridgeable gap between his forever "for now" and your forever "for always." In fact, as you eventually find out, it's a veritable abyss. When the relationship begins to crack once the honeymoon phase ends, you feel confused and wounded. What happened to all his promises of love and commitment? Were they offered in a parallel universe? You never realized that his "for life" really meant "for as long as you give me a buzz" or "for as long as I feel like it." Given all those nice words, flattery and promises, and especially given the emotions, time and energy you've invested into the relationship, you couldn't tell that he dwells in the shallowness of a perpetual present; that momentary sensations, desires and objectives is all that counts for him.

When one's "love" has the lifespan of a butterfly—to use Picasso's metaphor—one must find other flowers to pollinate. Given their restlessness and shallowness, psychopaths need to secure multiple sources of novelty, pleasure and excitement. And they're quite good at lining them up. They place several women in reserve, filling their lives with back-ups to their back-ups. That way as soon as one relationship sours, it's no big deal. They quickly move on to another. Besides, no woman will be pleasant and obliging every minute of every day. When one woman's tired, unavailable or in a bad mood, a psychopath can always fall back on another one to console him. He feels entitled to it. After all, in his mind, he's perfect all the time!

Picasso, for one, isn't shy about sharing with Gilot the main intention behind his machinations. He wants to destroy the self-esteem of women who previously had a positive image of themselves: "'For me, there are only two kinds of women—goddesses and doormats.' And whenever he thought I might be feeling too much like a goddess, he did his best to turn me into a doormat.'" This constitutes the *raison d'être* of just about any psychopath. As we've seen, an emotional predator's goal is *not* to build a healthy and enduring relationship with his partner. Rather, it's to amuse himself and feel more powerful by undermining her dignity before moving on to his next target. Picasso sampled several different types of women. He idealized each one at first as a "goddess," but eventually treated all of them like a "doormat." Gilot perspicaciously identifies the dualistic mindset behind using a woman as a temporary fantasy (the idealized new girlfriend) to displace another woman who represents mundane reality (the current devalued partner):

[Marie-Thérèse] haunted his life, just out of reach poetically, but available in the practical sense whenever his dreams were troubled by her absence. She had no inconvenient reality; she was a reflection of the cosmos. Marie-Thérèse was very important to him as long as he was living with Olga because she was the dream when the reality was someone else. He continued to love her because he hadn't really taken possession of her: she lived somewhere else and was the escape hatch from a reality he found unpleasant. But once he had, in order to take fuller possession of that form of hers for which he had such an insistent desire, sent Olga away, then reality suddenly switched sides. What had been fantasy and dream became reality, and absence became presence. Along came Dora Maar to take photographs of Pablo, and Pablo became very interested in her (235-6).

She goes on to recount how, following the same logic of turning each previously idealized "goddess" into a devalued "doormat," Picasso discarded Maar once she, herself, caught his eye. Gilot realizes that there's a certain predictable pattern to the way Picasso perceives his relationships with women. She sees that if she doesn't escape of her own free will, he's bound to step all over her as well.

11. *The Devaluation and Abandonment Phase.* As a matter of fact, that's exactly what he sets out to do. Once Gilot moves in with him, Picasso begins to treat her as he did all of the other women who shared his life. Once she's under his control, he becomes bored with her, cheats on her, bullies her and lies to her. He also imposes upon her humiliating double standards, which we'll shortly examine in greater detail. He demands that her whole existence revolve around fulfilling his every need, yet nothing she does pleases him for long. At the same time that he controls every aspect of her life, he also begins to distance himself from her to pursue other affairs and flings. When Gilot confronts him with her warranted suspicions, Picasso becomes downright indignant. He refuses to admit the truth about his infidelities:

> From the time I went to live with him in May 1946 until his trip to Poland with Eluard and Marcel, Pablo and I had never been apart a single day. After his return from Poland he began taking short trips to Paris without me.... Once when he didn't come home... I dragged a mattress out onto the balcony and stayed there, sleepless, until I saw the car pull up in front of the garage just before dawn. When Pablo came up the stairs, he flew into a rage, accused me of spying on him and said he was free to come in whenever he wanted to—all this without my having said a word to him.... "Instead of sleeping in bed where you belong, you're out here waiting for me. It's obvious to anybody that you're trying to take my freedom away from me" (336).

Never mind that Gilot can't do anything without Picasso's knowledge and approval, let alone travel by herself or engage in extramarital affairs, as he does. No doubt, Picasso's attitude reflects the epoch's double standards for men versus women. But it's also a symptom of a psychopath's sense of entitlement. It reflects the view that he's far superior to his mate and therefore deserves to do whatever he wishes while she's to remain under his thumb. The "doormat" phase of the psychopathic bond has clearly arrived for the former "goddess." Gilot offers a moving description of her own devaluation: "In the weeks that followed, I saw that both spiritually and physically he was erecting a wall between us. At first I couldn't believe it possible that he should want to stay apart from me at the very moment I was making the greatest effort to be close to him" (336).

If one takes into account the clinical information on psychopathy, however, the fact that Picasso loses interest in his partner precisely at the point when she's most emotionally invested in him doesn't seem like a coincidence. As we've seen, once a psychopath hooks a woman emotionally, she no longer presents a goal to him. He regards her as his rightful possession while feeling entitled to pursue other challenges by seducing other women. To psychopaths and narcissists, having such double standards is as natural as breathing. Which leads us to our next point.

12. *The Psychopath's Double Standards.* A psychopath will happily and with great ease leave his current partner for another woman or just because he feels like it. But he's not likely to be as cavalier about a break-up when his partner chooses to leave him instead. That's not, of course, because he loves her and would miss her. It's because, as Roger Melton explains, psychopaths are narcissistic controllers. Being left by their partners wounds their inflated egos. Although he cheated on Gilot and neglected her towards the end of their relationship, when she finally decides to leave him, Picasso feels furious. Since the honeymoon phase of their relationship is long over, this time he doesn't couch his argument in phony other-regarding terms. Instead, he explicitly reminds her of her inferior position: "Your job is to remain by my side, to devote yourself to me and to the children... Whether it makes you happy or unhappy is no concern of mine" (355).

Picasso attempts to prevent Gilot from leaving him not only to reassert his power over her, but also because, as we've seen, psychopaths like to have numerous pawns at their disposal. They dwell in what's been called in literary studies, following René Girard, "the triangulated space of desire," or more aptly, of duplicity. They need to be cheating on someone to enjoy a given target. They need to gossip with the woman they're chasing about the woman they're dumping. They need to find yet another woman to deceive the girlfriend with and enjoy the double, triple or even quadruple duplicity. Each relationship is triangulated. It consists of the psychopath, his current target to whom he's criticizing his previous victim, who's now become his back up.

Feeling confused? Then try putting yourself in the poor psychopath's shoes! If there's nobody to gossip about, nobody to complain about, nobody to deceive, nobody to conquer from another man, nobody to cheat on, nobody to hurt, nobody to malign, then sexual relationships lose their spice. Romantic partners become as familiar as old shoes. Normal life, believing in moral standards, having genuine emotions and lasting relationships is really boring from a psychopath's perspective.

13. *The Emotional Vacuum.* If ultimately Gilot can no longer be persuaded by Picasso's arguments to stay with him, it's because his actions have spoken louder than his occasional declarations of love. After all, it's very easy to tell a woman that you love her. It's much harder and more meaningful to prove your love by treating her with the consideration and respect that she deserves. Initially, when Gilot saw how Picasso mistreated his former partners, she found some comfort in the hope that he would treat her better. She believed his claim that he loved her more and that she was more compatible with him than any other woman in his life. But after awhile, Gilot realized that she wasn't the exception that confirmed the rule. She was just another link in his pattern of idealizing, devaluing and discarding women:

> They all had different kinds of failures, for different reasons. Olga, for example, went down to defeat because she demanded too much. One might assume on that basis that if she hadn't demanded too much and things that were basically stupid, she wouldn't have failed. And yet Marie-Thérèse Walter demanded nothing, she was very sweet, and she failed too. Then came Dora Maar, who was anything but stupid, and artist who understood him to a far greater degree than the others. But she too failed, although, like the others she certainly loved and believed in him. So it was hard for me to believe in him completely. He had left each of them, although each of them was so wrapped up in her own situation that she thought she was the only woman who counted for him, and that her life and his were inextricably intertwined. . . There was no means, ever, of really coming close to him for long (340).

Understandably, once she confronts the sad reality that Picasso is no more capable of loving her than he was of caring about any other woman, Gilot becomes visibly depressed. Even when he sees the suffering he's caused her, however, all Picasso thinks about is how he can use her sorrowful expression for his paintings. "I cried a good bit of the time," Gilot recalls. "Pablo found it very stimulating. 'Your face is wonderful today,' he told me while he was drawing me. 'It's a very grave kind of face.' I told him it wasn't at all a grave face. It was a sad face" (337). Not only is Picasso impervious to Gilot's pain, but also he criticizes her for having lost weight due to the hardships he imposed on her. He tells her, "You look like a broom. Do you think brooms appeal to anybody? They don't to me" (337). While his cruelty towards the woman he supposedly loves is nothing short of astonishing, when it comes to his own suffering, with characteristic double standards, Picasso expects from her the utmost compassion and devotion.

By this point, however, Gilot can no longer offer him anything but discouragement and sadness. She sees the writing on the wall. She senses their mutual alienation. She also realizes that her usefulness to him has nearly expired, just as it did for all her precursors. Robert Hare and Paul Babiak document in *Snakes in Suits* that when psychopaths have used up their targets, they manifest an emotional emptiness that's almost beyond description or comprehension. Their tone and behavior become mechanical. Their demeanor becomes cold and distant. Months or even years of shared experiences become effaced from their minds, as if they never existed.

Some women feel so emotionally invested in their psychopathic partners that they take refuge in denial. They cling to false hopes, refusing to acknowledge the palpable alienation. Gilot, however, courageously confronts it: "But our relationship continued to deteriorate to the point where the usual personal and emotional fulfillment a woman derives from a man's love was no longer possible" (338). Unfortunately, it takes her two more years of suffering, from 1949 to 1951, to fully absorb this realization and leave him.

14. *Deception and Gaslighting.* Like most psychopaths, Picasso was a master of gaslighting. Even though, as mentioned, he repeatedly cheated on Gilot, he vehemently denied having affairs. He even called her "crazy" for suspecting him of infidelity. Martha Stout and Robert Hare both state that a psychopath can be so convincing in his dramatic denials that his victim begins to question her knowledge of the truth and even doubt her own sanity. The classic strategy of gaslighting plays itself out in the following scene between Gilot and Picasso: "When Pablo returned, I asked him if he waned to tell me about the change in his feelings toward me. I said we always had been very frank with each other and I felt we should continue on that basis. Deciding, doubtless, that too much talk on the subject would complicate things for him, he said, 'You must be crazy. Nothing at all is going on.' He sounded so convincing, I believed him, preferring to think that perhaps the journalists had been badly informed" (345). Yet once Picasso's infidelities intensify and become more flagrant, Gilot can no longer accept his lies. She finally wakes up from the psychopathic spell: "I had been under his spell, but I was no longer. I had waked up and I was disenchanted" (348).

15. *The Psychopath's Rage.* As we've seen, psychopaths regard their partners as their personal property. While they reserve the right to juggle multiple relationships and find pleasure with others, they become downright furious when their devalued partners dare to move on with their lives as well. Picasso expresses his possessiveness quite bluntly when he tells Gilot: "I prefer to see a woman die, any day, than see her happy with someone else" (351). By the time Gilot decided to leave him, Picasso was already practically living with his new girlfriend, Jacqueline Roque, whom Gilot describes as slavishly submissive to him. But the fact that he had already replaced her did not in any way prevent Picasso from viewing Gilot as rightfully his: "'You owe me so much,' he said, 'This is your way of thanking me, I suppose. Well, I've just got one thing to say. Anybody else will have all of my faults and none of my virtues. I hope your life is a fiasco, you ungrateful creature'" (366).

Picasso's statement would ring true only if Gilot would have replaced a talented psychopath like him with a garden variety psychopath—your ordinary Loser—who lacked his ambition, accomplishments and abilities. But, in fact, she didn't trade one kind of psychopath for another. She replaced Picasso with a real, functioning man who truly loved her. Psychopaths hate the sense that they have not succeeded in destroying their former partners. They don't want "their" women to regain their strength and lead much happier lives without them.

Picasso admits as much when he tells Gilot, "Every time I change wives I should burn the last one. That way I'd be rid of them... You kill the woman and you wipe out the past she represents" (349). In fact, he partially accomplished this goal. He more or less succeeded in psychologically destroying all of his former partners: except, that is, for Françoise Gilot. No matter how hard he tried, he could not conquer her. He experienced her freedom as a betrayal. In his article on narcissistic controllers, Melton explains that psychopaths and narcissists don't understand betrayal the way normal people do. They don't regard it as a violation of mutual trust. After all, they don't trust others and aren't trustworthy themselves. Instead, they view betrayal as an assertion of independence by those who were formerly under their control:

> For most people, betrayal usually means a deep violation of trust inflicted by someone with whom a close, personal relationship exists. But, to a Narcissistic Controller, betrayal simply means that someone stopped pandering to his every want and need. In other words, when someone breaks away from his control, he feels betrayed. Since Narcissists do not have the capacity to develop close, trusting personal relationships, there can be no deep violation of real trust. When a Narcissistic Controller feels betrayed, contempt dominates his facial and verbal expressions. The insolent, aloof sneer commonly accompanies expressions such as, "He didn't know who he was dealing with!" Or, Doesn't he know who I am?" His real complaint—if he had the ability to see it—should be, "Don't you know who I think I am?" ("Romeo's Bleeding: When Mr. Right Turns out to be Mr. Wrong," *obgyn.net*).

To reassert dominance, Picasso attempts to undermine Gilot's self-esteem, so that she'll lack the confidence to leave him for good. He tells her that she's nothing without him. He asks her, "You imagine people will be interested in you?" as if the very idea were preposterous (355). Fortunately, however, this time she doesn't believe his insults. She chooses instead to believe in herself. She doesn't see herself as only his shadow. Perhaps her own lucidity saves her. Most people made exceptions for Picasso's bad behavior because he was, indeed, such an exceptional artist. Because Gilot saw who Picasso was as a human being—the emptiness within him—she moved on to a better life without him. Ultimately, Picasso didn't rob her of real happiness with another man. He also didn't succeed in making her bitter towards the rest of humanity, or even towards him, for that matter. Instead of hating her former lover and rejecting their past together, Gilot saw her years with Picasso as a painful learning experience that enabled her to mature. They gave her an inner strength that lasted for the rest of her life:

Pablo had told me, that first afternoon I visited him alone, in February 1944, that he felt our relationship would bring light into both our lives. My coming to him, he said, seemed like a window that was opening up and he wanted it to remain open. I did, too, as long as it let in the light. When it no longer did, I closed it, much against my own desire. From that moment on, he burned all the bridges that connected me to the past that I shared with him. But in doing so he forced me to discover myself and thus to survive. I shall never cease being grateful to him for that (367).

I can only hope that those who read Françoise Gilot's moving autobiography take away from it her message of survival, resilience and strength. Her account of her relationship with Picasso also illustrates that one can run across evil individuals in every wake of society and life. If you expect psychopaths to be the ugly monsters you see in thrillers rather than the cultivated, charming and seemingly sensitive artists, doctors, scientists, teachers or lawyers that they sometimes are, then keep on watching them in movies and reading about them in novels. But remember to also watch out for them in all their guises, talents and professions in real life, which is where you're likely to encounter them.

Chapter 5

The Psychopathic Seducer in Literature:
Benjamin Constant's *Adolphe*

There have been a number of great novels written about seducers, some of which are about psychopathic seducers in particular. Of course, the tantalizing tales of Don Juan and Casanova set the standard. But it's Laclos' *Dangerous liaisons* (1782), an eighteenth-century French epistolary novel that we know now mostly thanks to John Malkovich's and Glenn Close's excellent performances in the 1988 movie, that explores the emotional emptiness and the game-like ruses inherent in the process of psychopathic seduction. *Dangerous liaisons* focuses mostly on the machinations of the seducers themselves. There are also a few classic novels that sketch the psychological profile of the women who are seduced by them. To offer one notable example, Flaubert's *Madame Bovary*, first published as a serial in *La Revue de Paris* in 1856, generated a scandal. Flaubert was charged with the corruption of public mores. Many novels depicted with relative immunity middle-class men cheating on their wives with courtesans, mistresses and prostitutes. But the theme of a middle-class woman cheating on her husband shocked the public at the time. Flaubert was nonetheless acquitted in 1857. His novel became an instant best seller and remains to this day a popular nineteenth-century classic. Tolstoy broached the same theme in *Anna Karenina*, my personal favorite. He published it in installments in *The Russian Messenger*, between 1873 and 1877. His novel was extremely successful and didn't cause a scandal. Unlike Flaubert's morally ambiguous and cynical *Madame Bovary*, Tolstoy's novel was presented as a morality tale. *Anna Karenina* masterfully expressed a popular, if somewhat tired, message. For middle-class women, the novel implied, cheating on their spouses and pursuing passion instead of familial duties results in suffering and an untimely death.

Out of all the novels on seduction I've read, I believe that Benjamin Constant's Romantic classic *Adolphe* captures best the insidious process of psychopathic seduction in particular. Although this novel is somewhat less well known internationally than *Madame Bovary* and *Anna Karenina*, it was an instant hit in France. It was first published in June 1816 and reprinted quickly thereafter in three more editions—in July 1816, then again 1824 and 1828—due to its popularity. Part of what made this novel so successful was the fact that it was seeped in gossip. Readers interpreted the work as a roman-à-clef. They believed that Constant described in *Adolphe* his tumultuous long-term affair with one of the most famous women of the times, Germaine de Staël, as well as aspects of his on/off relationship with the devoted Charlotte von Hardenberg.

In the preface to the second edition, however, the author vehemently denies any connection between his love life and the characters of his novel. In fact, Constant goes so far as to chastise critics and readers alike for having reduced a complex work of fiction to personal intrigue. The author also claims that his sense of tact and devotion to his friends would preclude him from translating his life into fiction. He explains that his novel shows what happens when love is asymmetrical: when one partner loves too much and the other not enough. Although some literary critics still interpret Constant's novel as largely autobiographical, I'd have to agree with the author that the personal angle is not the most interesting aspect of this work. I believe that *Adolphe* stands the test of time above all because of its penetrating insight into pathological relationships.

Constant claims that Adolphe, the (anti)hero of the novel, is too weak to escape a relationship that got too deep too fast with Ellénore, a woman whom he no longer loves. The novel's detailed and nuanced exploration of human pathology, however, leads me to sketch a different psychological profile of Adolphe. I don't see him as a weak and sensitive man who got in over his head, as the author claims. Rather, I see him as an emotional predator. Adolphe represents the kind of man who is incapable of genuine love. He regards the seduction and destruction of women as an entertaining way to pass time and to alleviate boredom. As realistic as this novel is in depicting a psychopathic seducer, it's even more accurate in its depiction of the kind of women who fall in love and stay with psychopaths long after the relationship with them has grown cold and their so-called "love" has turned into indifference.

From a certain perspective, the plot bears out the author's reading of his own text. Adolphe, the protagonist and narrator of this unhappy romance, is the son of a government minister. He leads an aimless and solitary life until a friend's success in love induces him to seek a comparable diversion. At a party, he meets Ellénore, a beautiful aristocratic Polish immigrant. She's the mistress of a certain Comte de P, with whom she has two children. Upon seeing her, Adolphe instantly decides to seduce her. He uses his charm and manipulation skills to achieve this goal. Ellénore resists at first—rather half-heartedly—but eventually gives in to his advances. For her, their physical relationship translates into real emotional bonding. For him, it doesn't. The difference in their attitudes motivates the plot of the novel, moving it towards its fatal conclusion. The more Adolphe withdraws emotionally from Ellénore, the more she struggles to regain his initial affection. In the end, the heroine is reduced to the shell of the person she once was. True to the Romantic tradition, Ellénore dies of sorrow, feeling unloved and rejected by the lover for whom she has sacrificed everything: her partner, her children, her social connections, her reputation and, ultimately, her whole identity. Although now somewhat neglected in the canon of European literature, Constant's novel helped consolidate Romanticism in France. It also paved the way for psychological fiction, which would later be pursued by Henry James and Marcel Proust.

For decades, literature has been interpreted by literary critics through the optic of psychology. That's not, of course, because literary characters are real. It's because they can represent character traits, motivations, interactions and emotions that drive real human beings. Often, however, such interpretations tend to be archetypal or, more generally, theoretical. Psychoanalytic criticism relies upon Freudian, Lacanian, Jungian and other kinds of broad, and generally abstract, frameworks to read general patterns of behavior, desires, emotions and drives. Rarely are the theories applied to literature drawn directly from current pragmatic psychology, meaning from contemporary research on and experience of real, suffering human beings. In my estimation, reading literature in light of actual human experience, disorders, struggles and problems can be illuminating. They shed light upon pathological characteristics that exist in real human beings and that affect our lives deeply. We have a lot to learn about human nature and behavior from good psychological fiction without erasing the boundaries between fiction and life. Constant's fictional depiction of the process of psychopathic seduction—from its promising beginning to its pathetic ending—is strikingly modern and, as I hope to show by relying on the latest research on psychopathic seduction, remains relevant to this day.

Since they lack the capacity to form emotional bonds with others, from a very young age psychopaths experience a nearly constant state of restlessness and boredom. They also generally lack the patience to complete any of their tasks, seeking meaning in temporary diversions. Young Adolphe, the narrator of the novel, fits this profile. "Distracted, inattentive, bored, I couldn't notice the impression I created, and I divided my time between studies that I frequently interrupted, projects which I didn't complete, pleasures which didn't really interest me, when an apparently very frivolous circumstance produced in my disposition an important revolution" (*Adolphe*, my translation, 41). Although a misanthrope by his own admission, Adolphe needs others for entertainment. Almost by accident he stumbles upon a solution to the emptiness he feels within. He observes with interest the excitement of an acquaintance that has fallen in love. Before meeting any actual woman, Adolphe falls in love with the idea of falling in love. "The spectacle of such happiness made me regret not having tried it yet; I didn't have any affair of the heart that could have flattered my self-love; a new future was revealed to me; I felt a new need at the bottom of my heart" (42). From the very beginning, the narrator regards love as a fantasy of conquest. He doesn't view it as a shared emotional experience that may result in finding a potential partner in life. As Sandra L. Brown's research illustrates, psychopaths attach to their targets in order to control them.

With this goal in mind, Adolphe quickly spots his target. He zeroes in on Ellénore, the Polish mistress of Comte de P, one of his father's friends. From the outset, he assesses her weaknesses and needs. He sets out to seduce her by appearing to provide whatever has been missing from her life. He takes note of the fact that Ellénore's current lover, with whom she lived for ten years and with whom she has two children, didn't marry her. In Adolphe's eyes, the refusal to legitimate her status reveals her partner's ambivalence towards her. He'll take full advantage of that division between the two lovers, and especially of Ellénore's unfulfilled need for more attention and a deeper commitment, to seduce her. Adolphe also notices that Ellénore doesn't quite fit into any culture. Polish by birth yet living in France, she's a partial outsider to both cultures. With predatory intuition, he focuses on her tenuous social situation and inner contradictions, which he fully intends to exploit: "Ellénore, in a word, was in a constant struggle with her fate. She protested, we may say, through each of her actions and words, against the class in which she found herself, and as none of her efforts changed anything about her situation, she was very unhappy" (44-5).

Ellénore may be discontented and needy, but she's by no means an easy prey. She's proud, well educated, still beautiful and enjoys the protection of a powerful count and his circle of acquaintances. Adolphe decides that this woman has just the right mixture of vulnerability and strength to represent a worthy conquest. "Presented to my attention at a moment when I needed love and my vanity sought success, Ellénore seemed a conquest worthy of me" (45). Although he explicitly reviews his target's weaknesses and strengths, the narrator qualifies that he's not assessing Ellénore in a cold and calculated manner. He claims to be genuinely drawn to her. The two attitudes don't necessarily contradict. As Robert Hare and Paul Babiak illustrate in *Snakes in Suits*, during the assessment phase, when psychopathic seducers measure up their targets, they also idealize them, to see them as objects worthy of their attention. In other words, for emotional predators, the calculated assessment phase and the process of idealization coexist.

In the beginning, Adolphe sees Ellénore both as a potential conquest, which he can dominate through his presence and charm, and as the fulfillment of his romantic dreams. "I thought I was taking, like a cold and impartial observer, a survey of her mind and character, but each word that she uttered seemed to be cloaked in an inexplicable grace" (46). He remains lucid enough, however, not to confuse his powerful obsession with love: "I didn't believe I loved Ellénore, but I couldn't accept not being liked by her. She occupied my mind constantly: I formed thousands of plans; I invented thousands of ways to conquer her" (47).

Psychopaths skillfully mimic, rather than actually feeling, human emotions. Adolphe knows how to flatter his target with simulated words of love, borrowed phrases from romantic novels and from other people's genuine feelings. He's stimulated above all by the act of simulation itself. He experiences the "duper's delight" that psychopaths commonly feel when they convincingly present themselves as something they're not or express sentiments they lack. "My lack of certainty in the success of my endeavor gave my letter an agitation which strongly resembled love. Heated up as I was by my own style, I began to feel, by the end of my writing, a little of the passion which I tried to express with as much force as possible" (48). The fact that Ellénore doesn't give in to his desires fuels Adolphe's artificial fire. For weeks, she refuses to see him. He states, "This response overwhelmed me. My imagination, irritated by the obstacle, took over my whole existence. The love which just an hour before I applauded myself for faking I thought all of a sudden I was experiencing with passion" (48).

The inadvertent cat and mouse game that Ellénore instigates through her initial resistance only increases Adolphe's predatory focus on her. He becomes consumed by the single-minded goal of seducing her: "I was surprised myself about what I was feeling... I was equally incapable of distraction or study. I walked around constantly by Ellénore's door... Impatience was devouring me. I checked my watch all the time" (49-50). His passion is intense yet hollow. Sandra L. Brown, M.A. explains that emotional predators can form intense attachments without connecting emotionally with their targets. Attachment means simply seeking proximity. Emotional bonding, on the other hand, implies greater depth: a real connection. Psychopaths are incapable of making real, emotional connections. The psychopathic bond is therefore an inherently mismatched relationship. Brown elaborates:

> So within the attachment phase of this relationship we have a woman who tests 97% higher in attachment than other people and who tends to trust automatically, and her partner, the psychopath, who has the equivalent of an adult attachment disorder who is trying to camouflage it by masquerading enormous amounts of zealous affection (*Women Who Love Psychopaths*, 156-7).

While psychopaths can't bond with others they can, like Adolphe, become obsessed with pursuing a given woman. For a period of time, they may desire to be in her company day and night. But this dogged pursuit of their target doesn't imply any feelings of caretaking. On the contrary, it exhibits an inherent lack of empathy and the pathological need to control another person by monitoring her activities. However, since psychopaths lack standards of comparison between genuine, deeper feelings of affection (which they can't experience) and their intense infatuations, they commonly mistake their temporary obsessions for real love. Adolphe recounts, "I passed the night without sleeping. There was no longer any question of calculation or plans; I felt myself, as sincerely as possible, truly in love" (53).

Not satisfied with admiring her from a distance, the narrator starts pressuring Ellénore to see him. Even in our days such ambiguous circumstances may be regarded as inappropriate. In early nineteenth-century France, this violation of social mores would have been flagrant. Adolphe manifests an obvious lack of empathy for how his behavior would compromise Ellénore in the eyes of her partner, her children and her social circle. However, he skillfully couches his selfish request in the flattering language of passionate love. When Ellénore rightfully objects that seeing him in private would tarnish her reputation, Adolphe switches the focus to himself: "I'm terribly unhappy," he complains. "I don't have the strength to endure such prolonged unhappiness; I hope for nothing, ask for nothing, except to see you: but I must see you to survive" (53). Ellénore buys into this inflated rhetoric and agrees to see him. Adolphe, in turn, reassures her that this initial boundary violation will not result in further transgressions that could compromise her reputation and ruin her family life. In other words, he deceives her.

To readers, Adolphe's promise appears like a transparent ruse to get her alone so that he can make his advances on her. But to Ellénore, who's yearning for attention and affection, such a request seems relatively innocuous. She relents, but imposes upon him the condition that they see each other only in public. When she gives in to his wishes, Adolphe initially rewards her with further declarations of love and flattery. Shortly thereafter, however, he's no longer satisfied with this level of control. He needs more. Consequently, he pushes the envelope further, demanding new boundary violations from her. Each time Ellénore gives in to his will, the line she drew in the sand becomes erased. Consequently, her values and boundaries lose meaning. The heroine reflects the psychological profile of women who love psychopaths. Brown's research suggests that such women are eager to please. They also trust the psychopath's words rather than paying attention to his actions. In general, women involved with dangerous men tend to be too cooperative with their partners' desires, even when those go against their best interests. Brown documents, "She feels the magnetic pull into an emotional and sexual vortex that she can't free herself from. She mistakes intensity for love and passion for bonding. It doesn't take the psychopath long to test the depths of her love (and tolerance) and to figure out he has a lot of wiggle room in the relationship to abuse" (*Women Who Love Psychopaths*, 213-4). Soon, Ellénore and Adolphe see each other more frequently, nearly every day. Rather quickly, she becomes addicted to her lover's lavish flattery, to his intense focus on her as well as to his professed love.

Once their dominance bond is consolidated, Adolphe feels sufficiently confident to ask that they see each other in private. This carries with it the obvious implications of physical intimacy. Wisely, he doesn't make his request explicit. Instead, Adolphe couches his need for sexual conquest in the more comforting language of an amitié amoureuse, or the ambiguous but supposedly chaste friendship between men and women that was common in France at the time (granted, probably far more common in theory than in fact). He also turns social mores on their head. He asserts that in being cautious and proper Ellénore is actually being frivolous and superficial. "One would say that in asking you to see me, I obtained the same favor for the whole universe. I swear, in seeing you so prudent, I never thought you'd be so frivolous" (55).

Already used to Adolphe's daily presence and accustomed to giving in to his requests, Ellénore violates her boundaries yet again. By now, she's emotionally hooked on Adolphe. She's not prepared to risk losing him by refusing to fulfill his wishes. The emotional predator senses that he's got his prey firmly in his grasp. He coolly observes, "The idea of breaking up no longer occurred to her: she consented to see me sometimes alone" (55). Inch by inch, Adolphe erodes Ellénore's boundaries and approaches his goal. Soon enough, she not only accepts his inappropriate declarations of love, but also reciprocates them. At first, Adolphe rewards Ellénore for each concession, to gain her trust. "I spent several hours at her feet, declaring myself the happiest man on earth, giving her thousands of assurances of tenderness, devotion and eternal respect" (56). Of course, in compromising her reputation, Adolphe isn't manifesting even temporary and conditional respect, much less the eternal, unconditional love he professes. But like so many victims of psychopathic seduction, by now Ellénore feels too attached to her lover to examine his inappropriate actions: especially the disconcerting succession of violated promises.

As they become more intimate, they exchange confidences. Adolphe pays close attention to everything Ellénore reveals about her background, experiences and needs. He wants to find out as much as possible about his target's vulnerabilities to discover more ways in which he can control her. He also tells her exactly what she wants to hear and gives her the kind of attention she always craved but never experienced before. Adolphe notices, with satisfaction, Ellénore's growing emotional dependency on him. By now, she listens for his footsteps, hoping that he'd visit her several times a day. Ellénore helps the seducer's assessment process along by openly admitting to him that she's obsessed with him. She confesses to Adolphe that she thinks of practically nothing and nobody else. As is the commonly case with psychopaths, however, the more power the seducer gets over his target, the more he wants from her in order to feel the same degree of pleasure from her conquest. Adolphe now wants to possess Ellénore completely, body and soul. Once again, he camouflages his sense of entitlement—the attitude that he should get whatever he wants when he wants it simply because he wants it, no matter what the cost to others—in flattering, romantic terms. "Ellénore, I wrote her one day, you don't know at all what I suffer. Close to you, far from you, I'm equally unhappy. During the hours which separate us, I walk aimlessly, hunched over from the burden of an existence that I can no longer tolerate" (57).

In *The Sociopath Next Door*, Martha Stout states that the phony pity play constitutes one of the give-away signs of psychopathy. Psychopaths make everything in life be about them. By representing themselves as sensitive victims, they induce others to ignore their own needs and obligations in order to cater to theirs. Adolphe hints that Comte de P, Ellénore's partner, poses an unacceptable obstacle between them. For as long as the count remains in her life, he implies, their romantic future will be precarious. To overcome that barrier, Adolphe suggests, she must belong only to him. "Close to you, I still fear some obstacle, suddenly placed between you and me" (58). He's careful not to ask Ellénore more explicitly to leave the count. Instead, he relies upon his skill for manipulation to instill in her the anxiety that she might lose his devotion if she doesn't leave her partner of her own "free will." Isolated from the count, her family and her social circle, Ellénore will be fully under her predatory new lover's control and at his mercy. Which is exactly where Adolphe wants her.

As we've seen, psychopaths commonly foster their victims' dependency in order to control them. They tend to move very fast, in a race against time. Brown exposes the strategic logic behind this seemingly passionate rush:

> The rapid pace that psychopaths are known to have in relationship skill build-ing will move her quickly into gorilla-glue bonding at lightning speed (*Women Who Love Psychopaths*, 156).

Any fast-paced romantic relationship with a psychopath inevitably turns into a train wreck. Ellénore's affair with Adolphe is no exception. Unfortunately for her and those who care about her, the heroine gives in to her lover's unre-lenting pressure. Like Mme Bovary and Anna Karenina, seen from the external perspective of the implied reader, Ellénore is not a particularly sympathetic character. She readily abandons her values and obligations to others for the sake of ephemeral pleasures with a cheap seducer. She falls victim not only to Adol-phe's machinations, but also to her own vanity and selfish tendencies. Psycho-paths intuitively know how to use their victims' character flaws against them. Like so many women seduced by emotional predators, Ellénore is addicted to the narcissistic supply that only her lover gives her, which, during the seduction phase, makes her feel more special, more desirable and more interesting than other women. Adolphe sees that his persistence and false promises have paid off. "Ellénore never knew until now this passionate sentiment, this feeling of another being lost in her existence, which even my anger and frustration proved to her" (59).

Just as he's open-eyed about his target's vulnerabilities, Adolphe remains lucid about the fact that the process of seduction itself excites him, not Ellénore herself. He observes, "Her resistance intensified all my sensations, all my thoughts: I experienced anger which frightened her and moved her to submis-sion, tenderness and idolatrous veneration" (59). Only Ellénore confuses her lover's intense pursuit and bullying persistence with genuine caring. More gen-erally, she misconstrues his goal of seduction for the goal of building an endur-ing relationship together. Acting upon this false assumption, "she abandoned herself completely" (59).

While Adolphe experiences casual fondness for his new mistress and takes pleasure in her company, his attachment to her is only temporary and superficial. Emotional predators tend to view sex as their preferred vehicle of exercising dominance. For a psychopathic seducer like Adolphe, once the conquest is over, so is the thrill of the chase. The lesser pleasure of ownership replaces the intense rush of seduction: "I walked with pride among men; I looked them over with a domineering glance" (59).

Psychopaths live passion only in the moment. At this point in the narrative, Constant gives voice to the most lyrical description I've read of the psychopathic bond: of this highly contingent and conditional yet often intense form of passion that makes the present seem eternal. The narrator declares, "Love is nothing but a luminous point of light, and yet it seems to extend throughout time. A few days ago it didn't exist, soon it won't exist anymore; but, for as long as it lasts, it spreads its clarity upon both past and future" (56). For a psychopathic seducer, however, the present moment casts very little light upon the past and the future. Memories of wonderful times shared together or of overcoming common hardships don't sediment for such shallow individuals. Therefore, they also don't create a foundation of real intimacy. Likewise, hopes for the future mean nothing to them without the intense pleasures of the moment. When you remove the significance of a common past as well as future commitment from human experience, all you have left is a tainted, and increasingly tedious, present.

Once no longer distracted by the goal pursuing Ellénore, Adolphe feels inconvenienced by his new mistress' demands. He remains flattered by her love. But her excessive attention has an obvious downside now, which never bothered him before, when he was euphoric with the rush of pursuing her. As Ellénore's attachment to him grows with contact, Adolphe's attraction to her proportionately diminishes. The narrator observes, "Her attachment to me seemed to increase from the sacrifice she made me. She never let me go without trying to retain me. When I left, she asked me when I'd return… It was sometimes inconvenient to have all my steps measured in advance and all my minutes counted" (59). What turns out to be most "inconvenient" for the seducer is the fact that he has to break up with most of his "acquaintances"—code word for his other lovers and flings—since Ellénore is a much more high-maintenance mistress. To his chagrin, she demands most of his time and attention in exchange for her devotion.

At this point, Adolphe is still "in love" with Ellénore. But there's a palpable difference between the cool satisfaction he feels now and the hot passion of his initial pursuit. He depicts the distinction eloquently and succinctly when he states, "Ellénore was no doubt still a lively pleasure in my life, but she was no longer a goal, she was a bond" (62). That's not a very good thing to be, at least from the perspective of a psychopathic seducer. A bond is someone or something that restrains his behavior. Psychopaths want to enchain others and gain total control of their lives. But they, themselves, need to remain free. Love bonds can be exclusive because they're grounded in mutual caring. By way of contrast, the dominance bonds psychopaths establish with their targets aren't exclusive. Once a psychopathic seducer conquers a woman, she also loses most of his interest.

Unfortunately for their unsuspecting victims, psychopaths rarely admit the selfishness, malice and cynicism that motivate their relentless pursuit of women. While during the seduction phase they commonly argue in favor of violating social mores, once they tire of their targets they appeal to the very norms that they repeatedly transgress and don't even believe in. Conveniently, Adolphe rationalizes his diminished interest in Ellénore in terms of his concern for her social reputation: "I feared moreover compromising her. My constant presence must have astonished her servants, her children, who could see me. I trembled at the idea of unsettling her life" (62). Funny that he should think of his mistress' reputation only now, after having used her. It never occurred to him to consider Ellénore's partner, her children and her place in society before, when she was pointing out to him all these factors as reasons not to get romantically involved. As we recall, at that time Adolphe viewed them as nothing more than obstacles in his path.

It's not exactly a cosmic coincidence that once a psychopath attains his goal, he suddenly changes rhetoric and becomes conventional. The narrator makes it transparently obvious that once seduced, Ellénore no longer attracts him. He attempts to detach himself from his mistress so that he can be free, once again, to pursue other women. Being emotionally hooked on him and believing in his disingenuous love, however, Ellénore holds on to her lover with all her might. Adolphe's impatience to move on is only mollified by the idea that the liaison with Ellénore is, after all, temporary: "At any rate the vague ideal that, by the nature of things, this affair couldn't last... served to calm me when I got tired or impatient with her" (62). Adolphe sees the end of their affair as the light at the end of the tunnel. By way of contrast, Ellénore views him as the light of her life.

Adolphe's diminished interest in his mistress after having seduced her doesn't necessarily prove that he's a psychopath. As many women will tell you, there are millions of emotionally unavailable or shallow men, who view "love" as a sequence of exciting hook-ups. Fortunately for the rest of society, however, most of them aren't clinically psychopathic. Usually, they're out to have a good time, not to control and emotionally destroy their targets. What makes a psychopath far more dangerous than your ordinary player is the fact that an emotional predator doesn't want his targets to escape from his clutches unharmed. Players may, more or less unwittingly, leave behind a trail of broken hearts. They're generally indifferent to the welfare of their "scores." Psychopaths, on the other hand, deliberately and maliciously harm their targets. They leave behind a trail of shattered lives.

On some level, psychopaths suffer from incurable addictions, even to the targets they no longer desire. Although he's grown tired of Ellénore, Adolphe can't detach from his own dominance bond with her. This establishes between them an unhealthy co-dependency, which becomes increasingly burdensome to him and extremely dangerous for her: "Her happiness was necessary to me and I knew I was necessary to her happiness" (62). Of course, what the narrator goes on to describe is anything but happiness. Because both characters seem unwilling (or unable) to let each other go, literary critics generally take the author at his word. They view Adolphe as a man who lacks the strength to break his mistress' heart, even after having fallen out of love with her. I don't see much evidence for this interpretation in the novel, however. Instead, I recognize in Adolphe's language and behavior the kind of rationalizations psychopaths commonly make for keeping their victims on the hook long after the thrill of seduction, and thus their so-called "passion," is nothing but a distant memory.

Adolphe's unwillingness to tell Ellénore the truth—namely, that he tired of her and wants to move on to someone else—functions as a form of psychological torture for her. She can't understand why she lost his "love." She therefore doesn't know what to do to prove herself worthy of Adolphe's devotion once again. Like many of the real women who love psychopaths, Ellénore clings to the memories of Adolphe's supposed passion. She refuses to confront his obvious lack of caring for her. Sandra L. Brown, M.A. attributes this bracketing of unpleasant realities in the psychopathic bond to the trance-like focus encouraged by the psychopath during the seduction phase: "Trance produces perceptual biases. That means if the psychopath is telling her wonderful things and she is euphoric with him, she tends to associate wonderful and euphoric things with the memory of him... even after he's turned into a monster" (*Women Who Love Psychopaths*, 181).

Trusting those misleading memories over real actions, Ellénore hopelessly struggles to reclaim Adolphe's affection. Yet nothing she does proves good enough for him. She abandons her partner. She leaves her children under the custody of Comte de P. She refuses the fortune the count offers her on the condition that she leaves her unprincipled lover. She gives up what's left of her social circle to follow her lover wherever he wants to go. She invites him to live with her at her expense in her native country, Poland, once she receives an inheritance from her father. The list of sacrifices she makes to regain the seducer's "love" goes on and on. By the end, it starts to resemble the absurdity of one of Voltaire's farces. Ellénore mistakenly believes that the more she gives up for Adolphe, the more he'll grow to appreciate her sacrifices. In fact, the opposite logic applies. The more she gives in to him, the more he asks of her. As she struggles to meet his new needs, these shift.

Seeking dominance rather than successful relationships, psychopaths enjoy watching their partners jump through hoops for them. They can't appreciate or reciprocate feelings of devotion, self-sacrifice or love. Consequently, they often prey upon women who play the martyr role, taking everything they give and offering them less and less in return. In fact, the more power a psychopath acquires over a given target, the less she interests him and, therefore, the fewer concessions he makes for her.

After the seduction phase, joint life between Adolphe and Ellénore turns into a game of simulation. He pretends to care about her while she, in turn, pretends to be happy with their increasingly distant relationship. The less effort the seducer makes to keep on his phony mask of charm, the more his true identity and ugly motives show through. As a result, their relationship degenerates into a series of explosive fights and mutual reproaches, punctuated by periodic reconciliations: "We exploded in mutual reproaches. Ellénore accused me of having misled her, of not having had for her anything but a passing infatuation and having alienated the count's affection, having placed her in the compromising social situation which she had tried all her life to escape" (65).

Susan Forward wittily states in her best-selling book on misogynist men, *Men Who Hate Women and the Women Who Love Them*, that when the honeymoon phase of a romantic relationship is over, it's over for both partners. One of them doesn't get to stay in Hawaii while the other one returns home. Both Adolphe and Ellénore become dissatisfied with their hollow relationship. Perfunctory reconciliations after fights can't erase the fact that they both realize that his feelings for her are gone. "We kissed: but the first blow was delivered, a first barrier was crossed. Both of us spoke irreparable words; we could remain quiet, but not forget them" (65). During such moments, even Ellénore opens her eyes to catch a glimpse of the unpleasant reality. She acknowledges her loss of status in her lover's eyes. What she refuses to confront, however, is the more disturbing fact that Adolphe never loved her because he's incapable of love.

Believing that she must have done something to lose his affection, Ellénore clings to her lover with all her might. Predictably, this leads him to withdraw further. "I complained about my constrained life, of my youth consumed by inactivity, of the despotism she exercised over my actions" (70). From the revered queen placed above all other women on a pedestal, Ellénore becomes a slave to her lover's wishes. She turns into an abject woman who's pathetically aiming to appease a psychopath so that he can stay in her life. Needless to say, Ellénore's desperate struggles don't reignite Adolphe's initial enthusiasm for her. They only weaken her further, increase his power over her and perpetuate the farce their life together has become. Once again, her behavior conforms to the real responses of many of the women who love psychopaths, who are weakened by their constant efforts to please their pathological partners. Brown documents, "By the mid-part of the relationship a woman who is normally dominant and resourceful may for the first time in her life feel 'fragile' or even 'mentally ill'" (*Women Who Love Psychopaths*, 214).

Although she keeps jumping through his hoops, Adolphe is not satisfied with the power he has over her. Deprived of any possibility of mutual love, their life together feels rehearsed: "Ellénore and I pretended with one another," the narrator recounts. "We said nothing about the only thought that obsessed us. We lavished upon one another caresses, we uttered words of love, but we spoke of love out of the fear of speaking of anything else" (70).

Tellingly, only when Adolphe encounters another obstacle—once his father banishes Ellénore and forbids him from seeing her—does he experience a spark of his former passion for his mistress: "I formed thousands of plans to rejoin Ellénore forever: all my heart came back to her; I was proud to protect her. I hungered to hold her in my arms; love repenetrated my soul, I felt a fever which overwhelmed my head, my heart, my senses" (77). This flicker of reawakened emotion, triggered by willfulness rather than love, is quickly extinguished. For once, Ellénore sees through its real motivation and confronts her lover: "She insisted on forcing the truth out of me; her joy disappeared, her face was covered by a dark cloud" (77).

Afterwards, Ellénore and Adolphe fall back upon the only thing they can do, given their pathological interdependency and the absence of mutual love: dissimulation and diversion. Irritated by her reproaches, Adolphe finally confesses to his mistress: "I will always be your friend, I will always feel for you the most profound affection... But love, this transport of the senses, this involuntary inebriation, this forgetfulness of all other interests and duties, Ellénore, I don't feel them anymore" (77). In admitting to her the truth, Adolphe isn't motivated by integrity, compassion or honesty. He allows his mask of charm to slip off once he feels that he's already used up Ellénore's value. He's now ready to initiate the discard phase. As Sandra L. Brown, M.A. elaborates, "Psychopaths enjoy power most when it is equated to, and produces, victimization" (*Women Who Love Psychopaths*, 39).

At this point in the narrative, if Ellénore were strong enough to accept this fact, she would have finally understood that Adolphe's passion for her was predatory, shallow and ephemeral and moved on with her life. But that wouldn't make for such a poignant story. It also wouldn't be as psychologically realistic. Current research on the psychopathic bond shows that many women stay with their dangerous partners and persevere in toxic relationships even after they see the psychopaths for what they are and even after their pleasure and joy together are gone. Instead of letting go of her malicious lover, Ellénore continues trying to resuscitate their comatose relationship. Predictably, none of her strategies work. Adolphe aptly summarizes the emotional vacuum he senses between them: "We lived, if one could call it so, in a kind of memory of the heart, sufficiently strong so that the idea of separation was painful to us, but too weak to give us any pleasure in being together" (85).

To alleviate their mounting tension, Adolphe and Ellénore throw themselves into social life. They also resort to playing mind games with one another. She tries to make him jealous by flirting with other men. "This cold and reserved woman [...] seemed to suddenly change personality. She encouraged the feelings and even the hopes of a crowd of young men" (99). But her plan predictably misfires, since having already had her, Adolphe no longer wants to possess her. In addition, he sees through her transparent ploys. Although not genuinely jealous, Adolphe exerts control over his unhappy mistress for its own sake. He asks Ellénore to stop flirting with other men. She instantly obeys, hoping, as before, that her concessions will buy her his love. They don't, of course. On the contrary, Ellénore's constant submission to his will bores Adolphe. A defeated, passive conquest presents no further challenge to a psychopathic seducer. The narrator recounts, "Everything around us resumed a normal existence but we were even unhappier. Ellénore thought she had new rights over me; I felt weighed by new chains" (102). The downside of establishing such dominance bonds, at least from the psychopath's perspective, is that they also constrain the seducer himself.

To make matters worse, Adolphe is blinded by his own delusional narcissism. He imagines that without being tied to his current mistress, he'd be great, rich, successful, sociable, beloved, wealthy and desired by far more distinguished aristocratic women: even though he wasn't doing anything productive with his life before having met Ellénore. "As stingy men see in the treasure they amass all the goods they could buy with them, so I saw in Ellénore the privation of all the successes I could have without her. It's not just one career that I regretted. As I hadn't tried any of them, I regretted them all. Having never used my talents, I imagined them to be limitless; I wished that nature would have made me weak and mediocre to spare me the regret of having sunk so low voluntarily" (89-90).

Having already devalued his victim, Adolphe sets the groundwork to discard her with immunity by criticizing her to others. He damages Ellénore's tainted reputation further by making misogynist comments to mutual acquaintances. His interlocutors correctly interpret such jabs as aimed at his mistress, not at women in general. "People reproached her for not having inspired in her lover more consideration for her gender and more respect for romantic bonds" (71). He then proceeds to complain about Ellénore more directly to a man who is a friend of his father's—and thus already biased against her—as well as to his mistress' best friend. The psychopath's smear campaign works. Both acquaintances fall for Adolphe's fake pity play. They spread more nasty rumors about Ellénore.

After having demeaned his mistress and isolated her from everyone who cared about her, the seducer abandons her. When Ellénore discovers a letter Adolphe wrote to his father's friend, in which he maligns her and promises to leave her, she falls seriously ill. She finally realizes that she has sacrificed everything and everyone in her life for a man who doesn't even love her. Only then does Adolphe also see that he'll soon lose the only being over whom he exercised total control. He's not particularly concerned about Ellénore's failing health. He worries instead about finding himself alone, deprived of such a willing and malleable target: "I broke the only being who loved me; I broke this heart, this companion, who persisted in devoting herself to me with indefatigable tenderness; already a sense of isolation overcame me. Ellénore was still breathing, but I could no longer confide in her my thoughts, I was already alone in the world, I no longer lived in this atmosphere of love that spread itself around me... The whole of nature seemed to tell me that I ceased to be loved forever" (113-4).

Readers need not worry about Adolphe, however. We can be confident that psychopathic seducers like him will always find plenty of willing victims to attract, use, manipulate and destroy. The death of Ellénore is not a tragedy, just as the story of this failed love affair is not a romance. As much as it's difficult to believe in Adolphe's sorrow at the end, it's difficult to mourn the death of Ellénore. Even though she's a more sympathetic character than Adolphe, her self-absorption, the neglect of her obligations towards her previous partner and children and her obsessive need for an empty man's manipulative attention caused her undoing. Yet in some respects, like Emma Bovary and Anna Karenina—two comparably imperfect heroines—Ellénore is an emotionally compelling character that deserves some sympathy. She reflects with stark realism the psychological devastation of victims of emotional predators. She illustrates how psychopaths turn strong and healthy individuals into effigies of their former selves. It's difficult to comprehend this horrible experience if you haven't felt it on your own skin. How can anybody have sympathy for someone whose moral framework and dignity have been so seriously undermined that she willingly accepts such a humiliating asymmetrical arrangement and even pines for it when the psychopath inevitably grows tired of her and discards her?

The only way I can answer this question is by suggesting that we should not look at "voluntary" relationships only in terms of a reductive voluntarism. I'll offer an analogy to explain my point. When the women in Afghanistan "choose" to cover their whole bodies except for their eyes in burkas, when they "choose" a religious ideology which regards them as the property of men in their culture, when they "choose" to forgo education and even basic medical care, it's because their options of gaining respect in that society are severely restricted. Basically, their "voluntary choice" is to be respected as a proper Muslim woman or not at all. Our choices aren't open-ended among infinite possibilities. We make life decisions largely based on our temperaments, circumstances, values and, above all, the information we have at our disposal.

When dealing with psychopaths, however, you're dealing with a steady flow of misinformation, compounded by phony yet often compelling behavior, which distorts your perception of reality and hampers your ability to make rational decisions. Lack of knowledge about personality disorders, false or partial information, brainwashing and the creation of unrealistic expectations all play a significant role in determining women's poor choices once they're trapped in psychopathic bonds. Furthermore, with each step they take to get closer to their psychopathic partner and strive to gain his approval, such women become increasingly entangled in a web that narrows the range of their freedom and diminishes the quality of their lives, as Adolphe did for Ellénore. Like her, they can end up prisoners of an unrequited love.

Why is this phenomenon relevant to a general audience and not just to those who have been burned by psychopathic seducers? Because just about anyone can be ensnared by emotional predators. As we'll see in my discussion of the current research on the women who love psychopaths, psychopathic seduction can happen to anyone, not just to women predisposed to masochism or to those who lack self-esteem. Constant's novel illustrates that psychopathic seduction happens gradually and in ways that are disguised as true love and mutual caring. Current research shows that it happens to moral and religious women as well as to those with more liberal values. It happens to women of every age, social background and range of education. Information about psychopathy and relationships with emotional predators is the best way to protect yourself against them. Without this information, you may not realize that you're involved with a dangerous man until it's too late: until, like the misfortunate Ellénore, you've invested far too much for far too long into that toxic relationship. How much are some women willing to sacrifice in the name of "love"? Both fact and fiction tell us that the answer is astonishingly much. Sometimes even everything.

Chapter 6

The Women Who Love Psychopaths

Sandra L. Brown, M.A. published a very informative book on the psychological profile of the women who love psychopaths, to which I've alluded frequently in previous chapters. It's called, descriptively, *Women who love psychopaths: Inside the Relationship of Inevitable Harm with Psychopaths, Sociopaths and Narcissists* (Mask Publishing, 2009). This is a timely and groundbreaking book. Although there are many books about domestic violence as well as numerous clinical studies of psychopaths and psychopathy, this is the only book I found that focuses on the female victims from both a clinical and lay perspective. It combines victim testimonials with a clear psychological explanation of how psychopaths operate, their victims' perspectives and their damaging effects. Given that the victims far outnumber the psychopaths themselves, it's very important to understand their behavior as well. I'd like to summarize here some of Brown's findings by using the structure of addressing common misconceptions. You can also find out additional information on this subject by visiting her website, saferelationshipsmagazine.com.

As previously mentioned, Robert Hare, who elaborated the clinical standards of evaluating psychopathy/antisocial personality disorder used in prisons and elsewhere, estimates that between 1 and 4 percent of the population suffers from this personality disorder. The bad news about this statistic is that there are millions of psychopaths in this country alone who negatively impact tens of millions of lives. The good news is that it's still a relatively small percentage of the population. You have no doubt met a few psychopaths during the course of your life. But chances are that they weren't your husband, your lover, your son, your daughter or your sibling. Perhaps they were your colleague, your teacher, your acquaintance or your boss: essentially, people with whom you've had relatively superficial contact. We already know that in casual contact psychopaths come across as absolutely wonderful. They can be charming, cool, eloquent, sweet and sociable. They love to be the center of attention and bask in public approval and applause. This means that you probably won't be able to relate to the degree of malicious damage that psychopaths inflict upon their partners and their families.

Most people have encountered jerks. We've met people who cheat, lie or steal. But those individuals aren't necessarily psychopaths. They may feel remorse for what they've done wrong. They may not harm others deliberately, to inflict maximum damage. They may be capable of love and empathy. Most people have also run across people with narcissistic tendencies. We probably met individuals who are very full of themselves and consider themselves superior to others. These people are annoying and, in some respects, ridiculous. But they're usually capable of remorse and of respecting moral boundaries. They can love others. They just don't know how to express their feelings because they're too focused on themselves.

Most people have also run across people with psychological problems, such as neuroses, depression, anxieties or mood swings. Those individuals are generally more harmful to themselves than to others. Moreover, they're usually capable of empathy. Many women have at some point been burned by players, or men who are either sex addicts or just plain promiscuous. If you're looking for commitment and emotional depth, these men certainly spell trouble. But they generally don't engage in the degree of malicious deception that psychopaths do. They rarely try to convince you that you're the love of their life. They don't usually tell you that they want to marry you and spend the rest of their days with you. If anything, your ordinary players give you very clear signals that they run around with many women, that they don't want any commitment and that you're one of many to them. You either accept this unpalatable arrangement or you refuse to engage with them. But at least with your ordinary players you generally know what you're getting yourself into. With psychopaths you don't.

Consequently, if you've been the partner of a psychopath, most people won't relate to your experiences. They won't understand why your suffering is so extreme and why it takes you so long to get out of that relationship and to get over it once you leave him. Many people whom you tell about what's happened to you— once you clarify that you're not dealing with your ordinary jerk or player—go to another extreme. They erroneously assume that psychopaths are obvious predators who are very easy to detect. Because it's mostly psychopathic murderers who make it on the news, they may also mistakenly associate all or most psychopaths with notorious serial killers like Ted Bundy, not with your seemingly ordinary, charming husband or boyfriend who is a teacher, a lawyer or a doctor: the man you live with day to day, who appears to be healthy, devoted and normal. They can't understand what it's like to have spent your intimate life with someone who creates the illusion not only of normalcy, but of hyper-normalcy: namely, of being far better than your average man and of being engaged in an extraordinary relationship with you. It's very difficult to explain to most people that in a long-term romantic relationship with a psychopath, you feel not only cheated, but also emotionally raped. In other words, a close relationship with a psychopath is, fortunately for most people and unfortunately for the victims, beyond the pale of normal human experience and comprehension. The seventy-five women who participated in Brown's study all report being deeply traumatized by their interactions with psychopaths (*Women Who Love Psychopaths*, 231).

Just as people tend to have false assumptions about psychopaths, they also have correspondingly false assumptions about the kind of women who become ensnared by them. Since they believe that the signs of psychopathy are either mundane (such as a jerk or a player) or obvious (a serial murderer), they assume that the women who fall for such men are gullible or, worse yet, just as corrupt as the psychopaths themselves. Brown's research helps dispel these false assumptions. Granted, in some cases, it may be true that the women targeted by psychopaths are not very deep or that they're disordered as well. But usually that's the kind of women whom psychopaths target for more superficial contact, such as flings and one-night stands. Psychopaths, as we've seen, depend on double standards. For longer-term relationships, they generally select moral women who won't do unto others as is done unto them. These women tested particularly high in empathy, which is the emotional underpinning for moral behavior. Psychopaths only abused their partners' empathy. "Just what can too much empathy do in the hands of a psychopath?" Brown asks. "He can keep her tied to the relationship way past the point of sanity" (*Women who Love Psychopaths*, 135). Sandra L. Brown's research also reveals that the women whom psychopaths select as their partners—meaning their wives or long-term girlfriends—tend to be educated, independent and accomplished. As we know, psychopaths enjoy a challenge. The challenge, in this case, consists of taking a healthy, strong, high functioning woman and turning her into a puppet. "To some degree," Brown elaborates, "this is the ultimate power play for a pathological to take someone strong and slam them to the mat emotionally. This is the totality of psychological triumphing for the psychopath" (*Women Who Love Psychopaths*, 229).

If you think about it, there'd be no challenge for the psychopath if the woman he selected as a partner were as bad as he is. There'd be nothing to corrupt and nobody to fool. A link between two psychopaths occurs sometimes. In fact, it's the subject of one of my favorite French novels, from whom I borrowed the title for this book: *Dangerous liaisons*. But such relationships are rare and don't last long. Two psychopaths in a couple is one too many. Each tries to outdo the other in wrongdoing, promiscuity and harm. Neither can dupe the other because they're equally well versed at the art of manipulation and deception. So two psychopaths "in love" are likely to part ways rather quickly. They may enter into a provisionary corrupt agreement, like the Count of Valmont and Mme. de Merteuil do in *Dangerous liaisons*, to compete for how many people they can seduce, dupe, use, etc. But even in those cases, as in Laclos' novel, the two psychopaths eventually turn upon each other. As we've seen, psychopaths have no loyalty to anyone but themselves.

But if the women who fall in love with psychopaths are usually decent, intelligent and moral individuals, as Brown's study indicates, then why don't these women get away from the disordered person who becomes their partner? This question leads us to a second false assumption that people tend to have about the women who love psychopaths: insofar as they think about the subject at all, of course. They assume that these women are very insecure and weak if they put up with the kind of abuse a psychopath is likely to dish out. Brown's research reveals that this hypothesis is partly true, but largely false. It's true that if you've been in a long-term relationship with a psychopathic husband or boyfriend, you'll have adjusted psychologically to the manipulation, the lies and the domination. No doubt, your confidence and self-esteem have suffered as a result. But it's factually false that you were therefore a weak and unconfident person initially, when you first had the misfortune to meet the psychopath and the misjudgment to become involved with him.

Throughout her book, Brown describes the women who fall in love with psychopaths as successful professionals: doctors, lawyers, teachers, therapists and nurses. This information may seem counterintuitive. We know that psychopaths want control. Logically, it's much easier to control weak individuals. But keep in mind that psychopaths enjoy power games. They're not sufficiently entertained by dominating a person who is already meek and passive. Where's the fun in pushing against an object that offers no resistance? You're not going to exercise your muscles by doing that, just as you're not going to exercise your manipulation skills against malleable and gullible targets. As Brown goes on to explain, psychopaths tend to be attracted to women with strong personalities and high relationship investment. They prefer tenacious individuals who will engage in their power games and stick it through the inevitable difficulties they create in the relationship. As Brown documents, for such a woman, "… her trust, tolerance, and hope will win out keeping her loyal even in the face of betrayal" (*Women Who Love Psychopaths*, 141).

So then where does this false assumption about the weakness and naïveté of the women who love psychopaths come from? It comes, once again, from most people's limited knowledge and experience, which mercifully excludes intimate involvement with a psychopath. To most people who lead normal, healthy lives, the signs of domination and abuse are obvious. Abuse means hitting one's partner. It means rape. It means verbal insults. The more sophisticated psychopaths, however, don't necessarily engage in such behavior. More commonly, charismatic psychopaths deceive and manipulate very charmingly. They generally present their machinations to you (and others) as doing you a favor rather than as sabotaging your life.

Research shows that psychopaths' brains are constructed without the capacity to form emotional bonds. Yet such individuals tend to be very clever, particularly when it comes to Machiavellian maneuvers to get what they want. Most of their mental resources are channeled into strategies of manipulation, deception and disguise. Which leads me to my next point related to why it's not so easy to recognize psychopaths. As we've seen in previous chapters, such individuals are natural chameleons. They change their personality traits and interests to appear compatible with any woman they want to seduce and use. They don't necessarily fake interest. Temporarily, their interest in you may be quite genuine when they wish to pursue you. By extension, so is their interest in everything you care about. For this reason, psychopaths initially appear to be highly compatible with their partners not only from the outside, but also from their partners' own perspectives as well. Moreover, as my analysis of *Adolphe* illustrated, their abuse is often subtle, gradual and presented as for your own good. Psychopaths are great salesmen. They pan off evil as goodness and their selfish interest as yours. By the time you wake up and realize that you've been emotionally conned, you've already slid down a slippery slope.

Sandra L. Brown, M.A emphasizes that the women who love psychopaths share an eagerness to please others. Such malleability leads them to engage in constant compromises with their increasingly demanding partners. This, of course, conforms perfectly to his plan. "For the psychopath, this level of tolerance is a pretty good guarantee she'll be around for quite a while...no matter what!" (*Women Who Love Psychopaths*, 137). However, the author also reminds us that such women give in to the psychopath out of empathy and tenaciousness rather than out of weakness. The effect, however, is the same. Excessive tolerance and misplaced empathy leads these women to repeatedly bend to the psychopath's will. Each time they do so, it diminishes their power and increases the psychopath's hold on them.

The one thing that is usually true about the assumption that women who fall prey to psychopaths are "weak" is that psychopaths tend to select strong women at their most vulnerable moments. It's as if their predatory instinct—plus all the information that you, yourself have disclosed—tells them that you're going through difficulties. You may be suffering from marital problems, or a death in the family, or a broken relationship, or anxiety, or depression, or any kind of trauma that clouds your judgment. At the lowest points in your life, psychopaths can pounce upon you. They initially promise to fix whatever problems you're experiencing. If you've gone through a painful divorce as a result of a cheating husband, then the psychopath presents himself as a faithful and trustworthy guy. In the beginning, when in your company, he has eyes only for you. When not in your company, well, that's a different story, whose plot you can imagine. If you're experiencing financial problems, the psychopath may offer you loans. If you have self-esteem issues, he will copiously flatter you: but only during the honeymoon phase of the relationship, of course. Afterwards, during the much less amusing devalue and discard phases, you're made to feel far less attractive and accomplished than you actually are.

So, contrary to popular misconceptions, the women who fall in love with psychopaths tend to be strong, independent and resourceful women at the beginning of the relationship. By the end, however, these women have been duped, mistreated, maligned and controlled so much that their self-confidence is severely impaired. Sometimes they leave their jobs as a result of the psychopath's direct pressure. At others, the psychopath's constant criticism and drama leads them to lose their jobs. Because of the severe strains of the psychopathic bond, some of the women involved with psychopaths became mere shadows of the strong and independent women they once were. Fortunately, however, many of those women took charge of their lives after putting an end to their toxic relationships. They become stronger and wiser individuals as a result of their traumatic experiences, better able to distinguish real people with genuine emotions from their psychopathic counterparts.

Chapter 7

Coping Mechanisms for Staying with a Psychopath

In the hit song *Fifty ways to leave your lover*, Paul Simon gives a man advice about how to break up with his lover. His advice would serve well any person who becomes intimately involved with a psychopath. There are at least fifty thousand great reasons to leave a psychopathic partner and not one good reason to stay with him.

Once you confront this basic truth, you run away from the psychopath in the opposite direction without ever looking back. In fact, if psychopaths generally have short-lived relationships, it's not just because they get bored with their partners and leave them. As we've seen, such men tend to save women as back-ups to their back-ups. By their logic, the more the merrier. But after the psychopaths' mask of sanity comes off, many of the women they're involved with can't stand the persons they see underneath. Psychopaths are often surprised by the degree of ice-cold contempt many of their former partners experience towards them. They can't believe that their cheating, lying and malicious manipulations could ever lead those women to reject them utterly and completely, for the rest of their lives. One explanation for their surprise is, of course, that psychopaths lack empathy. Yet this reason is a kind of psychological shorthand and not entirely accurate. As sadists, psychopaths certainly do experience a perverse form of empathy. This twisted emotion enables them to sense and relish the pain they cause others. But their capacity to envision other people's suffering is limited by the shallowness of their own feelings.

In other words, psychopaths can't fully imagine how deeply they've hurt others. They therefore can't understand how complete and irreversible those individuals' rejection of them can be. Nor do they care. To return to my initial point, the natural response of most women involved with a psychopath once his thin layer of charm peels off is to not only leave that lover, but also to feel only disgust and contempt for his behavior, for him and for every shred of memory of him. Everything about the relationship—including the seemingly good moments—becomes irreversibly tainted once you see the real psychopath. What's far more intriguing and puzzling, at least from a psychological point of view, is why some women choose to remain with a psychopathic partner even after his mask of sanity falls off and his real identity is revealed. Dating a psychopath briefly may be the product of chance or bad luck. But staying with him, I'm convinced, is the result of a long series of self-defeating choices. As we've seen, psychopaths test the limits of their partners' patience, love, loyalty and capacity to tolerate mistreatment. In this chapter, I'll explore the issue of why some women choose to stay with psychopaths from the perspective of narcissism, which lies at the core of the psychopathic bond.

In his book *Malignant Self-Love: Narcissism Revisited*, Samuel Vaknin explores in depth the malignant narcissist/psychopath side of the equation. He states that a malignant narcissist "is never whole without an adoring, submissive, available, self-denigrating partner. His very sense of superiority, indeed his False Self, depends on it." The main difference between a narcissist and a psychopath, I would add, is that the narcissist experiences fundamental insecurities that trigger his demand for constant validation. Consequently, he's more likely to be transparent in his egocentricity. He also usually lacks the psychopath's glibness and charm. A narcissist seeks praise from others so desperately that he's not likely to mask his disorder. He often appears pompous and even ridiculous to others. A psychopath, on the other hand, isn't needy. Although he also requires others to agree with his self-assessment as smarter, hotter, cooler and more interesting than others, unlike the narcissist, if they disagree or criticize him, he's not hurt at all. As we've seen, psychopaths are too emotionally shallow to experience genuine self-doubt. Their egos enable them to absorb praise and to deflect criticism, as if protected by a natural shield. In other words, for psychopaths, everything feeds and nothing disturbs their view of themselves as superior to others.

Vaknin goes on to describe the other half of the equation. He focuses on the kind of woman who stays with a psychopathic or narcissistic partner: "First and foremost, the narcissist's partner must have a deficient grasp of her self and of reality. Otherwise, she (or he) is bound to abandon the narcissist's ship after the honeymoon phase is over. The cognitive distortion is likely to consist of belittling and demeaning herself—while aggrandizing and adoring the narcissist." Vaknin characterizes their complementary relationship in terms of the polarity of sadism (on the part of the psychopath or malignant narcissist) and masochism (on the part of his adoring partner): "The partner is, thus, placing herself in the position of the eternal victim: undeserving, punishable, a scapegoat." The author acknowledges, however, that the "masochistic" partner's position isn't always self-denigrating:

> Sometimes, it is very important to the partner to appear moral, sacrificial and victimized. At other times, she is not even aware of this predicament. The narcissist is perceived by the partner to be a person in the position to demand these sacrifices from her partner, being superior in many ways. . . The status of professional victim [or martyr] sits well with the partner's tendency to punish herself, namely: with her masochistic streak.

I'd like to pause here for a moment. In reading the rest of Vaknin's book, I'm left feeling like the rewards for the so-called "masochistic" partner are being glossed over. The author suggests that any woman who stays with a malignant narcissist or with a psychopath lacks self-confidence. But the research on women who love psychopaths indicates that this is not necessarily the case. From the external perspective of an observer looking in on the relationship between a psychopath and his partner, she may appear to be weak or masochistic. Otherwise why would any woman willingly choose to stay with a man who routinely mistreats her and who's incapable of reciprocating anyone's love? Yet from an internal perspective, meaning from her own point of view and experience, the psychopathic bond appears more rewarding and complex. As we've seen, such a woman, who truly believes that her psychopathic partner is superior to other men and that therefore their relationship itself is extraordinary, also feels superior to others by association with him. Thus staying with a psychopath is not just a matter of being masochistic or of having an inferiority complex, though such tendencies may exist. It also involves having a superiority complex.

Now I'd like to take one of Vaknin's comments a step further. The author states that the women who stay with narcissists and psychopaths play the role of "professional victim" because they wish to redeem the psychopath at all cost. I'd argue, however, that such a martyr complex implies a sense of one's own moral strength and superiority. Women who cling to psychopathic or narcissistic men know enough about their partners' misdeeds and deficiencies to feel superior to them and to wish to reform them. A huge incentive—and constant challenge—for women who stay with dangerous men is the struggle to "save" them. Masochism and having an inferiority complex have little to do with this aspect of the psychopathic bond. On the contrary, being with a psychopath can make a woman who does have a moral compass feel needed and, in some respects, better than her dysfunctional partner. While the psychopath may have excessive self-confidence, he's emotionally and morally immature. His partner may believe that he needs to "grow up" by following her example and learning how to love. Thus, in some respects, the women who stay with psychopaths adopt a maternal attitude towards their comparatively childish partners. So if one wishes to apply Freudian categories, the Electra complex fits their relationship better than the masochism-sadism duality.

I'd like to dwell on the superiority complex, since I believe it explains best the tenacity of women who stay with psychopaths. Such women tend to feel superior not only to the morally deficient psychopath, but also to other women: especially to those who left or were left by the psychopath. I've mentioned earlier that the psychopath's inflated view of himself rubs off on his partner. She comes to believe that she's in a superior, unique and special partnership with him. Furthermore, if she's the only woman who's capable of having a long-term relationship with him (because the other women left him or because he left them), she may also feel like that she's privileged in his eyes. Consequently, she justifies her misguided tenacity in positive terms. She assumes that other women lacked the qualities necessary to retain the psychopath's long-term "commitment" or the patience to guide him towards moral and emotional growth. She thus convinces herself that she's far more devoted and other-regarding than them. In her own mind, staying with a psychopath in spite of all the difficulties he causes in their relationship reveals her strength of character.

Brown draws the same conclusion from the research on women who love psychopaths. She notes that persistent and strong-minded women, rather than weak and unconfident ones, refuse to give up the fight against their partner's personality disorder. This only works in the psychopath's favor. Brown states, "Her high relationship investment in a situation like this can do nothing but benefit the psychopath, while his low relationship investment has disaster written all over it for her" (*Women Who Love Psychopaths*, 120). Out of love and tenacity, they foreground all the positive aspects of the relationship. They relegate the negative aspects, as much as possible, to the background. By saying that the women who stay with a psychopath consider themselves in some respects superior to their deficient partner, I'm not suggesting that the relationship itself doesn't remain fundamentally hierarchical, tipped in his favor. Of course it does. Being narcissistic and control driven, psychopaths dictate the parameters of their relationships. But abiding by a given hierarchy, however unfair it may be, doesn't have to imply weakness or low self-esteem. That would mean that all women who participate in cults, where the cult leader is clearly at the top of the totem pole, or women who accept gender hierarchies in more traditional cultures, are necessarily passive, masochistic or submissive. They aren't. Anthropological studies have shown that such women often regard themselves as strong, feminine and ethical individuals. They also consider themselves superior to women who don't observe the same cultural norms and complimentary and necessary to the men who govern their lives.

Yet one's still tempted to ask, how can any confident, rational and sane woman ever believe that black is white? How can she possibly interpret the psychopath's negative behavior in a positive manner? She can, indeed, if she herself feels superior to others by association with her psychopathic partner, whom she considers so special. In other words, she can if she herself gains some kind of validation from the relationship. As we recall, psychopaths depict not just their own selves as superior, but also the romantic relationship with them as unique and special. They inculcate in their partners an "us versus them" mentality.

Just as they justify their negative behavior (the cheating, lying, etc.) in positive terms, they also justify your deviant behavior as a couple in positive ways as well. If they foster your pathological dependency and distrust so that you follow them around like a puppy, they explain it as a form of extraordinary intimacy. Other couples don't spend as much time together because they're not as close, not because they have more autonomy as individuals and more warranted trust in each other. If they demand that you have sex in public or in perverted ways, they argue that normal couples don't engage in such activities because they're less sensual and less attracted to each other, not because most other couples' sexual behavior is not dictated by the perverse desires of a psychopath. When you're deeply immersed in the psychopathic bond, especially one that lasts for several years, your partner's self-aggrandizement and his narcissistic justifications for his behavior tend to rub off on you. You get some validation, and thus begin to feel superior yourself, by being involved with such an "extraordinary" man and by participating in such a "unique and special" relationship, which normal people can't even imagine, much less experience.

At this point in my explanation, however, all the negative reasons come into play as well. Because how can a strong and sane woman continue to find the positive image established by the psychopath plausible over time, when there's so much overwhelming evidence to the contrary? The false image of the psychopath as an extraordinary man and partner, rather than the subhuman person he is and the pathological relationship he establishes with you, sticks only if he's isolated you from others and undermined your moral boundaries and identity. If you need his praise to feel good about yourself; if you need his company to feel complete; if you need to remain his partner to feel adequate in the eyes of others, then it will be very difficult to detach yourself from the psychopath no matter how much he mistreats you.

The psychological and emotional chains of dependency can be stronger than physical chains. They're internal to how you define yourself and to who you have become. In that case, it may take years of further abuse by the psychopath, or even being left by him, to confront the harsh and, in many ways, obvious reality: that any man who repeatedly cheats on you; who lies with great ease and no compunction whatsoever; who hurts both you and others; who deceives and manipulates all those who love and trust him and who undermines your efforts to become a stronger individual, can't possibly be better than other men, uplift you or build with you a fulfilling relationship. Such a man can only bring you down. Whatever validation you might have gotten from staying with a psychopathic partner was hollow, tenuous and short-lived. What's more, you've probably paid for each good moment, loving word and compliment from him with years of humiliation, betrayal and abuse. If you're one of the women who chooses to stay with a disordered partner even once his true self has been revealed to you, just remember that everything good about that man is pure illusion and, by extension, so is everything positive about your relationship with him: past, present and future.

In life, you can apply your strength to worthy objectives or to futile ones. Fixing a psychopath and your relationship with him constitutes a self-defeating goal. So why do so many strong women continue to bang their heads against the wall of this personality disorder? I'd like to outline below some of the coping mechanisms that enable such women to accept the fiction that a psychopath can grow to love them and that the problems in their relationship can be improved:

1. *Denial.* The most common defense against any unpleasant reality is denial. Each time you have a suspicion that your partner is being unfaithful or lies to you, you push it towards the back of your mind. It often resurfaces in the form

of anxiety, insecurity, depression, neuroses, insomnia or bad dreams. When your partner offers you implausible excuses for his lateness or absences, you accept them because you want to believe him. When others try to tell you about his misdeeds, you refuse to listen to them. To deflect blame away from him, you focus on their flaws rather than his. When you read about psychopathy, you push that information aside. Nobody can really understand the depth of your relationship with him. You keep on believing that because you're so special, moral, patient and kind and, above all, because you love him, you can be the exception that confirms the rule. You consider yourself to be the only person who truly understands him and who can "save" or reform him.

2. *Isolation.* If your narcissistic or psychopathic partner has succeeded in isolating you from others, you miss out on getting external points of view. You're also cut off from potential confidants who might be able to offer a more realistic perspective on your relationship with him and genuine emotional support.

3. *Superiority Complex/Narcissistic Tendencies.* I've covered this point previously. In some respects, you feel superior to other women in his eyes and in your own as well. If other women left the psychopath, it's because they were less moral, less kind, less generous, less forgiving, less everything than you. You believe that your unwavering loyalty to him reflects your exceptional qualities. Others can't appreciate just how special you, he and your relationship really are.

4. *Doublethink.* George Orwell coined this term to describe how people cope with mind control in totalitarian societies. They're brainwashed to believe that black is white. But they still know in the back of their minds that white is white and black is black. This concept also sheds light upon the dualistic and contradictory mindset of individuals who survive in cults or in intimate relationships with psychopaths and malignant narcissists.

As Sandra L. Brown, M.A documents, many of the women who choose to stay with psychopaths are far from naive. They know in the back of their minds that their partners are cheating and lying to them. They know in the back of their minds that their partners lack a moral compass. They know in the back of their minds that one can't blame only other women for the endless string of affairs. They recognize when their partners' lies and excuses sound so implausible that they're utterly ridiculous. But they survive in the relationship with the psychopath through a kind of doublethink. They believe two mutually exclusive sets of assumptions. On the one hand, they think that their partner is great, honest, loving, faithful, devoted and in many respects the ideal man. On the other hand, they also realize that he's a lying, conniving, cheating Loser who can't love anybody and who can't be trusted at all. In any logarithm, one couldn't possibly accept both sets of premises. But the human mind is far more complex than any logical framework. Emotions, hopes, fantasies, defense mechanisms and desires enrich our mental landscape. They also enable us to reconcile incompatible assumptions and thus, in this case, to cope with dangerous men and to adapt to pathological relationships.

At the risk of sounding too rational, however, I'll say that lucidity about who you are, who he is, what your relationship is and, more generally, educating yourself about personality disorders offers a far better self-defense than the coping mechanisms I've described above. These trap you in a series of double-binds: between masochistic and sadistic tendencies; between inferiority and superiority complexes; between contradictory assumptions (or forms of doublethink); in denial strategies that reject reality, which nonetheless resurfaces through negative psychological and physical symptoms, such as depression, insomnia, anxiety or various neuroses. However difficult it may be to confront the truth about the psychopath, and however resilient you may wish to be, giving up on a hopeless relationship is not the same thing as accepting defeat. In fact, the real defeat consists of wasting your entire life with an irredeemably bad human being who will never give you anything positive in return for your irreversible sacrifice. After all, you only have one life to live. How will you choose to live it?

Emotional Abuse and Stockholm Syndrome

We usually recognize physical abuse because it often leaves external marks: bruises, broken bones, wounds, gashes or disfiguration. Because such abuse tends to be objectively identifiable, we're not only likely to recognize its signs, but also to sympathize with the victims. Some of the great novels of modern and contemporary literature focus on victims of (statutory) rape, battery and other forms of physical abuse. I'm thinking, above all, of Nabokov's incomparable *Lolita* which, without any trace of sentimentality or moralism, offers a multidimensional characterization of the victim as well as a realistic portrayal of the remorseless pedophile. Wally Lamb's *She's Come Undone* and Anna Quindlen's *Black and Blue*, two of my favorite contemporary novels, give a compassionate portrayal of the victims. If readers readily sympathize with the heroines of these novels, it's partly because the victims are as innocent as it gets and partly because their physical abuse (rape in one case, battery in another) is obvious. Yet, as I've tried to convey here, in many situations in real life the abused isn't as morally pure (because she colludes with the abuser) and her abuse isn't necessarily so obvious (because it may be emotional rather than physical in nature). Some psychopaths, especially those who also suffer from borderline personality disorder, may, indeed, spin out of control and engage in acts of physical violence. But many are subtler in the damage they inflict upon others.

As we've seen, charismatic psychopaths present to the outside world and even to their partners an impeccable image of self-control, sanity, kindness and charm. Such psychopaths sometimes pose a greater danger than those who engage in overt acts of physical violence because their personality disorder is better camouflaged. Unfortunately, so are the symptoms of their abuse. Which brings me to my main point here. Just as outsiders may fail to identify and sympathize with the signs emotional abuse, the victims may as well. In her article "How Can I Get My X Away from the Psychopathic Con Artist?" Liane Leedom explains that psychopaths escalate their control over their partners gradually, BITE (behavior, information, thoughts, emotions) by BITE (*lovefraud.com*, September 7, 2007). Psychopaths intuitively tighten the screws at the moment when they feel they can get away with it. Over time, the victim becomes used to each new form of abuse as well as to the on-going manipulation and deceit. Charismatic psychopaths poison you softly, while pretending to love you and act in your best interest.

To offer an analogy, I've watched several episodes of *Forensic Files* where a man has poisoned his wife by introducing small doses of a toxic chemical into her food. She eventually died after months of gruesome suffering. Most psychopaths don't literally poison their spouses. But they achieve a similarly toxic effect on a psychological level. They introduce tiny doses of emotional poison into their partners' daily lives.

Your life with a psychopath can turn into a constant state of anxiety and self-doubt. You may develop neurotic habits, eating disorders and depression. Furthermore, the abuse can be so underhanded that you may not even realize that the person causing you all these negative symptoms is your own partner, the supposed love of your life. Consequently, saving yourself from a charismatic psychopath entails, first and foremost, recognizing his pattern of emotional abuse. After all, you can't fix a problem until you identify its cause.

Definition: Emotional abuse constitutes a pattern of behavior over time that is designed to control another human being through the use of manipulation, deceit, threats, intimidation, emotional blackmail, verbal abuse, insults, gaslighting, coercion or humiliation. Even normal people occasionally engage in some of these behaviors. But the key term here is a "pattern" of such behavior over time. Emotional abuse functions as a form of brainwashing. The strategies I will describe below are commonly used in prisons, labor camps, by the Secret Police of totalitarian regimes and cult leaders. They're extremely effective and very destructive. They can reduce a healthy and strong human being to the mere shadow of her former self. After months or years of such mistreatment, the victim may develop Stockholm Syndrome and, like Ellénore, cling desperately to her abuser, even after he's satisfied with the fact that he's psychologically destroyed her and moved on to new targets.

1. *Abusive Expectations*. Emotional abuse occurs in asymmetrical relationships, where one partner strives to meet the expectations of the other, while he constantly raises the bar. In a healthy relationship, expectations are reasonable, fair and balanced. Both partners strive to please each other and treat each other with mutual respect.

2. *Threats*. A psychopath maintains control of a relationship through the use of implicit or explicit threats and the inculcation of fear or anxiety. He may tell

his wife that she needs to lose weight, or move to another state with him, or change her interests and habits, or leave her job in order to keep him. Otherwise, he implies, he'll cheat on her or even divorce her. A sword hangs over the victim's head if she doesn't meet the psychopath's incessant demands and unreasonable expectations. However, even when she meets his demands he still cheats, lies and actively seeks other opportunities. Meeting a psychopath's demands accomplishes nothing constructive. It only weakens the victim and places her further under his control.

3. *Verbal Aggression.* This includes name-calling, blaming or commanding. Psychopaths rely upon such tactics to assert dominance. Verbal abuse transforms what should be an equal and mutually respectful relationship into one where the psychopath is on top. His partner fears to disappoint him or do anything that might trigger his anger.

4. *Condescending Attitude.* Charismatic psychopaths often couch their aggression in a condescending attitude towards their partners. For instance, a psychopath may act as his partner's spiritual guide or life coach. He may pretend to alleviate the symptoms of the psychological problems that he, himself, has caused her. If she develops anxiety attacks, insomnia or an eating disorder because of his ongoing deception, manipulation and mind games, he might paternalistically act as her guide, as if to help alleviate these negative symptoms. The underlying assumption in such a relationship is that the psychopath is healthier, more sane and superior to his partner. She should strive to approximate his level of mental, physical and emotional health. This cultivates her dependency on him and fosters a sense of helplessness. More importantly, it masks the underlying source of her psychological problems, which is *him* and *his* harmful behavior. It's kind of like the husband who puts poison in his wife's soup while pretending to be loving and concerned. When you get rid of the psychopath in your life, who's poisoning your existence, you also alleviate the symptoms of whatever psychological and physical ailments you developed while being involved with him.

5. *State of Uncertainty/Emotional Chaos.* A psychopath derails his partner by keeping her in a perpetual state of uncertainty. She doesn't know what to do to please him. She constantly struggles to keep him from engaging in various misdeeds or abandoning her. Psychopaths who also have borderline personality disorder transform daily life into a battlefield with occasional truces. A charismatic psychopath, however, poses a more hidden threat. He preserves the external appearance of being calm, collected and loving while periodically hinting that the perfect picture of the relationship you struggle so hard to preserve is highly precarious. Anything you might do—or fail to do—can destroy it. In reality, of course, nothing you do or refrain from doing meaningfully affects his behavior. I've never read about (or met) a psychopath who didn't do exactly what he wanted.

6. *Denying your Needs.* Being completely narcissistic, a psychopath won't prioritize your needs unless they coincide perfectly with his or cultivate your dependency on him. Consequently, he's bound to discourage you from any pursuits that solidify your bonds with others or make you stronger, more successful and more independent. His motive is clear. The less self-confidence and meaningful contact with others you have, the more he has you under his thumb and can mistreat you however he wishes. Moreover, if you dare complain that he doesn't satisfy your basic emotional need for caring or communication, he's likely to become dismissive, sarcastic, derisive or even aggressive. In his mind, everything and everyone should revolve around him.

7. *Domination.* Psychopaths establish control over their partners through a ratchet. They automatically get their way on everything when their will is not contested. When you challenge them and express your own needs, they may sometimes compromise with you, to appear fair. This image of equality is misleading, however. When you look at the whole picture of your relationship over time, you notice that it's systematically determined by the desires of the psychopath. Such an asymmetry constitutes a form of domination, which should be unacceptable to any woman who considers herself equal to her partner and worthy of the same consideration and respect as him.

8. *Invalidation.* To psychopaths, what other people think, want and feel is, to use the vernacular, "bull crap" (they commonly use such vulgar language). If you disagree with a psychopath, he's likely to invalidate your arguments and insult you. Psychopaths tend to be stubborn and persistent. Even when a psychopath momentarily relents, in the long run he returns to the same issue to "win" the match by getting his way. If your partner consistently dismisses what you know, feel, want or believe, it's obviously a very bad sign. It means that he doesn't have any genuine respect or love for you.

9. *Minimizing and Gaslighting.* If you tell a psychopath that you're hurt by his actions—such as his constant lying and cheating—he'll either deny that behavior (i.e., lie to you yet again) or minimize it by saying that you're being hypersensitive or paranoid. He'll argue that you misinterpreted the matter, or that you're exaggerating, or that it's just a misunderstanding, or that you're being a drama queen. If he calls you "crazy" and tells you that you're imagining things when you accuse him of the bad deeds he's actually done, then he's also gaslighting you.

10. *Arbitrary Reactions.* Psychopaths and narcissists commonly use arbitrary reactions to establish dominance over others. If you can't anticipate how your partner will react, then you're always on edge, trying to figure out what to do or say to please him. In addition, if you care about his opinion, your moods and self-esteem will oscillate like a yo-yo, depending upon his approval or disap-

proval. A psychopath can keep his partner completely focused on his needs by toying with her emotions in this seemingly arbitrary fashion. This despotic behavior leads his partner to feel unhinged, anxious, depressed and powerless.

11. *Sarcasm, Irony and Humiliation.* Because they prefer to cultivate a nice external image, charismatic psychopaths may not verbally abuse their partners in a blatant fashion. They may opt for more subtle techniques—such as sarcasm, irony and humiliation—to make their victims feel bad about themselves. If you're involved with a psychopath, you may have noticed that while he makes fun of you and others, any joke or wry comment about him is unwelcome and not considered amusing. Psychopaths establish double standards in practically all aspects of their lives: fidelity, honesty, freedom and even the hidden weapons of sarcasm and humor. While they routinely humiliate their partners to weaken their self-esteem, they demand nothing but the utmost respect for themselves.

The only way to reclaim your dignity when you've suffered the pattern of emotional abuse I've just described is to go straight to the source. Uproot the psychopath from your life. If you stay with him, he'll continue to mistreat you and undermine your self-esteem as he's done so far.

When you Love your Abuser: Stockholm Syndrome

So far I've used the word "victim" to describe the women who suffer at the hands of psychopaths. Yet I don't really like this word for several reasons. It tends to imply a certain passivity, as if the woman herself had nothing to do with the decision to get involved with the psychopath or, worse yet, to stay with him even once his mask of sanity started to slip. It's rare that a psychopath physically coerces a woman to get involved with him or to stay with him. Although he intimidates and brainwashes her, generally the victim cooperates.

This isn't to imply, at the opposite end of the spectrum, that the women who get involved with psychopaths are "guilty" or deserve the mistreatment. In fact, that's the other main reason why I don't like the term "victim." It evokes certain notions of moral purity that put the victim on trial. There used to be a conventional prejudice, for example, that if a victim of rape dressed in a provocative manner or walked around alone at night, then she wasn't really "innocent" and somehow "asked for it."

We realize now that this perception is false and prejudicial. Women can be targeted and abused without being perfect angels themselves. Analogously, one shouldn't have to have to prove one's perfection in the court of public opinion to gain sympathy for being used and abused by a psychopathic partner. Nobody capable of empathy and love deserves the kind of brainwashing, intimidation, lying, cheating, manipulation and distortion of reality to which a psychopath routinely subjects his partner. Despite the fact that I don't like some of the connotations of the word "victim," however, I use it because I believe that the women who become involved with and stay with psychopaths of their own free will are, in some respects, being victimized. To illustrate how you can be victimized while colluding in your own victimization, I'll rely upon Dr. Joseph Carver's explanation of Stockholm Syndrome in his article "Love and Stockholm Syndrome: The Mystery of Loving an Abuser" (*drjoecarver.com*).

Carver states that he commonly runs in his practice into women involved with psychopathic partners who say something to the effect of, "I know it's hard for others to understand, but despite everything he's done, I still love him." While cultivating feelings of love for a partner who repeatedly mistreats you may seem irrational, it's unfortunately quite common. Psychological studies show that molested children, battered women, prisoners of war, cult members and hostages often bond with their abusers. Sometimes they even go so far as to defend them to their families and friends, to the media, to the police and in court when their crimes are brought to justice.

This psychological phenomenon is so common that it acquired its own label: "Stockholm Syndrome," named after an incident that occurred in Stockholm, Sweden. On August 23rd, 1974, two men carrying machine guns entered a bank. They held three women and one man hostage for several days. By the end of this ordeal, surprisingly, the victims took the side of their captors. They also defended them to the media and to the police. One woman even became engaged to one of the bank robbers. Another spent a lot of money for the legal defense of one of the criminals. Those who suffer from Stockholm Syndrome develop an unhealthy positive attachment to their abusers. They come to accept the abuser's lies and rationalizations for his bad behavior. They sometimes also assist the abuser in harming others. This psychological condition makes it difficult, if not impossible, for the victims to engage in behaviors that facilitate detachment from the abuser, such as turning him in, exposing his misconduct or leaving him.

This unhealthy bonding solidifies when the abuser alternates between the carrot and the stick conditioning, as we've seen in the case of Drew and Stacy Peterson. He interlaces the abuse—the lying, the cheating, the implicit or explicit threats and insults, and even physical assault—with acts of "small kindness," such as gifts, romantic cards, taking her out on a date to a nice restaurant, apologies and occasional compliments. Needless to say, in any rational person's mind, a cute card or a nice compliment couldn't erase years of abusive behavior. Yet for a woman whose independent judgment and autonomy have been severely impaired by extended intimate contact with a psychopath, it can and often does. Such a woman takes each gift, hollow promise and act of kindness as a positive sign. She mistakenly believes that her abusive partner is committed to changing his ways. She hopes that he has learned to love and appreciate her as she deserves. She wants to believe him even when the pattern of abuse is repeated over and over again, no matter how many times she forgives him.

A victim of Stockholm Syndrome irrationally clings to the notion that if only she tries hard enough and loves him unconditionally, the abuser will eventually see the light. He, in turn, encourages her false hope for as long as he desires to string her along. Seeing that he can sometimes behave well, the victim blames herself for the times when he mistreats her. Because her life has been reduced to one goal and one dimension which subsumes everything else—she dresses, works, cooks and makes love in ways that please the psychopath—her self-esteem becomes exclusively dependent upon his approval and hypersensitive to his disapproval.

As we know, however, psychopaths and narcissists can't be pleased. Relationships with them are always about control, never about mutual love. Consequently, the more psychopaths get from their partners, the more they demand from them. Any woman who makes it her life objective to satisfy a psychopathic partner is therefore bound to eventually suffer from a lowered self-esteem. After years of mistreatment, she may feel too discouraged and depressed to leave her abuser. The psychopath may have damaged her self-esteem to the point where she feels that she wouldn't be attractive to any other man. Carver calls this distorted perception of reality a "cognitive dissonance," which psychopaths commonly inculcate in their victims. He elaborates:

> The combination of 'Stockholm Syndrome' and 'cognitive dissonance' produces a victim who firmly believes the relationship is not only acceptable, but also desperately needed for their survival. The victim feels they would mentally collapse if the relationship ended. In long-term relationships, the victims have invested everything and 'placed all their eggs in one basket.' The relationship now decides their level of self-esteem, self-worth, and emotional health (*drjoe-carver.com*).

I stated earlier that the only way to escape this dangerous dependency upon a psychopath is to remove yourself permanently from his influence. Any contact with him keeps you trapped in his web of manipulation and deceit. In some respects, however, this is a circular proposition. If you have the strength to leave a psychopath and the lucidity to reconsider your relationship with him, then you're probably not suffering from Stockholm Syndrome. You may have been temporarily lost in the fog of the psychopathic bond, as I was. But those who suffer from Stockholm Syndrome find themselves lost in a dark tunnel. They don't know which way to turn anymore. They probably need outside help to see the light and save themselves. So what can family and friends do for them?

Liane Leedom addresses this question in an article called "How Can I Get My X Away From the Psychopathic Con Artist?" (*lovefraud.com*, September 7, 2007). She advises a subtle intervention rather than clobbering the victim with accusations against her abuser, which may put her on the defensive. As we recall, psychopaths establish control of their victims BITE by BITE, like emotional vampires. Once again, "BITE" stands for "behavior, information, thoughts and emotions." Psychopaths attempt to control all aspects of their partners' experience of reality.

To counteract their dangerous influence, you need to BITE back. Give the victim a true perception of reality and real emotional support. If and when she complains about her psychopathic partner, don't rush to join her in criticism. She's likely to start defending the psychopath again. Instead, be a good listener. Draw out calmly and rationally the implications of the actions which upset her. Show her that you understand and support her. This way she'll have a standard of comparison between her partner's abusive behavior and your genuine caring. As we've seen, a psychopath is bound to make his partner feel insecure and pathologically dependent on him. Encourage the victim to find other sources of satisfaction in her life, which are not motivated by the desire to please him.

The issue of motivation is key. Psychopaths' partners commonly lose weight, dress better, find better employment, pursue more interesting hobbies, all of which may appear to be positive signs. But they're not if these self-improvements remain motivated by the desire to gain the psychopath's approval or avoid his disapproval. The quest for his validation keeps the victim—and her self-esteem—enchained to a disordered human being whom she can never satisfy and who doesn't have her best interest at heart. Above all, Leedom suggests that family and friends of the victim should make it clear that they will be there for her once she disengages from the psychopath. She won't find herself lost, unloved and alone, as the psychopath probably leads her to fear in order to keep her under his control.

Sometimes, family and friends of the victims notice similar behavior from the victim as from the psychopath himself. Both, for instance, may lie. Leedom and other psychologists state that, sadly, this phenomenon is also quite common. We've seen that contact with a psychopath tends to be contagious and destructive, like a virus. It distorts your perception of reality, corrupts your moral values and diminishes your empathy for others. According to Leedom,

> This is what happens when you have any association with a psychopath, no matter how you know them and whether or not you live with them. This is why I strongly encourage family members to cut the psychopath off. Psychopaths' whole way of relating to the world is about power and control. This need for power and control is *very personal*. They do it one person at a time, one victim at a time. They do it very systematically with malice and forethought. When they succeed in hurting someone or getting another person to hurt him/herself or others, they step back, revel in it and say "I did it again, shit, I'm great!" (they use a lot of foul language also) (*lovefraud.com*).

Just as most people experience a visceral pleasure in making love, or eating chocolate, or seeing their children's team win a game, so psychopaths experience great pleasure when they hurt others. They enjoy corrupting their partners so that they too become manipulative, deceptive and callous like them. For a psychopath, destroying his partner from the inside/out—her human, moral core, not just her daily life—represents a personal triumph. Psychopaths identify, pursue, isolate, corrupt, devalue and eventually discard one victim at a time. By this I don't mean to suggest, of course, that they're faithful to anyone. But they focus their energy in a single-minded fashion on destroying one life at a time, one person at a time. Women seduced by psychopaths enter what psychologists call a "hypnotic state." They shut out any aspects of reality that would reveal the truth. They focus instead only on the parts of reality that conform to the distorted perspectives presented by their partner. This logic often applies to the psychopath's family members as well. I've already mentioned that Neil Entwistle's parents supported their son even after he was convicted of murder. Parents who behave this way, Leedom explains, "want to have the perfect family as much as anyone else. They therefore normalize and justify all of the psychopath's hurtful controlling behavior" (*lovefraud.com*). Of course, when parents go so far as to either ignore or justify murder, their behavior crosses the line into pathology.

Yet no matter how much love and support you may offer the victim of a psychopath, like individuals who suffer from other kinds of addictions, she can only save herself. Ultimately, it's up to her to find the inner strength to confront the truth about the psychopath. Psychologists state that, generally speaking, the longer a woman stays with the psychopath, the less likely she is to recover from that harmful relationship. Her tortured love for him may last for the rest of her life. But it's highly unlikely that the psychopath will stick around for that long. If you don't leave a psychopath, chances are that he'll eventually leave you to mine for new opportunities elsewhere. Leedom adds, "The question here is whether this will take so long to run its course that the victim will lose herself completely. When that happens there is great risk of suicide when the relationship falls apart" (*lovefraud.com*). Hopefully, the more information we spread about psychopathy, the easier and sooner victims will recognize the symptoms of this personality disorder. This information can give them the strength to escape psychopathic seduction and control before it's too late.

Fascination with Evil: Addiction to a Psychopath

One of the main reasons why some women knowingly choose to stay with dangerous men that I haven't yet discussed in greater detail is a perverse attraction to evil. Many of us are fascinated with evil, primarily because it's caused by human beings who are fundamentally different from the rest of us. Just as it's impossible for psychopaths to relate to what's good about human nature—they see conscience, empathy and love it as weaknesses—it's almost as difficult for most people to understand what motivates psychopaths to harm others. The film *The Dark Knight* was a box office hit largely due to the popularity of the evil character. The Joker kills not in order to become richer, as do the other outlaws in the movie, but solely for the sport of it. His characterization as a psychopath is plausible: except perhaps for the unfortunate fact that most psychopaths are much harder to identify. They usually don't look as repulsive and don't act as obviously crazy as the Joker does. Similarly, Dracula novels remain international best sellers for a similar reason. In spite of ourselves, we're drawn to human vampires who feed upon our lives, to weaken and destroy us. Even crime shows that feature psychopaths are very popular. Evil individuals also tend to monopolize the personal interest and crime stories featured on the news.

Because most of us are capable of empathy and love, and thus can't identify with those who completely lack these capacities, we imagine evil people to be far more complex and intriguing than they actually are. We may be initially mystified by the contradiction between a psychopath's apparent charm and his underlying ruthlessness. But once we realize that the charm of evil people is purely instrumental, to get them whatever they want at the moment, this contradiction is resolved and ceases to intrigue us. In reality, normal people are far more interesting and less predictable than psychopaths. The depth and range of our emotions complicates, nuances and curbs our selfish impulses and desires. For psychopaths, however, nothing stands in the way of their absolute selfishness. Each and every one of their actions, including seemingly other-regarding acts, can be plausibly explained in terms of their quest for dominance.

Evil men may appear to be masculine, self-confident and in charge. They seem to know what they want from life and how to get it. Keep in mind, however, that it's so much easier to know what you want when you're considering only your own desires and are willing to sacrifice everyone and everything to satisfy them. Even animals manifest deeper emotions. They care about their young and bond with others. Psychopaths don't. If decent men sometimes hesitate, it's because they're more thoughtful and other-regarding. They put other people's needs into the equation before reaching a decision. Thus, paradoxically, it's only because of their deficiencies and simplicity with respect to normal, more multidimensional, human beings that we consider evil individuals our "Others" and are intrigued by them.

This perverse logic applies all the more to the women who choose to stay with dangerous men. Although they're repeatedly traumatized by their disordered partners, they must also, on some level, enjoy the challenge of "taming" a bad man. They may be hooked on the constant manipulation, second-guessing and other kind of mind games in which psychopaths engage on a daily basis. Many also become love addicts. After living with a psychopath for years, where every exchange is strategic and where each day brings on a new power struggle, such women may have grown so used to playing mind games that they may be bored by decent men. They may not know how to appreciate men they could trust, who would love them deeply and who would stand by them in difficult times. Such "normal" men are far more interesting than the one-dimensional and irredeemably selfish psychopaths. Living with them, however, doesn't present the insurmountable challenges that living with a psychopath does.

If you're drawn, in spite of your better judgment, to constant risk, to danger, to living on the edge in the fear that you'll be left or replaced at any moment, to histrionic shows of emotion rather than genuine feelings, to second-guessing manipulation and lies rather than honest and straightforward communication, to hide-and-seek games rather than mutual trust, then that may mean that you're too fascinated with evil to escape your addiction to the psychopath. In my opinion, it's best to leave these human monsters for the movies and fiction while enjoying your real life with a partner who loves you and who treats you right.

PART III.

HOW TO SAVE YOURSELF FROM PSYCHOPATHIC SEDUCTION

Chapter 1

Escaping the Psychopath

On her website *lovefraud.com*, Donna Andersen has several entries on how to leave a psychopath, step by step. She states that it's important to build up your social network of family and friends and to establish financial autonomy in advance. It's also advisable to rely upon external resources—such as a women's shelter and counseling—so that you don't go through this difficult and potentially dangerous process on your own. Andersen counsels victims to work up to the goal of *no contact* with the psychopath. Any communication with him will leave you vulnerable to his continuing manipulation and perhaps even retaliation. Sandra L. Brown M.A. also has a lot of helpful information for victims of dangerous men on her website, *saferelationshipsmagazine.com*, including a list of resources and centers they can contact. I'd like to focus here, however, on a different kind of escape: one that is in some ways more difficult and takes more time. It's one thing to get the psychopath out of your life. But how do you get him out of your heart and mind?

Some psychopaths become extremely angry and abusive when their partners leave them. They regard those partners as possessions, as women they own, whom they've marked and who belong to them forever, long after they, themselves, have tired of them. No matter how badly the psychopath has treated you—he may have cheated on and lied to you; he may have undermined your self-confidence; he may have stolen your money; he may have physically abused you—it's clear that he can't feel genuinely sorry for the harm he inflicted. He can only offer you histrionic shows of regret and empty promises that he won't hurt you again.

If you take him back out of love, it establishes a precedent in his mind. He will believe that you're too weak to let him go. Each time you take him back, you give him the opportunity to mistreat you even worse. Given his bad character, he will take full advantage of it. For this reason, Martha Stout advises, "Do not try to redeem the irredeemable. Second [...] chances are for people who posses conscience. If you are dealing with a person who has no conscience, know how to swallow hard and cut your losses" (*The Sociopath Next Door*, 161). Some people improve after hurting their loved ones. Some people feel genuine remorse. Many of us grow from traumatic experiences, including those that we, ourselves, inflict upon those we love or upon innocent strangers. But all the experts on the subject say that psychopaths don't. They can't feel empathy for you. Consequently, they don't feel genuinely sorry for hurting you. They see your love as a sign of weakness, not generosity. They will exploit you for as long as you let them.

Although I've said that some psychopaths become furious when you leave them, most don't. You weren't important enough to them. Because they form only shallow attachments, psychopaths also detach very easily. They can replace you with someone else within a matter of days, if not hours. Besides, chances are that by the time you decide you've had enough, it's usually when the psychopath has grown tired of the relationship as well. As we've seen, once psychopaths lose interest in you, they no longer bother to put in the effort to disguise themselves. Consequently, they're no longer as charming and "nice" as they were when they wanted you or something from you. Once they unmask themselves, they show their lack of contrition, their coldness, their selfishness and their heartlessness. It's a very chilling experience to look at a psychopath unmasked. No matter how attractive some of them may be on the outside, all psychopaths are horrifically ugly people on the inside, which counts much more.

Yet it's still difficult to escape the psychopath in your life, even once you realize that he's not the sweet, loving person you thought he was. As we've seen, psychopaths exercise a hypnotic control over their partners. Brown documents in *Women Who Love Psychopaths* that they often talk in a smooth, mesmerizing manner, using rhythmic repetitions, like music, like an incantation (*Women Who Love Psychopaths*, 174-186).

We've also seen how psychopaths condition you, through offering and withdrawing approval and affection, to pin your self-worth upon their validation. They separate you from your family and friends, or at the very least discourage meaningful contact with people who genuinely care about you. They undermine your self-esteem, sometimes through overt criticism, at others more insidiously, through subtle disapproval. Throughout the relationship, they have played all kinds of mind games with you. They also filled your life with lies. After awhile, you're no longer sure of your own beliefs and perceptions of reality.

They also trained you in the beginning of the relationship to expect over-the-top affection, attention and flattery. Now you're always looking for that kind of pathological interdependency. Normal relationships seem to pale by comparison. In addition, most people are kind enough to give others the benefit of the doubt and second chances in life, especially if they love them. Nobody's perfect. Most people make mistakes. Many people lie and cheat without being monsters. The problem is that psychopaths are different types of people. They never deserve a second chance. They didn't deserve the first chance in the first place. Every relationship with them is a failure: a mistake that will cost you everything you choose to invest in it.

As we've seen, like other natural predators, psychopaths depend on the isolation of their victims. They require secrecy and loyalty to them. You don't owe the psychopath any loyalty. Record his behavior and share it with others. Not as a form of gossip, but as a form of truthful information and therapy. The free therapy you give yourself. You also owe yourself the truth. Reevaluate the relationship for yourself, on your own terms, rather than accepting what he wants you to believe. See if reality conforms to his image. See, above all, if his actions conform to the devotion he sometimes professes, when convenient. All this is common sense, of course. But in a relationship with a psychopath you lose common sense, especially when it comes to evaluating your bond with him. Your world becomes a little box of skewed reality he's created. By extension, you become someone who continually aims to pacify, impress and please him. You focus your energies on struggling to save the precarious, fragile relationship with him from imminent destruction. Escape that box, which exists above all in your own mind. Shatter the false construct of reality he's gotten you to accept as real.

Notice that the psychopath doesn't want you to get out of the box he's built around you. It's the mental prison that keeps you under his control. Only you have the key to get out. And you will do it only when you're strong enough and ready. Nobody else can free you, no matter what they say about him and what information they reveal about his personality disorder. It will be up to you to decide when you will take no more mistreatment. Only you can tell when you feel confident enough to see that your life can continue, far better and happier, without him. People who care about you, or those who have been through similar experiences, can only help you once you're good and ready: once you, yourself, have decided to get out of the box.

When you become more critical of the relationship, discuss it with others or seek counseling. Psychopaths tend to discourage sharing information. To them, therapy is useless psychobabble. Shrinks are crooks. What others say about them and their behavior is garbage. As we've seen, psychopaths believe that they're not only healthy, but also better than everybody else. They're proud of who they are and of what it gets them in life. However they acted towards you, they rationalize it in their own minds. They believe that you deserved the mistreatment, even if they may occasionally offer disingenuous excuses or apologies, to continue the relationship for however long they wish to maintain it.

Psychopaths want you to accept their unacceptable behavior. They want you to find it normal and appropriate, just as they do. That's why they disapprove of your efforts to seek support, information and psychological help elsewhere. But you need it, even if you're a strong and sane person. If you've been intimately involved with a psychopath, he's toyed with your emotions and messed up your mind. He's stretched your boundaries of acceptable behavior. He's even altered your perception of truth and falsehood, since so much of what he told you was either a distortion of reality or an outright lie.

A therapist, your family, books that describe his disorder, the internet as a source of helpful information, support groups, all threaten to expose the false version of reality he's created and diminish his hold on you. Which is precisely why these are also the avenues for you to regain your sense of self and win back your freedom. Write down the facts. Record his behavior. Google his personality symptoms. Reconnect with family and friends. Trust them, and your own intuitions, not him. Above all, be willing to be honest with yourself. Perhaps that's the hardest thing to do once your mind has been hijacked by this alien force, by this human being who isn't fully human. To escape the psychopath in your life, you need to escape the one in your mind. That may take the longest time. Because so many of us who have fallen in love with a psychopath really want to believe in the illusion of the perfect partner and of the ideal relationship he initially created. Escaping the psychopath requires, as a first and last step, escaping that fantasy.

Chapter 2

Understanding the Science Behind the Disorder

Since the early 1940's, when Hervey Cleckley conducted his study of psychopathy, psychologists have tried to understand the physiological basis for this dangerous personality disorder. During the nineteenth century, psychopathy used to be called "moral insanity." It could also be called "the malady of lovelessness," since it's caused by shallow emotions. Robert Hare shows that the root of the problem lies in the fact that for psychopaths *neither* side of the brain processes emotion properly. To psychopaths, emotionally charged statements such as "I love you," "I'm sorry that I hurt you," "I'll never do it again," mean absolutely nothing. They're just words they use to deceive and manipulate others. Of course, they're not random words. Psychopaths see that other people attach a special meaning to them. They notice that when they say "I love you," "I'll always be faithful to you" or "You're the woman of my life," they get a positive reaction. These hollow phrases help them seduce others, establish their trust and use them for their own selfish purposes. Psychopaths lack the capacity, however, to experience, and thus to fully grasp, the meaning behind emotionally charged words. Hare observes:

> Like the color-blind person, the psychopath lacks an important element of experience—in this case, emotional experience—but may have learned the words that others use to describe or mimic experiences that he cannot really understand (*Without Conscience*, 129).

To verify these findings, Hare and his research team conducted experiments on psychopaths versus non-psychopaths. They connected their subjects to an EEG machine, which records the electrical activity of the brain. Then they flashed on a screen strings of letters. Some of them formed real words while others formed only gibberish. They asked their subjects to press a button as soon as they identified a true word. A computer measured the time it took them to make the decision. It also analyzed their brain activity during the performance of this task. They found that non-psychopathic subjects responded quicker to emotionally charged words—such as "death" or "love"—than to non-emotional ones, such as "tree." By way of contrast, emotionally charged words had no effect whatsoever on psychopaths. Hare elaborates:

> For most of us, language has the capacity to elicit powerful emotional feelings. For example, the word 'cancer' evokes not only a clinical description of a disease and its symptoms but a sense of fear, apprehension, or concern, and perhaps disturbing mental images of what it might be like to have it. But to the psychopath, it's just a word" (*Without Conscience*, 133).

According to both psychological and physiological research, psychopaths function far below the emotional poverty line. They're much shallower than what we generally call "superficial" people. This has a lot to do with the faulty wiring in their brains. Hare explains that in most people the right side of the brain plays a central role in processing emotion. By way of contrast:

> Recent laboratory evidence indicates that in psychopaths *neither* side of the brain is proficient in the processes of emotion. Why this is so is still a mystery. But an intriguing implication is that the brain processes that control the psychopath's emotions are divided and unfocused, resulting in a shallow and colorless emotional life (*Without Conscience*, 134).

The shallowness of their emotions explains why psychopaths are so callous as to use and abuse even those closest to them: their partners, their children, their parents, their lovers and their so-called friends. It also clarifies why they can't see anything wrong with their mistreatment of others. Even when they rape and murder, psychopaths feel no remorse. Their theatrical apologies and promises to reform are as empty as their vows of love. When they cry in court after having been sentenced to prison for their crimes, they either feign emotion to gain sympathy or cry about the fact they got caught. While research shows that psychopaths are incapable of real emotional bonding with others, this doesn't imply that they're out of touch with reality. When they harm others, even when it's opportunistically and in the heat of the moment, they're cold-blooded and deliberate about their actions. They're also aware of the fact that their misdeeds are considered morally wrong by society. But, fundamentally, they don't care. In fact, breaking the rules (without suffering any consequences) is the name of their game. As Hare clarifies:

> As I mentioned earlier, psychopaths do meet current legal and psychiatric standards for sanity. They understand the rules of society and the conventional meanings of right and wrong. They are capable of controlling their behavior and realize the potential consequences of their acts. The problem is that this knowledge frequently fails to deter them from antisocial behavior (*Without Conscience*, 143).

Whenever any discussion of criminal or deviant behavior takes place, the age-old debate between nature versus nurture tends to come up. The question thus arises: are psychopaths bad because of their social environment or are they born that way? The simple answer to this question is: they're born that way and they can be made worse by a bad environment. Unfortunately, they can't be made significantly better by anything at all. Psychological and sociological research shows that, in fact, psychopaths are much *less* influenced by their environment than non-psychopaths. This conforms with the general finding that psychopaths have rock solid egos, which are more or less immune to negative input. As we've seen, although they enjoy affirmation and praise, as all narcissists do, they don't care when they're criticized or punished. While a corrupt environment and abuse is unlikely to cause psychopathy, it can lead a psychopath to express his constitutive emotional callousness through violence (*Without Conscience*, 175).

Martha Stout seconds Robert Hare's conclusions that nature—or the physiological incapacity to experience and process emotion properly—has much more to do with psychopathy than nurture. Stout observes, "In fact, there's evidence that sociopaths are influenced less by their early experience than are nonsociopaths" (*The Sociopath Next Door*, 134). She elaborates:

> The sociopaths who have been studied reveal a significant aberration in their ability to process emotional information at the level of the cerebral cortex. And from examining heritability studies, we can speculate that the neurobiological underpinnings of the core personality features of sociopathy are as much as 50 percent heritable. The remaining causes, the other 50 percent, are much foggier. Neither childhood maltreatment nor attachment disorder seems to account for the environmental contribution to the loveless, manipulative, and guiltless existence that psychologists call psychopathy (*The Sociopath Next Door*, 134).

In other words, psychopathy constitutes a physiological deficiency that causes shallowness of emotions and all the negative implications which stem from it that we've explored so far. This deficiency is genetically inherited only half of the time. The other half of the time it may be caused by accidents, brain damage, drugs or other, unknown causes. The saddest implication of the scientific research on psychopathy is the fact that there's no cure for it. No medication or treatment has yet been discovered that can give a psychopath the neurological capacity to process emotion properly. Consequently, nothing can turn him into a functioning, caring human being. In other words, nothing can transform a psychopath into a non-psychopath.

It's up to you to decide if you wish to sacrifice the rest of your life to a man who, at best, may become somewhat less impulsive and dangerous with medication, but who was, is and will always remain incapable of appreciating you and of reciprocating your love.

Psychopaths and Therapy

By now it should be quite obvious that a psychopathic partner will agree to go to therapy with you only if he believes that there's something in it for him, not because he actually cares about you or values your relationship. Perhaps you offer him a useful income, a home, or the cover of normalcy he needs to better manipulate you and others. Or perhaps he hasn't yet secured another target who's as willing to tolerate his abuse as you are. Keep in mind that psychopaths always have self-serving motives, even when they appear to be other-regarding and willing to please. If you still want to save the relationship with a psychopath, it means that you have not yet accepted the fact that you're dealing with an evil human being who can't be fixed through love, kindness, compromise, medication, therapy or understanding. As one of the regular contributors to *lovefraud.com* wisely stated, no matter how much you may pet a snake, it won't grow fur and become a puppy. Sooner or later, perhaps when you least expect it, it will strike against you. Your attempts to redeem the irredeemable will therefore prove as futile as your efforts to please him have been. However, since psychopaths cultivate highly addictive relationships and since they can be charming when it suits them, you may not be willing to abandon the impossible goal of saving him and your relationship with him. You may need to undergo further humiliation and abuse to hit bottom, as therapists say about alcoholics and drug addicts.

Robert Hare begins *Without Conscience* with a telling anecdote. As mentioned in the previous section, he and his students did research "to monitor electrical activity in the brains of several groups of adult men while they performed a language task" and submitted their article to a well-regarded professional journal. The editor of the journal rejected their article. He stated, "'Frankly, we found some of the brain wave patterns depicted in the paper very odd. Those EEG's (electroencephalograms) couldn't have come from real people'" (*Without Conscience*, 1). Hare objected that he and his research team certainly didn't do their experiments on aliens. They conducted them on "a class of individuals found in every race, culture, society, and walk of life. Everybody has met these people, been deceived and manipulated by them, and forced to live with or repair the damage they have wrought. These often charming—but always deadly—individuals have a clinical name: psychopaths" (1).

But you don't need to conduct neurological research to know if your partner is likely to be a psychopath. If you notice a consistent pattern of deception, cheating and manipulation—all masked by supposedly good intentions and a thin, but often compelling, layer of charm—you have sufficient information to know that you're dealing with a dangerous man. Since research shows that psychopathy is partly due to a genetic deficiency that can't be cured in adults, the only reason why you'd go into therapy with a psychopathic partner is because you haven't fully accepted, on an emotional rather than just rational level, the seriousness and permanency of his personality disorder. You may also be exactly the kind of partner a psychopath seeks: someone who's willing to do everything possible to hold on to him. Steve Becker argues that the effort to please a psychopath is futile and self-defeating. Such a disordered individual doesn't seek a successful relationship with anybody. Instead, he's looking for a scapegoat whom he can use, manipulate and humiliate. Becker notes:

> I'm often surprised in my work by the tenacious investment exploited partners make in solving the needs and complaints of their self-centered mates. Of course, they'll never succeed, but as long as they continue owning the exploiter's blame for the latter's discontent, they can keep trying, keep striving to be a better mate—to become, finally, the good-enough mate the exploiter has claimed to deserve all along. Let us emphasize the futility of this scenario—the exploiter really doesn't want a satisfying or, for that matter, even a perfect, partner; rather what he or she wants is a partner who, in his or her insecurity, will continue to accept on some level blame for the exploiter's unending, habitual exploitation. The exploiter, in other words, is looking much less for the perfect partner than the perfect scapegoat (*lovefraud.com*).

Furthermore, the psychopath may manipulate the therapist or take advantage of the structure of couples' counseling itself. Counseling generally functions under the assumption that both partners have flaws and need to make an equal effort to improve themselves and their relationship. This symmetrical structure is unlikely to address the fundamental asymmetries of the psychopathic bond. For as long as you seek ways of improving your relationship with a psychopathic partner, you'll continue to run around in circles like a gerbil on a spinning wheel. As Becker observes, not only will you fail in your efforts to save the relationship, but also you'll never be rewarded by the psychopath with any real appreciation:

> The exploiter is, of course, incapable of appreciating his or her partner's devotion. But even if not, he or she would intentionally withhold such recognition anyway; his or her object, remember, rather than to uplift his or her partner, is calculatingly the opposite—to engender hopelessness and depression in him or her. On and on the cycle goes, until the vulnerable partner, just as the exploiter has sought, finally feels so low, incompetent and disempowered that he or she can't seriously imagine a different future (*lovefraud.com*).

To imagine and actually live a different future, you need to end your relationship with the psychopath. Undergoing therapy with him won't improve your life. On the contrary, it will only propel you along the same downwards spiral that has undermined your dignity and happiness so far. Instead of undergoing therapy to save a harmful relationship with an inherently bad person, it's in your best interest to get individual counseling from someone who understands what you're going through and has your best interest in mind.

Chapter 3

The Two Phases of Mourning:
The Rational and the Emotional

Since I began working on this book, I've followed with great interest the testimonials of women who have been intimately involved with psychopaths, on the website *lovefraud.com*. Out of the dozens of life stories I've read there, not one woman—not a single one—claimed to have gotten over a relationship with a psychopath while she remained in close contact with him. Each and every communication with a psychopath gives him the opportunity to play upon your emotions. Although nobody gets over a psychopath while still with him, it seems that once they look up the symptoms of his disorder, victims realize, at least intellectually, that they're dealing with a sick man. As we've seen in the previous section, the first impulse of a woman living with such a person, once she discovers that the totality of his symptoms comprise a dangerous personality disorder, is to attempt to cure him through her love or with the help of professional counseling.

Her need to change him means that she only has an intellectual understanding of his personality disorder. But she hasn't yet absorbed the information on an emotional level as well. By "intellectual," I mean that having done some research, the rational side of her brain has put together the symptoms of her partner's behavior and seen them as signs of psychopathy. She may be horrified by this discovery. Perhaps a part of her wanted to believe that he was just a regular man, who made the mistake of cheating on her and is sorry about it, who lies sometimes, or who's impulsive and somewhat childish, but that's a huge part of his charm, after all. Once you do research on psychopathy you finally realize, on a rational level, the magnitude of his disorder. You also see how much more severe and damaging to others it is compared to "ordinary" cheating, lying or immaturity. You realize, rationally, that you're not dealing with someone who's extraordinary, as the psychopath encouraged you to believe. You're dealing with someone who's subordinary: with a person who lacks the main qualities that make us human.

When you finally reach this disheartening conclusion, instead of accepting or admiring the psychopath's behavior as before, you disapprove of it. You also no longer see the problems in the relationship as he presented them to you, as largely your fault. You realize, rationally, that his sex addiction has nothing to do with the fact that you're not sufficiently attractive or sensual. It has everything to do with his malady. You also see that his constant deception is neither harmless nor normal, as he would like you to believe. It's pathological and self-serving. Once you realize that the problems in your relationship have much more to do with his personality disorder than with your own deficiencies, you begin to mourn the death of the idealized image of him and of the special relationship you thought you had with him. You also start to ruminate. You obsessively turn over and over in your mind all the lies and inconsistencies he's told you. But this is not enough to get over the psychopath. You need to absorb this information on an emotional level as well in order to move on.

In her article "Do Psychopaths/Sociopaths Make Choices?" published on May 23, 2008 on *lovefraud.com*, Liane Leedom draws a distinction between *intellectual disagreement* with the psychopath's actions, which is largely a rational process, and *emotional disgust* with his actions and with him. When you mourn the end of the idealized image of the psychopath only rationally, by disapproving of his behavior, you're not likely to feel sufficiently repulsed by his identity to want to escape the relationship. You're more likely to focus instead on improving him, the relationship with him and maybe even your own self (since for as long as you stay with a psychopath, he'll continue to shift the blame unto to you). You therefore risk remaining under his spell and, therefore, under his thumb. Only once you pass to the second stage of mourning—that of experiencing visceral disgust—do you begin to get over the psychopath, escape his hold on you and move on with your life. Leedom states that you reach this stage once you realize that the sum of his actions is who he is. He is a pathological liar. He is malicious. He lacks empathy. He is completely narcissistic. His harmful actions aren't normal human mistakes. They reflect the bad person that he is and that he'll always be, no matter what false promises he makes and how much you may want to believe him.

Since the psychopath knows that, unlike him, you're a loving person capable of empathy and forgiveness, he may look you in the eyes like a penitent puppy and tell you that the love you feel for him is unconditional. Even though he's shown time after time that his own professed love for you is nonexistent. What he's telling you about your own love is, once again, false. It's a ploy intended to trap you in the toxic relationship with him. As the dozens of testimonials on *lovefraud.com* from women who have overcome psychopathic bonds illustrate, you don't have to love an emotional predator unconditionally. When you go through the process of emotional mourning, you stop liking, respecting and loving the psychopath.

After awhile, you no longer even experience anger towards him. Such an emotion still implies some traces of passion, a lingering attraction. He's sunk so low in your eyes that it's not even worth hating him. You finally see him as the trivial human being that he is. You're repulsed by his actions, by all of his malicious lies, by his manipulation of others, by his fake niceness and conditional gifts, by his predatory and perverse sexuality, by everything he does and by everything he is. You reject him deep within your heart, as utterly and completely as one human being can reject another. At that point—and only at that point—are you finally ready to escape the psychopath and the harmful relationship with him that has been your prison.

Chapter 4

Sharing Information with Others

Fighting the Psychopath's Smear Campaign

I have shown earlier how the psychopath, as a human predator, attempts to isolate you from your sources of validation and support so that you become emotionally dependent on him. He also sets others against you or persuades them, sometimes subtly, sometimes overtly, to devalue you. That way, like Adolphe did with Ellé-nore, he maximizes his chances of gaining sympathy from others when he mistreats or discards you. You can bet that if you're his wife and he cheated on you, he's told his girlfriend(s) negative things about you and positive things about his efforts to "save" the relationship.

Analogously, once their ruses are discovered, psychopaths become quite democratic in their lack of loyalty to women and, by extension, in their smear campaigns. They criticize their girlfriends in the same cowardly manner that they did their wives. They commonly present the girlfriends as temptresses without morals—essentially, as sluts—to generate rancor, contempt and spite against them and to exculpate themselves. Notice how unoriginal and caricatural their misogynist representations of women are when they rely upon the tired duality of the frigid prude (the wife) and the salacious whore (the mistress). More insidiously, as we've seen in the earlier discussion of gaslighting, psychopaths commonly depict their victims as "crazy" or "disturbed." That's partly because they take themselves to be the standard of sanity and perfection. Consequently, they view anyone who criticizes them as necessarily deranged. But it's also because psychopaths want to malign their victims. That way the valid charges against them won't stick. If the wife or girlfriend who tells others what the psychopath did to harm her can be persuasively portrayed as "crazy," the "real psychopath" (instead of him), "disturbed" or a "drama queen," then her word against his will carry much less weight. This is also why it's important to fight the psychopath's smears of you in a calm, honest and rational manner. You need to inform others about what he did and about his personality disorder factually, without flinging dirt back at him. Insults can't even reach his impenetrable ego. But they risk tarnishing your image in the eyes of others.

Since psychopaths enjoy manipulation and strife, as we've seen in the section on Picasso stringing women along, they set the wives against the girlfriends so that the women turn against each other. In addition, psychopaths are very adept at manipulating their own families. They give them false or incomplete information that bolsters their image as good but misfortunate people: essentially, as victims. So, if you've been intimately involved with a psychopath for an extended period of time, you've probably been smeared, criticized and depicted as somehow inadequate, not just to your face, but also to the friends and family members that could have been your support system. You need to reclaim their respect by telling them the truth. You will depend on them to recover from the damage inflicted by the psychopath. For this reason alone, you need to fight the psychopath's smears of you. Not in order to smear him back, since the psychopath prides himself on his bad behavior. Not in order to get revenge, since psychopaths have no depth of feelings. Solitary confinement may be the only thing that bothers them. They get painfully bored if they have nobody to use, deceive and manipulate. But since you're not likely to put the psychopath in solitary confinement, there's nothing you can do to hurt him back. You also can't make him feel sorry for what he did to you. In fact, he's gloating about it. Any complaint you express will only make him feel even better about himself, like he won the match. They say that the best revenge is living well. That's no doubt true, so that's what you need to focus on.

First and foremost, be honest with yourself about what the psychopath is and what he did to you and others. Inform yourself about psychopathy. Inform your family, his family, and your mutual friends about what he did: if and only if they're likely to be part of your support system. If he has already set his family against you, or if they're not likely to be reasonable people, forget about communicating with them about your negative experiences with him. In that case, the psychopath will only use them to his advantage, to smear you further. The last thing you need is more toxic people to poison your life. Share truthful information only with those who care about you and want to help you, at least by offering emotional support. You will inevitably run against a barrier, however. People who haven't dealt with such a sick human being may not understand you, or grasp the depth of betrayal you have suffered. Sometimes they'll tell you, even with the best of intentions, to get over it. The reason why you can't get over a psychopathic bond that easily is because practically nothing you have lived through your partner was real. It was all misleading and malicious. Woody Allen, the eternal pessimist, once said, "Expect the worst and you won't be disappointed." Although this cynical saying doesn't apply to most people, it applies one hundred percent to any intimate relationship with a psychopath. The depth and degree of betrayal hurts so much more than the natural degeneration of a normal relationship, where people grow apart or realize that they have "irreconcilable differences." Psychopaths have "irreconcilable differences" with the rest of the human species. No matter how charming they may seem on the outside, they're all misanthropes on the inside.

The magnitude of deception in a psychopathic relationship is very difficult to digest. But even if your family and friends can't fully identify with your experience, if you tell them everything that's happened, they will understand the essential truth. That he has mistreated you when you did not deserve it. That you are essentially a good person with a heart and he is not. That he cheated on and lied to you repeatedly. That even when you gave him second, third and fourth chances in life, he trampled all over you. If you've given the psychopath too many second chances, however, you're likely to lose some sympathy from others. They may believe that there's something's wrong with you if you've bent over backwards to stay with such an obviously bad man. At any rate, what's important is not to present yourself as flawless, since nobody is, but to establish the facts.

Since the psychopath probably involved you in some of his bad actions, and since he's acted in a way that's deeply humiliating, you may feel too ashamed to share with others what happened. Don't cower to him. Don't feel ashamed. Reclaim your power and your voice. If you spread truthful information about the psychopath and his personality disorder, you're not only setting the record straight, but also you may help others who are in a similar situation to yours. The more you hide the truth, the more you remain in the psychopath's grasp, on his terms, covered in shame. If anyone should feel deeply ashamed, it's the psychopath himself, but he's incapable of it. He's the one who deserves contempt, once people find out what he is on the inside, beneath the nice facade. Psychopaths don't feel any scruples themselves, yet they're very skilled in projecting blame unto others. Don't fall for it. The stronger and more self-confident you become, the better equipped you'll be to get the psychopath out of your life for good.

Sharing information with others also carries the additional benefit of depriving the psychopath of the mask he needs to keep his main sources of narcissistic supply—of love and admiration—close to him. As we know, psychopaths thrive in superficial relationships. They prefer promiscuous liaisons and casual acquaintanceships with people whom they can charm, use and discard rather quickly. But psychopaths also need others who care about them in order to feel more powerful. Who those others are doesn't really matter, since people are interchangeable to them. It can be a wife or a girlfriend. It can be one girlfriend or another. Without other people's love to feed on and abuse, psychopaths are just empty souls blown about from place to place, engaging in various excesses and misdeeds. Consequently, telling the truth about the psychopath in your life not only helps you reclaim your image in the eyes of others, but also chips away at the phony mask of decency that enables him to use and abuse all those close to him.

Telling the Other Woman (or Women) about the Psychopath

I've shown in a previous section how psychopaths use women against one another to string them along as back-ups and to play puppet master. The more subtle psychopaths also use them to keep their hands clean, so to speak. If a psychopath criticizes his wife to the girlfriend (to justify his cheating and prove his trustworthiness to her) and, once discovered, the girlfriend to his wife (to exculpate himself), then the two women are too busy fighting each other to focus on his wrongdoings. Aside from the entertainment value of jealous women fighting over him, the psychopath gets the additional advantage of not having to engage directly in a smear campaign. He allows the women, who now disrespect and maybe even hate each other, to do it for him. They can spread false or selective information to family members and friends, thus sparing him the dirty job of doing it himself. He's lied to them both and cheated on them both. He should be exposed, not only to the other women, but also to his own family members.

The tricky part is how to do it most effectively. Because such manipulative men antagonize women against each other, it becomes difficult to share information in a civil manner. Once she realizes that she's been mistreated and that something's seriously wrong with this man, how does the wife tell the girlfriend about it (and why would she do her rival such a favor?) or the girlfriend tell the wife? Both are likely to suspect the other of ulterior motives, such as wanting to get the man for herself or petty revenge against him. Moreover, the wife, or the psychopath's main partner, has been morally wronged most. The girlfriend with whom the psychopath cheated on her has wronged her almost as much as her own partner (except more impersonally). She's therefore not likely to respect the girlfriend (or girlfriends) enough to even want to communicate with her (or them).

I followed with interest the thread on *lovefraud.com* on this subject. Numerous women have shared their experiences of trying to tell the other women about the psychopath and his personality disorder, once they have opened their eyes. The contributors reported mixed results. Some of them were able to get through to their "rivals," which were really fellow victims. Others received further insult and abuse, only now from the woman or women they were trying to help. Obviously that didn't ameliorate the situation. The main reason, however, why some women reacted so negatively to the truth about the psychopath was not the rivalry he created between them, but the power he exercised over them. Victims of psychopathic seduction don't all awake from their spell simultaneously, like in a fairy tale. They don't all realize at the same moment that they've been duped and used, just as their rivals were. In addition, as we've seen, psychopaths generally undermine the boundaries and self-esteem of their long-term partners in a more profoundly damaging manner than they do those of their short-term girlfriends.

Trying to awake the girlfriend(s) from the psychopathic bond presents a different sort of challenge. Those women are probably being treated "better" than his long-term partner because the relationship is newer, because they don't have to live with a psychopath day-to-day and because they're being maintained for sex, entertainment and romance: meaning the most pleasant and light aspects of a relationship. Even psychopaths who are so stingy that they won't spend a dime on their wives often spend lavishly on their newest girlfriends. A woman who's been treated like a "princess"—wined, dined, pampered and romanced—is likely to be deeply under the haze of the psychopathic bond. How do you tell a girlfriend who's apparently treated well the sad truth? How do you let her know that she's only a temporary pampered pet who'll soon be devalued and discarded?

In my opinion, it's important to tell other women about what happened, but only in a way that doesn't hurt you or tarnish your reputation further. After having suffered the trauma of being involved with a psychopath, the last thing you need is more people insulting you or machinating against you. To determine whom to tell and how, follow your intuition. Timing is key. Obviously, you can't tell anyone about the psychopath unless they're willing to listen. If you catch them still in the honeymoon phase of the relationship, when the psychopath's acting like Prince Charming, you're not likely to convince them. If you catch them after they've been so severely psychologically damaged by their psychopathic partner that they're too weak or dependent to face reality, you won't get through to them either. You'll only get through to a person who retains enough autonomy and strength to face such devastating facts and who's been through enough unpleasant and disconcerting experiences with the psychopath to understand what you're talking about.

Relationship Boomerang: Why it's Hard to Get Rid of a Psychopath

Even if you manage to break up with a psychopath, you may still not be completely free of him. Relationships with a psychopath are usually like a boomerang. Even after you toss him as far away as possible, he may still swing back into your life. Years after breaking up with a psychopath, women commonly report that they're still cyber-stalked or somehow harassed by him, or that he's still testing the waters to see if he can worm his way back into their lives. So the question is: Why is it so hard to get rid of a psychopath?

Psychopaths are hoarders of women, even those they tired of and cast aside. They break up easily with their partners, of course. Psychopaths throw away old relationships with as little emotion or regret as normal people toss away their old shoes. But they rarely completely disappear from the radar, even years after the relationship with them is over. As they're pursuing their newest flames, psychopaths continue to keep tabs on their former girlfriends, sink their claws deeper into their current ones, put a few more women, which are on their way out, on the back-burner as they slowly simmer, wondering what they did to lose their attention and love. Hoarders accumulate junk; psychopaths accumulate broken relationships. Since possessing women (and men) reminds psychopaths of their dominance, the more ex-partners, current partners and potential future partners they can juggle, the more powerful they feel.

In *Women Who Love Psychopaths* (2009), Sandra L. Brown, M.A. describes the relationship cycle of psychopaths, as they juggle multiple partners in their tireless pursuit of their top goals: pleasure, dominance and entertainment (*Women Who Love Psychopaths*, 199-201).

1. *The Pre-stage.* During the early phases, a psychopath trolls for potential partners everywhere: at work, at clubs and bars, on the Internet, in the neighborhood, anywhere where he can meet sexual partners. Just because he has a wife, several girlfriends and a few casual relationships on the side doesn't mean the psychopath has stopped looking for other victims. Whatever his actual job may be, pursuing new partners is a psychopath's main occupation. He reads everyone's signal: from eye contact, attitude and what they verbally reveal about their lives. He zeroes in on those who express neediness, vulnerability, or just plain sexual willingness.

2. *The Early Stage.* A psychopath commonly has multiple email addresses (most of them using aliases), several cell phones, various means to juggle several partners and effectively hide that fact from his more "serious" pursuits. He tests the waters with dozens of individuals, but focuses his energies most on those whom he believes he can take to the next level.

3. *The Middle Stage.* He chooses to have full-blown relationships with multiple women and men (even psychopaths who claim to be straight commonly experiment with homosexual relationships, for variety). During this stage he woes more seriously the most promising targets: with romance, dinners out, exciting sex, loving words, etc. Many of these women believe they found their soul mate in him, the love of their lives. But while wooing and duping them, the psychopath keeps very busy. He still maintains a firm hold on a few relationships he's thinking about ending; keeps an eye out for fresh prospects; plus has innumerable sexual encounters on the side. Because your typical psychopath juggles so many relationships simultaneously, even during the honeymoon phase women start to experience some doubts. The psychopath may get calls from other girlfriends in the middle of their dates. He may be late to appointments or leave, inexplicably, for unaccounted periods of times. However, the wooing phase with a psychopath is so intense, fast-paced, sexually charged, flattering and romantic that women don't stop to think about those red flags or prefer to accept the psychopath's rationalizations and lies.

4. *The End Stage.* Once the excitement of the honeymoon period and the novelty of the conquest is over, the psychopath usually no longer invests much time and energy into a given relationship. He ends several relationships at the same time, just as he pursues multiple new ones simultaneously. Relationships with a psychopath typically end when the initial excitement and fun diminish; when the woman begins to see cracks in his mask of sanity and their fantasy

love; when the relationship becomes too high-maintenance and requires too much time and energy to sustain; or simply when he's found new relationships that are momentarily more exciting and entertaining. But, unfortunately, that doesn't mean that the psychopath moves on and out of your life forever!

5. *The Post++ Stage*. Because psychopaths can't relinquish power over anybody, they usually keep tabs on former girlfriends and periodically circle around them, like vultures, long after the relationships are dead. Even in the cases where they don't maintain physical contact, they may still send you nasty emails thinly disguised as spam or other unwanted communication. As Brown puts it, "Given both his boredom and excitement seeking, women must know that they, nor any other lover, ever really flies off his radar–for long" (*Women Who Love Psychopaths*, 201).

This is why it's so hard to get rid of a psychopath. The relationship cycle repeats itself, as the psychopath continually trolls for new partners, tires of current relationships, ends some of them, begins others, only to find his way back, like an unwanted boomerang, into his ex-girlfriends' lives.

Chapter 5

**Resisting Family/External Pressure
to Stay with the Psychopath**

If you have a psychopathic husband, you're likely to face not only internal pressure to stay in the relationship, but also external pressure, from your family, his family and your mutual friends. Psychopaths commonly use their family members and acquaintances as the support system that enables them to fool others (*Women Who Love Psychopaths*, 101-2). If your psychopathic partner relies upon such allies, it will take double strength to overcome both your own emotional investment and at the same time deal with all the external pressure to stay with him. Clearly, it's in your best interest to resist both internal and external pressures to stay with a psychopath. I've already covered some of the internal pressures. Now I'll address some of the external ones as well. In general, most of the external pressure stems from the fact that your family and friends may not comprehend that you're dealing with a severely disordered individual who can't be cured. It may take you, yourself, a long time to fully absorb this information. One can't expect people who know him less than you do and who aren't as well informed about psychopathy to realize just how dangerous he is. One might object that his own parents know him as well as you do. That's generally not the case, however. They probably haven't lived with him since he was a teenager. His parents know very well the child and adolescent psychopath. The main symptoms of his personality disorder, however, crystallized during adulthood.

Furthermore, it's easy to mistake the early symptoms of psychopathy—the pranks, the deception, the insubordination to authority figures (such as teachers and parents) and the emotional immaturity—for normal adolescent development. Most teens manifest some antisocial traits, especially towards their parents, as they struggle to assert their independence. His parents may have noticed that their son was particularly insubordinate or deceitful as an adolescent. But it's likely that they attributed his deviant behavior to other causes, perhaps even positive ones. They may have believed that the psychopath was brighter than other kids and misbehaved out of boredom. This generous explanation may have made some sense at the time. Psychopaths are, indeed, often smart and always easily bored.

One should keep in mind, however, that a lot of kids are bright. Yet they still thrive in their academic, extracurricular and professional endeavors. They don't all use their mental energies to deceive others and to undermine authority, as psychopathic children and adolescents tend to do. All this to say that his own parents do not, in fact, know the adult psychopath better than you. Consequently, they're unlikely to realize what you've been going through in your relationship with him. In addition, his family members probably haven't informed themselves about psychopathy. They may mistake his behavior—especially the cheating and the lying—as signs of "men will be men," i.e., of moral errors that are quite common and often forgivable. They probably won't grasp, just as it's very difficult for you to accept, that you've been, essentially, living with the enemy. The person whom you loved most and who claimed to love you in return made it his top aim in life to psychologically destroy you.

I'll offer an analogy to illustrate the underlying cruelty of psychopathic behavior. Imagine the following scenario: a boy who gets a puppy for Christmas. He pets him, feeds him, cuddles him, plays with him and even sleeps next to him at night. Then, six months later, after the puppy has bonded most with him and expects only nurture and affection from him, the boy takes a knife and slaughters him just for fun. That's exactly what a psychopath does, at the very least on a psychological level, to every person who becomes intimately involved with him. He carefully nurtures expectations of mutual honesty and love. Then he sticks a knife into her back through a pattern of intentional deception and abuse.

Let me now offer a second, more poignant, example. I remember many years ago being horrified when I read in the news about the rapes of Bosnian women by ethnically Serbian men. What troubled me most was a true story about a Serbian soldier who "saved" a Bosnian girl from gang rape by fellow Serbs. He removed her from the dangerous situation, fed her, protected her and talked to her reassuringly and tenderly for several days. Once he secured her trust, gratitude and devotion, he raped and killed her himself. Afterwards, he boasted about his exploits on the international news. This degree of psychological sadism exceeds that of the brutes who raped and killed women without initially faking niceness and caring. What he did to her was more insidious, duplicitous and perverse. All psychopaths behave this way towards their partners, at the very least on an emotional level. They gain your love and trust only to take sadistic pleasure in harming you. Each time you forgive their behavior and take them back, they enjoy the thrill of having regained your confidence so that they can hurt you again. How can you possibly make your parents, his parents and your mutual friends—all those who have had contact primarily or exclusively with the charming side of the psychopath—understand that you're dealing with such a deep and intrinsic level of perversion?

His parents are most likely to encourage you to stay with the psychopath because they probably care about him most. Once you inform them of his personality disorder, they may still hope that your love can help him improve. In fact, when he was a teenager, once they noticed some of the symptoms of his deviant behavior, they may have lavished a lot of attention and affection upon him. They may have done their best to encourage him to become a better and more empathetic person. Ironically, research shows that doting on a psychopath and being understanding and forgiving towards the symptoms of his malady—his impulsiveness, insensitivity, deceptiveness, manipulativeness, etc.—only reinforces them. The more you dote on a psychopath, the more you encourage him, admire him and treat him with compassion when he makes "mistakes," the more you feed his core narcissism and hence also his malady. This is why if his parents believe that your love will help cure the psychopath, they're definitely mistaken. Yet, as Liane Leedom documents, there's some truth to the assumption that, generally speaking, a psychopath is better off inside a stable marriage rather than outside of it. The regular, more orderly structure of family life diminishes his opportunities for engaging in the kinds of excesses and transgressions he's likely to pursue if left entirely to his own devices. Without any constraints and checks on his behavior, he may end up contracting a venereal disease, consumed by his addictions or in jail as a result of criminal activities. But keeping a psychopath out of trouble isn't a good reason for you to forfeit your own happiness. As you know, you won't be rewarded with any genuine love for your efforts and devotion. While it's understandable that his parents' priority might be to look out for their son, your top priority is to look out for yourself and your children, if you have any. Don't worry about the psychopath. He will look out for number one. He always does.

You may belong to a religion or a religious sect that disapproves of divorce. Divorce for trivial or immoral reasons—such as having an affair or because you got bored with your current partner—is wrong. Marriage should be taken seriously. But only a dogmatic and irrational interpretation of ethics would demand that you remain married to a person who abuses you. It's not your moral obligation to stay with a psychopath. Your moral obligation is to flourish as a human being and to stand by those who deserve and reciprocate your love. The psychopath doesn't fall into this category.

You may experience the mixed blessing of having children with the psychopath. Bringing a child into this world can be one of the most rewarding and meaningful experiences in human life. But having a child or children with a psychopath carries with it great risk. Since antisocial traits are partly genetic, your child or children can inherit those negative characteristics. Moreover, as we've seen, a psychopath is incapable of loving anyone. He regards all people, including his children, as tools to get what he wants and as his personal possessions. Like you, they represent objects he will manipulate and control. Like you, they confirm his virility and personal power. As he got tired of you and of every other woman he played with, he will quickly tire of your child, his newest toy.

No change in circumstances can ever alter a psychopath's underlying bad character for long. He is what he is and that's what he'll remain. Think back to the many second chances you've given him. Think back to all the times he shattered your hopes and abused your trust. You hoped that he'd change his cheating ways after you got engaged, but he didn't. You then believed that he'd take your commitment more seriously once you married, but he didn't. He just hid his perversions better and mastered the game of deceit. You hoped that a change of job or location would improve him, but it didn't. Instead, your repeated concessions to his will and willingness to swallow increasing doses of mistreatment made him more confident that you'd take whatever abuse he dished out. He turned your life into a game that has no rational or moral rules.

You played along with his arbitrary power games. You played along because you love him and because you want to believe that he loves you as well: in his way, on some level, you feel compelled to qualify. Sure, he left you for other women and he will leave you again. But you interpret the fact that he returns to you time after time as evidence of his love. In other words, you engage in wishful thinking and reject the obvious reality. He doesn't leave you because he loves anyone else more than you. Conversely, he doesn't return to you because he realizes how much he loves you, after all. He comes and goes as he pleases to whoever lets him because he's bored. Power over others fills his empty days. He's like one of those magicians that spin plates on poles. He wants to see how many women he can spin around at once and for how long he can cultivate for each one the illusion of perpetual motion, or of real love. Each time a plate falls to the ground and shatters, he enjoys it. Each life he destroys represents a personal triumph for him. With you and every other woman in his life he plays this sordid game. There's nothing inside of him that can love you or anybody else.

The same logic applies to having a child or children with him. If he cheated on you and wasn't there to support you meaningfully during the emotional and physical challenges of pregnancy, he'll remain equally unreliable and unsupportive as you raise your child. If he treated you with disrespect and even contempt before you had a child together, that's how he'll continue to treat you afterwards. If he shirked his professional and personal duties before, he won't be able to handle the most important responsibility of all, which is raising a child. And if he abused you, he will abuse your child, at the very least emotionally. The Loser will remain a loser no matter whom he attaches to because his evil actions reflect his true identity. He deliberately hurts others not because they're not right for him, as he claims to shift the blame, but because he's not right for anybody else.

Consequently, if you have a child or children with a psychopath, it's doubly important for you to protect not just yourself from his noxious influence, but also your children. Dr. Liane Leedom wrote a very informative book on this subject, called *Just Like His Father?* Her message is not purely cautionary, but also one of hope. She emphasizes that there's no chance whatsoever of having a mutually loving and respectful relationship with a psychopath. But there's a lot of hope for raising your child to be a healthy and empathetic individual who is *not* just like his father.

Your own family may pressure you to stay in such a destructive marriage. They may believe that the psychopath isn't all that bad (if they've mostly seen his superficially charming side). They may tell you that divorce would make them look bad. Or they may believe that a wife should stand by her husband no matter what he does. None of these are valid reasons to stay with a psychopath. You shouldn't destroy your life just to please others. Besides, if they truly care about you, your family members wouldn't want you to be unhappy.

This calls to mind a scene from one of my favorite comedies, *My Cousin Vinny*. A young man who was wrongly accused of murder objects that his mother would be upset if he fired the so far incompetent Vinny, his cousin, and chose another, better attorney to defend him. His friend counters: "Wouldn't your mother be more upset if you died?" The question is right on target and the answer is obvious. Once they come to understand the nature of his disorder, your family members would be far more upset if you continued to stay with a deranged man who makes it his life goal to make you miserable. In some ways, staying married to a psychopath constitutes a fate worse than death. It's being condemned to life-long psychological torture by the very person who's supposed to take care of you and love you most.

The Psychopath's Parents: A Process of Mourning

In almost every society and culture, parents view their children as, in some respects, a reflection of themselves. They're a biological reflection, since parents pass on some of their genetic qualities to their kids. They're also a social and moral reflection. Children can make their parents proud or they can bring shame upon their family. Some parents, however, carry the fact that a child reflects back upon their image to extremes. On the one hand, some parents have so much narcissistic investment in their children that even when those children are convicted of the most horrific crimes—such as killing their spouses—they still defend them. I'm thinking here of Scott Peterson's and Neil Entwistle's parents. They continued to claim that their sons are innocent even when it was proven beyond reasonable doubt in court that they were guilty of murdering their wives and babies. In such cases, as mentioned earlier, the parents themselves are either disordered or blind. They refuse to see their sons as anything but the perfect beings they want them to be.

At the other end of the spectrum, some parents go so far as to kill their children if they reflect badly upon their values. I have in mind some fathers in fundamentalist cultures who kill their daughters if they have premarital sex or become pregnant out of wedlock. They do so as a punishment and to preserve their image as perfect parents who instilled the right values in their children. In other words, just as some parents are willing to sacrifice their moral values to preserve an idealized image of their children, others are willing to sacrifice their children to preserve an idealized image of their moral values. These two extreme cases constitute chiasmic inversions of each other. In the first case, the parents idealize their children at all cost. In the second, they idealize their values at all cost. Yet both sets of parents follow the same logic of seeing the children's actions as a strict reflection of themselves.

Parents of psychopathic children are faced with the horns of the dilemma I've just sketched. Should they love their kids no matter what they do? Or should they reject them completely if their actions go against their own moral values? Unlike the fundamentalist fathers who sacrifice their daughters to their values, most parents feel that their love for their children is unconditional. At the same time, however, unlike Scott Peterson's or Neil Entwistle's parents, they would not go so far as to accept or ignore even the most atrocious behavior from their children. Most parents want their children to observe the ethical values they've inculcated in them. Yet they wouldn't go so far as to sacrifice their children to those values. Most parents would therefore adopt a middle ground position between the two extreme cases I've described. But what does such a middle ground actually mean when your child turns out to be a psychopath?

Finding out that your child suffers from an unfixable emotional and moral deficiency can be even more devastating for the psychopath's parents than it is for his spouse or partner. The wedding vows postulate staying together "for better or for worse." However, "for worse" doesn't include the psychological torture that psychopaths put their partners through. As we've seen, no partner is under the moral obligation to stay with a psychopath. Parents, on the other hand, face the social pressure, and perhaps even feel the natural inclination, to love their children no matter what. They're the only beings likely to offer something as close to unconditional love as humanly possible. I don't believe, however, that true unconditional love would be ethical or appropriate if your child makes it his life objective to harm others. If your parental love is truly unconditional, then you're also condoning the psychopath's immoral behavior towards others. In fact, parental love has to be conditional in some respects if the parents have any regard and compassion for the people whom the psychopath has hurt.

A psychopath's parents will somehow have to psychologically adjust to the fact that the adorable baby, toddler and boy whom they raised is a different person from the grown man who takes great pleasure in deceiving, using and hurting others. In other words, like his partner, they'll have to undergo a process of mourning. Those parents may always love the child they nurtured and raised. But they cannot, in good conscience, love in the same unconditional manner the bad person he's become. They can't endorse his immoral actions without violating their own principles and thus undermining their own humanity.

Many religions ask us to distinguish between a man's actions and his identity: to love the man but disapprove of his evil deeds. Since a psychopath is the sum of his actions, however, because those evil actions reflect his real character, the parents of psychopaths can't find much comfort in this theological distinction. If they wish to remain loving parents yet also maintain their integrity as individuals, they're obliged to always love (and mourn) the child they lost while at the same time condemning the man he became.

Chapter 6

Know your Worth:
A Healthy Self-Esteem is the Key to a Good Life

In an earlier chapter I explained how a psychopath controls his targets by exploiting their distorted self-image. Any woman may be initially hooked by a psychopath during the seduction phase of the relationship. But those who stay with him once his mask of charm comes off probably suffer from an unrealistic and dual image of themselves. The nature of their particular distortion doesn't really matter. It may be a woman who considers herself to be far more attractive than other women, but who doubts her own intelligence. Or, conversely, it may be a woman who believes herself to be more virtuous and competent than other women, but suffers from a low self-esteem about her looks and sex appeal. In both cases, the distortion is fundamentally similar in that it's exaggerated on both ends of the spectrum. In some respects, she has an inflated view of herself, in others a deficient one. Psychopaths can hook several such women for the long-term by manipulating their polarized view of themselves. They strategically flatter their partners' excessive vanity while also pouncing upon their insecurities. In other words, they play both sides of their ego like a fiddle.

Character distortions occur not only in psychopathic bonds, but also in narcissistic environments in general. As a scholar, I've participated in academic conferences in literary studies for nearly fifteen years. It would be laughable, if it weren't pathetic, to observe some scholars adopt a snobby attitude towards others just because they teach at elite institutions or because they've published a few articles or books that a handful of specialists consider "ground-breaking." Such narcissistic tendencies in certain academics (or writers, or artists, or actors, or models, or musicians, etc.) stem from an empty sense of self that requires inflated praise from others to feed it. In this sense, narcissists aren't all that different from insecure or "needy" people who require constant external validation. Yet no amount of praise can enduringly nourish such a person's voracious ego. If you research the lives of famous artists, writers, philosophers, scientists, actors or singers, you'll notice that none of them were actually made happy or fulfilled by the excessive adulation they got from others.

You gain peace and fulfillment from your own healthy self-esteem and from cultivating a respectful attitude towards others. This sense of balance is largely internal. Nobody else can give it to you. There are literally thousands of "how to" books on the market. They claim to help people find their inner balance in all sorts of ways: through yoga, Pilates, other mind-body exercises, improving their looks or increasing their sexual stamina. I suspect that most of them work about as well as the perennial miracle diets. They may produce some immediate results. But they rarely fundamentally change a person or improve the quality of his or her life in the long run. To improve yourself more enduringly, you need to cultivate a healthy perception of who you are and know what you want from life.

Dysfunctional lives and relationships often stem from character distortions, such as the ones I've described so far, which leave you dependent upon the perceptions of others to gain a sense of self-worth. Those most likely to exploit such neediness or vanity are not those who have your best interests in mind. They're likely to be individuals who want to use and control you. There's no magical step-by–step procedure that can give you a healthy self-esteem. Just as losing weight depends upon having a healthy, moderate attitude towards your body, so improving your self-image depends upon having a healthy attitude towards your mind. "Know thyself," the ancient Greeks advised. This, like so much of their practical wisdom, is sound advice. This is not to say that moderation, or what Aristotle called the mean between two extremes, is always the answer to everything. Nobody can be equally good and equally bad at everything. We all have a combination of weaknesses and strengths.

Knowing yourself, in my estimation, means using your strengths to improve your life and the lives of others rather than to appear superior to them or to gain their approval. Being an artistic or mathematical "genius," or being very popular and beautiful—however exceptional you may be in some respects—doesn't entitle you to special treatment. It also doesn't justify you mistreating others in any way. In other words, your strengths shouldn't feed your vanity, as they do for narcissists and psychopaths, just as your weaknesses shouldn't cripple you.

Reaching an inner balance also requires having the right motivation for your endeavors. For instance, don't create art to impress others or to become famous. Create to offer yet another instance of beauty and meaning to enrich your life and perhaps also the lives of others. Don't write books to become rich or consecrated. Write to express a talent that makes you happy and that may contribute some human wisdom that is best expressed more creatively. Don't give to charity or behave nicely to others to be considered generous and kind. Help those in need and be a genuinely decent human being. If you have a healthy self-image, your strengths and talents will radiate primarily from within. They will give energy to others rather than being absorbed from without, by depending upon their external validation. Similarly, having a healthy self-esteem entails working on your weaknesses without allowing them to haunt you, to become deep-seated insecurities that malicious individuals can exploit. Such a healthy attitude towards yourself and your life therefore implies some detachment from the views of others: from how they perceive you, what they expect from you and what they say about you.

Of course, none of us live in a vacuum. We're all partially influenced by the views and expectations of our partners, our families, our colleagues, our friends and society in general: as we well should be. But those with a healthy self-esteem are not determined primarily by others. For as long as they behave decently to other human beings, they don't fold under when their partners, family members, friends or peers criticize them. They also don't lose their self-esteem when they fail at some of their own goals. Conversely, they don't feel superior to others just because some people praise them or because they attain some level of success or even fame. Success and fame, like the criticism and praise of others in general, comes and goes. Knowing who you are and what you have to contribute can last a lifetime.

The only thing that can save you from a psychopath—or from any other manipulative person who wants to take over your life—is cultivating a healthy self-esteem. This may seem like a truism. Unfortunately, it's the kind of common sense that many know but fewer actually practice. Any therapist will tell you that he or she stays in business largely because of people's unrealistic perception of themselves. Character distortions not only damage our self-confidence, but also taint our relationships. They make us excessively vain, or needy, or inflexible, or too willing to bend over backwards just to please others. More seriously, character disorders, such as psychopathy and malignant narcissism, are unfixable in adults.

Fortunately, however, most people don't suffer from such constitutive emotional and moral deficiencies. More commonly, we suffer from distorted perceptions of ourselves. This puts us at risk of falling into the clutches of controlling individuals. To find your compass you need to look within, as the Greeks wisely advised. Ultimately, nobody else can save you. You can save yourself by living well, which depends upon knowing your worth—neither underestimating nor overestimating it—and pursuing with a mostly internally driven self-confidence the path you want to take in life.

Conclusion

Reclaiming Your Life:
Asserting Your Agency and Your Boundaries

Many of the women who love psychopaths intuitively know that they're dealing with a sick man. Yet they feel like they have invested too much for too long into the relationship to give up on him. In addition, as we've seen, their self-confidence and sense of reality have been severely undermined. They may tell themselves, hoping against hope, that their love and patience will fix the dangerous man. Or that after spending fifteen years with him, they can't throw away the entirety of their youth, as if those years together were all for nothing. In *How to Spot a Dangerous Man Before You Get Involved*, Sandra L. Brown, M.A. addresses this reasoning with a rhetorical question that is actually quite meaningful. She asks: what will the next fifteen years of your life look like with the psychopath?

The answer to this question can't possibly be positive, given that abuse gets worse over time and that his disorder is not fixable. In previous chapters we've seen that psychopaths prefer to seduce extraverted, accomplished and confident women. They could easily prey upon passive and weak women. But they prefer the challenge of destroying a strong person. We've seen how psychopaths use their partners' strengths against them. They use women's trust to deceive and cheat on them as well as, more generally, to play mind games. They isolate previously sociable women. They undermine the confidence of women with high self-esteem by focusing on their real or imaginary weaknesses. It's not unusual to develop neuroses, post-traumatic stress disorder and eating disorders while involved with a psychopath. He will even cultivate those maladies, and lead you to focus obsessively on them rather than on your strengths and achievements, to keep you under his thumb.

We've also observed how psychopaths brainwash women who have common sense and psychological perspicacity. Once again, they select intelligent women to naive ones because such individuals present more of a challenge in their sadistic power games. We've seen how psychopaths use women's capacity to love and their tenacity—their high emotional investment in the relationship—to keep them on the hook. They lure them with strategic withdrawals and empty promises to improve, which are belied by consistent, though often hidden, abuse. They dangle whatever women want most in life before their eyes—true love, fidelity, commitment, a happy life together, returning to the romantic and exciting honeymoon phase of the relationship—only to make conditional demands, that erode their partners' dignity and self-respect.

To counteract these strategies and reclaim your life, you need to reassert your agency, your strength and your boundaries. You need to recognize that you're not just a passive victim of the psychopath's control, even if you were, indeed, victimized by him. You have agency. You willingly began the relationship with the psychopath. You willingly stayed with him despite seeing red flags early on in the relationship. You may have willingly taken him back after discovering that he repeatedly cheated and lied. You may have also engaged in some immoral behavior to keep him in your life. You may have hurt or neglected those who loved you for his sake. Each step you took as a couple was not just his own doing. It was also yours. Sandra L. Brown, M.A. points out that seeing yourself as an agent in your life decisions doesn't imply denying the fact that the psychopath has hurt you or minimize the extent of your pain. It just shows you that you have the power to determine your life choices. Just as you chose to become involved and stay with a psychopath, you also have the power to disengage from him for good (*How to spot a dangerous man*, 32).

To understand why you made such poor and self-defeating choices, you need to assess realistically both your strengths and your weaknesses. In earlier chapters, I identified some of the potential weaknesses of women who get involved with psychopaths, which led them down a self-destructive path. The main one is an unrealistic and dichotomous view of themselves, which is narcissistically inflated (as better than other women) in some ways, and too weak (as less than other women) in others. You don't need a psychopath to identify your qualities and flaws. You don't need his manipulative criticisms that undermine your self-confidence. You don't need his fake and conditional flattery to feel good about yourself. You know who you are. And, deep inside, after so much mistreatment at his hands, you also know that it's clearly in your best interest to leave the dangerous man and end the sick relationship with him. Your self-preservation, not just your self-esteem, is at stake.

Exercising your agency also implies reasserting your strength and your boundaries. If you stayed with a psychopathic partner it's because he undermined the strength that he originally admired in you and that drew him to you, like a parasite to its host, to destroy you. You can find that inner strength again to live your life free of him. The longer you will be away from his noxious influence, the stronger you will grow. The psychopath has strung you along by eroding your boundaries: your moral sense of right and wrong, your sexual boundaries and your empathy. When you draw the line and say *no more* and mean it, the psychopath loses and you win. By way of contrast, each time you do what he tells you, each time you override your intuition to believe his lies, each time you violate your sense of right and wrong, each time you neglect or hurt those who care about you, each time you engage in perverse sexual acts just to please him, *he wins* and *you lose*.

The women who stay with psychopaths may be strong women, as Sandra L. Brown's research indicates. Yet many of them lack sufficiently strong boundaries. They may be strong in other areas of life. But they become weak as far as their personal relations with the psychopath are concerned. These, unfortunately, become the fulcrum of their existence. Staying with a psychopath indicates that they're willing to compromise their values, their relationships and their standards to please a disordered man.

To reclaim your autonomy and your strength, you need to reassert your boundaries. The negative experience with the psychopath has no doubt made you more aware than ever of what you stand for since you were repeatedly pressured by him to lower your standards and to violate your principles. Each time you did that it hurt because you lost not only part of your values, but also—and more importantly—part of yourself.

Asserting the limits of the person you are and of what you stand for constitutes an essential step towards rejecting the psychopath. Most likely, he won't even stay with you if you assert yourself and don't give in a single inch to him anymore. As a narcissist, he can't tolerate any real equality in a romantic relationship. He has to be "top dog." He constantly reaffirms this status through the power he exercises over you, his family and his acquaintances. Because he doesn't regard you (or anyone else) as his equal, the psychopath can't offer any genuine respect for your values, your activities, your needs and your identity. His fake charm, his controlling and possessive attention, his disingenuous and manipulative flattery and the empty romantic gestures he made (mostly in the beginning of the relationship) are *not* the same thing as genuine love, mutual caring and respect.

As we've seen, a psychopath is incapable of having a caring and equal relationship with anyone. For this reason, psychopaths seek women who are strong but exceedingly flexible; women whose boundaries they can erode and whose identities they can distort. If you regain your sense of identity and boundaries, you become much less vulnerable to psychopathic seduction and control. Psychopaths are parasites who want to suck the lifeblood—the emotions, confidence and strength—out of you. They violate your sense of self, through what psychologists call "enmeshment." As your identity blends into his, your whole life revolves around meeting his ever-changing needs. The more you violate what you stand for and who you are to please the psychopath, the more you dissolve into the dangerous relationship with him. As Sandra L. Brown, M.A. states:

> Boundaries are indicators of where we start and end, and where other people start and end. We set limits—or boundaries—in relationships to protect our bodily selves and dignity. . . Drawing your identity from a dangerous man. . . can have disastrous outcomes (*How to spot a dangerous man*, 201).

Not every misfortunate experience has a silver lining. Some, like fatal illnesses, may be purely tragic. Fortunately, overcoming a relationship with a dangerous man is one of those life experiences that does have a silver lining. After having been involved with a psychopath, for whom "love" means conquest, ownership and dominance, a normal relationship with a decent, respectful and honest partner will seem almost miraculous by comparison. Nothing about healthy human bonds can ever be taken for granted again after one has experienced the worst life has to offer.

Clearly, in choosing a psychopath you lost part of yourself and wasted part of your life. Such a destructive relationship came at a cost. Fortunately, you still have the power of choice as to how your life will continue. You don't have to throw away the rest of your life to him. This experience may have weakened you in some respects. But if you utilize it the right way, it can also make you a much stronger person. Whatever time, energy and emotion you spent on the psychopath weren't completely wasted. They have taught you how to know and defend the limits of your identity and values. They have taught you who to appreciate and love in life and who to reject and keep out. They have revealed your strengths and your limitations. They have made you more independent, since you've seen how flattery and criticism by others can function as a form of mind control.

It's now up to you to decide if you will allow the psychopath to continue to undermine your dignity and the quality of your life or if you will rely upon your strengths and true emotional bonds with others to live the kind of moral, honest and fulfilling life that you deserve. The psychopath has kept you under his control by narrowing and intensifying the range of your experiences. You consequently focused only on him and on how to twist yourself, like a fish on a hook, to please him. You can reverse this process. You can broaden the sphere of your existence by expanding your interests and focusing on those who deserve your affection. In fact, you can do more than that by helping inform others suffering at the hands of psychopathic partners about this dangerous and camouflaged predator. Making a clinical diagnosis of personality disorders is, of course, only up to experts. But identifying potentially dangerous traits isn't just for experts. Any of us can be adversely affected when we allow disordered individuals into our lives. Therefore, knowledge is the most essential form of self-defense for all of us.

Widespread information about physical and emotional abuse has saved millions of people from domestic violence. Spreading information about psychopathy may help save millions of additional lives from harm. Ironically, the disordered man who wanted to destroy you both morally and emotionally can give your life a higher, more other-regarding purpose. In the past, you may have relegated too many of your decisions to the psychopath. But, ultimately, the power of choice in what you do with the rest of your life lies in your hands, not his.

Notes

Introduction

In other words, these men are psychopaths. For all practical purposes, I use the terms "psychopath" and "sociopath" interchangeably. They essentially refer to the same personality disorder. The difference between these two terms has to do (mostly) with hypotheses about the physiological and/or sociological causes of the disorder rather than with its manifestations or effects. Generally speaking, I use the term "psychopath" to underscore the partly physiological basis of this personality disorder. However, I also cite experts on the subject who prefer to use the term "sociopath," to emphasize its social or environmental causes.

They say all the right things to reel you in. Almost all of the women involved with psychopaths interviewed by Brown commented on the psychopaths' extraordinary smoothness and charm. Brown observes, "The difference between other types of dangerous men and predators is that real predators don't fumble" (*How to Spot a Dangerous Man Before You Get Involved*, 183).

They're incapable of forming real love bonds with others. Brown distinguishes mere "attachment" from emotional "bonding." Psychopaths can form intense attachments with the targets with whom they're temporarily obsessed. However, they can't bond emotionally with anyone, in the sense of genuinely caring about them and their needs. Brown explains: "I agree with other researchers that the psychopath *does not bond*, however I believe the psychopath *does attach*... Psychopaths seek others because it is through human contact that they get to experience dominance" (*Women Who Love Psychopaths*, 166).

Are rebels without a cause. This characterization comes from Robert Lindner's study of psychopathy in *Rebel Without a Cause* (New York: Grune and Straton, 1944). His book became the inspiration for the popular James Dean movie by the same name. Lindner states: "The psychopath is a rebel, a religious disobeyer of prevailing codes and standards... a rebel without a cause, an agitator without a slogan, a revolutionary without a program; in other words, his rebelliousness is aimed to achieve goals satisfactory to him alone; he is incapable of exertions for the sake of others. All his efforts, under no matter what guise, represent investments designed to satisfy his immediate wishes and desires" (2).

To control others, psychopaths seduce them. In the beginning of a relationship, psychopaths rely on their charm to seduce others. Initially, they appear to be kind, loyal, fun, easy-going, interesting and respectful. They exhibit many of the desirable qualities one looks for in a potential partner, colleague or friend. Martha Stout observes, "One of the more frequently observed of these traits is a glib and superficial charm that allows the sociopath to seduce people, figuratively or literally—a kind of glow or charisma that, initially, can make the sociopath seem more charming or more intense or somehow more complex or sexier than everyone else" (*The Sociopath Next Door*, 7).

The narrow definition of "seduce." See *Collins Essential English Dictionary*, second edition. New York: *Harper Collins*, 2004.

The etymological root of seduction signifies. See *The American Heritage Dictionary*, Fourth Edition. New York: Houghton Mifflin, 2000.

Nor did Stalin exhibit any loyalty towards his supposed friends and allies. Allan Bullock documents Stalin's political shifts in *Hitler and Stalin: Parallel Lives*: "The first began in 1923 while Lenin was still alive but incapacitated and ended in 1925. In this, the troika of Zinoviev, Kamenev, and Stalin was ranged against Trotsky. The second, Stalin and Bukharin against Zinoviev and Kamenev, in 1925-26, runs into the third, Stalin and Bukharin against the United Opposition of Zinoviev, Kamenev, and Trotsky 1926-27. The final act of the drama, 1928-29, with the United Opposition defeated, sees Stalin turn against Bukharin, Rykov and Tomsky."

Blinded by the illusion of the perfect love. In general, when we fall in love, during the initial infatuation phase, we tend to have on romantic blinders. We experience the euphoria of discovering a new person and the hope of finding the right relationship. This normal idealization phase is all the more heightened by the skillful manipulation and deception of emotional predators. As Susan Forward elaborates, "It's not easy to see clues about someone's past relationships, problems, and irresponsibilities when that person makes you feel terrific. Blinders serve the function of eliminating from your vision any information that might cloud or spoil your romantic picture" (*Men Who Hate Women and the Women Who Love Them*, 23).

They gloat about it. Psychopaths fool and hurt people for the sport of it. To them, damaging the lives of others constitutes a highly entertaining game. Robert Hare and Paul Babiak note, "Psychopathic manipulators seem to experience a gamelike fascination in fooling people, getting into other people's heads and getting them to do things for them. They love control. This ability to win psychological games with people seems to give them a sense of power and personal satisfaction" (*Snakes in Suits*).

For a while, I believed that he was a warm, generous, attractive and sensitive man who was stuck in the wrong marriage. This, of course, was sheer naïveté and wishful thinking on my part. Sandra L. Brown, M.A. offers the following rule of thumb: "Men who are unfaithful with you will be unfaithful to you. His issue is not that he is with the 'wrong woman' it's that he has the wrong character" (*How to Spot a Dangerous Man Before You Get Involved*, 108).

To offer one of the latest examples, Phil Markoff was arrested on the charge of being the alleged Craigslist killer. For more information regarding this case, see Joe Dwinell's *Boston Herald* article of April 17, 2009.

Markoff appeared to be a very likable, clean-cut, charming and well-adjusted young man. In fact, their extraordinary ability to disguise their malicious natures and bad intentions makes such charismatic, bright and well-educated psychopaths exceptionally dangerous. Susan Brown observes, "As mentioned, emotional predators' number-one feature is their unbelievable charm. They have an ability to be a great date and to initiate rapid emotional intimacy..." (*How to Spot a Dangerous Man Before You Get Involved*, 185-6).

Enjoying time together becomes isolation from others. We've seen that controlling men want power, not love. To take charge of your life, a psychopath will do his best to isolate you, eliminate your contacts with others and narrow your outside interests. In other words, he will attempt to reduce your existence solely to your relationship with him. Susan Forward describes this insidious process as follows: "This process often begins in a subtle, indirect, benign way, which may even be experienced as flattery. For instance, suppose you have been taking a class one night a week. Your partner lets you know how he counts the hours until you come home and how lonely and miserable he is while you are gone. This can sound liken an expression of true love—he needs you with him all the time! But it's only a short hop from that kind of 'devotion' to possessiveness over many aspects of your life... How much of yourself must you renounce in order to prove your love?" (*Men Who Hate Women and the Women Who Love Them*, 55).

The ability to love and moral reasoning. For a detailed explanation of how psychopaths are lacking in impulse control, moral reasoning and the ability to love, see Liane Leedom's *Just like his Father?* (New York: Health and Well-Being Publications, 2006).

Of course, female psychopaths exist. More detailed information about Melissa Huckaby and her alleged crime can be found in the April 10, 2009 article on the subject published by the *Associated Press.* Subsequent articles cover her theatrical displays of emotion and excuse making. Recently, Huckaby attributed her horrendous behavior to having been raped by an officer. This claim may or may not be true. But, at any rate, it doesn't in any way justify her behavior towards an innocent girl. Psychopaths notoriously fail to take responsibility for their wrongdoings. They're also very adept at fake displays of emotion and at what Martha Stout calls the "pity play."

What I say here about male psychopaths applies to female psychopaths and male victims. That's because psychopaths have much more in common with each other than with normal human beings. Their inherent lack of conscience and heartlessness distinguishes them from the rest of humanity. As Martha Stout observes, "The presence or absence of conscience is a deep human division, arguably more significant than intelligence, race, or even gender... What distinguishes all of these people from the rest of us is an utterly empty hole in the psyche, where there should be the most evolved of all humanizing functions." (*The Sociopath Next Door*, 10)

In addition, research shows that 80 percent of the homicides of women are perpetrated by their husbands or boyfriends, which is to say, by the men they know and trust. For more information on how to spot red flags in dangerous relationships, see Sandra L. Brown's *How to Spot a Dangerous Man Before You Get Involved* (Alameda, CA: Hunter House, 2005).

As psychotherapist Steve Becker explains. From his article "Differentiating Narcissists and Psychopaths," posted on the website *powercommunicating.com* and *lovefraud.com*.

Psychologists call psychopathy "pathological." As we've seen, Sandra L. Brown, M.A. describes a relationship with a psychopath, or what she calls an "emotional predator," as "the pinnacle of poisonous and pathological dating choices" (*How to spot a dangerous man*, 179). She also explains why pathology, or a severe personality disorder like psychopathy, is unfixable. She states, "Most experts agree that there is very little permanent change that can occur to make such individuals 'less pathological'" (*How to spot a dangerous man*, 17). Individuals with pathological disorders, such as psychopathy or malignant narcissism, can't change because the disorder is part of their brain wiring as well as, in some cases, of their early social development. It's therefore engrained in their personalities.

It's the result of a faulty brain wiring. Psychologists stipulate that psychopathy has both genetic and environmental causes. But, ultimately, for the (potential) victims, the only thing that should matter is that it can't be cured in adults. From the perspective of those involved with psychopaths, the causes of this personality disorder are far less relevant than its harmful effects. Brown emphasizes, "The only thing that should concern you is deciding what to do when you face a man who you figure out is dangerous or pathologically ill" (*How to Spot a Dangerous Man Before You Get Involved*, 21).

Blame for the problems that occur in the relationship. Sandra L. Brown, M.A. states: "A woman who believes an abuser when he says it is her fault, he will change, he will never do it again, he will go to counseling, he will go to church, he only does it because she makes him, or he does it because she needs or deserves it is a top choice for a violent man" (*How to spot a dangerous man*, 165).

They're often deeply in love. Women who love psychopaths tend to be blinded by a toxic combination of fantasy, hope and denial. They refuse to face the truth about their partners' unfixable personality disorder. They want to believe that their love and patience will be able to cure them. But this is an impossible goal. As Sandra L. Brown, M.A. indicates, "Disaster can be the only outcome when a woman tries to conform to a pathological and abnormal relationship" (*How to spot a dangerous man*, 18).

It will also help heal your pain and set you free. See the witty and wise article "The Truth will set you free—but first it will piss you off," featured on *lovefraud.com* on July 28, 2008. This title is itself based on a quote by Gloria Steinem, the famous Women's Rights Activist. The contributor argues that, "in reference to sociopaths, truer words were never spoken. When we finally learn the truth about these people, after months, years or decades of deception, we are hurt—but we are also enraged. Then, as we try to dig ourselves out of the hole, we learn more infuriating truths about the inability of other people in our lives, and of society's institutions, to help us."

Part I. What is a Psychopath?

Chapter 1. Charismatic Psychopaths: Mark Hacking and Neil Entwistle

Charismatic psychopaths rely upon their natural trademarks. Sandra L. Brown, M.A. describes charismatic psychopaths, or "emotional predators," as follows: "They say all the right lines that the men in the past could never verbalize. They are brilliant and insightful about what you need. They seem to know exactly every pain you have suffered" (*How to Spot a Dangerous Man Before You Get Involved*, 185).

Wishing they too could have such romantic partners. Sandra L. Brown, M.A. elaborates on the emotional predator's seductive skills: "A predator wants to move in with you or marry you quickly, because time is against him. To move the relationship along and become indispensable to you, he must act helpful, comforting and generous" (*How to Spot a Dangerous Man Before You Get Involved*, 185).

And the vain hope that they can somehow recapture it. Women who stay with psychopaths even once they begin to see their dark side tend to believe that they can save their dangerous partners. They also hope to be the one exception to the rule. Yet, unfortunately, they never are. As Sandra L. Brown, M.A. cautions: "I can't stress the following enough: Your experience with a pathological man will *not* be the exception to the rule. A personality disorder is a virtual guarantee against any possibility for long-term change in an individual's core self" (*How to Spot a Dangerous Man Before You Get Involved*, 24).

His image of perfection is only a mask, set up to ensnare his target into a vision of her dream come true, which eventually turns into a nightmare. Psychopaths wouldn't be able to seduce anyone if they showed their real, ugly natures from the very start. Consequently, they initially present themselves as the opposite of what they really are (*Women Who Love Psychopaths*, Chapter 11: "Deceive and Believe: the Luring and Honeymoon Stage, pp. 187-201).

Constitutes their only real purpose in life. Some individuals—such as doctors or soldiers—are trained to curb their empathy in the context of their professions, to perform more effectively. This doesn't make them psychopathic. By way of contrast, psychopaths experience a total and constitutive lack of empathy towards everyone and in every context. Robert Hare observes: "Psychopaths, however, display a general lack of empathy. They are indifferent to the rights and suffering of family members and strangers alike. If they do maintain ties with their spouses or children it's because they see their family members as possessions, much like their stereos or automobiles" (*Without Conscience*, 45). This underlying mentality also enables some psychopaths to kill their family members or lovers as easily as normal people may toss away an old, broken stereo.

Fooling their families, their lovers, and their colleagues. Deception not only comes naturally to psychopaths, but also it's a big part of the fun for them. They can convince their spouses, their lovers and even their therapists or lawyers that they're innocent and kind-hearted people. They often present themselves as the real victims. When caught in a lie, they smoothly make up another story or change their narrative to incorporate the false information. Throughout the entire process, they remain more cool and collected than normal people do when they're telling the truth. Robert Hare notes, "Lying, deceiving, and manipulation are natural talents for psychopaths... When caught in a lie or challenged with the truth, they are seldom perplexed or embarrassed—they simply change their stories or attempt to rework the facts so that they appear to be consistent with the lie" (*Without Conscience*, 46).

Or, when caught, that they feel genuine remorse or have been victimized themselves—offers the extra bonus. Beware of the pity play, especially when it's undeserved. Female psychopaths are especially prone to dramatic displays of helplessness, remorse or acting like they're the real victims, usually of invented or exaggerated abuse. Empathy makes us capable of love and different from the heartless psychopaths. But misplaced empathy makes us dupes, vulnerable to psychopathic manipulation. Martha Stout advises readers, "Pity is another socially valuable response, and it should be reserved for innocent people who are in genuine pain or who have fallen on misfortune. If, instead, you find yourself often pitying someone who consistently hurts you or other people, and who actively campaigns for your sympathy, the chances are close to 100 percent that you are dealing with a sociopath" (*The Sociopath Next Door*, 160).

Lori and Mark Hacking. For more information on Lori Hacking's murder by her husband Mark, see Rachael Bell's article on the subject on trutv.com (http://www.trutv.com/library/crime/notorious_murders/family/mark_hacking/index.html).

Rachel and Neil Entwistle. For more information regarding this case, see Keith Ablow's article on the subject, "Inside the Mind of Neil Entwistle," published on July 26th, 2006 by Fox News. See also Katherine Ramsland's article on the same subject on *trutv.com*, where she describes Neil's pathological lying as "white lies" that went too far. The most accurate psychological profile of Neil Entwistle I found is sketched by Harrison Koehli in his article, "Neil Entwistle: Psychopath" (sott.net, July 2, 2008).

Their flashes of anger are as shallow and fleeting as their infatuations. Robert Hare indicates, "Psychopaths seem to suffer a kind of emotional poverty that limits the range and depth of their feelings. While at times they appear cold and unemotional, they are prone to dramatic, shallow, and short-lived displays of feeling" (*Without Conscience*, 52).

Chapter 2. What is a Psychopath? Close Readings of Cleckley's *The Mask of Sanity*

Where they're constantly punching in a new destination. Their constant pursuit of new goals relates both to their low impulse control and to their underlying lack of empathy. Robert Hare explains that psychopaths "have little resistance to temptation, and their transgressions elicit no guilt. Without the shackles of a nagging conscience, they feel free to satisfy their needs and wants and do whatever they think they can get away with" (*Without Conscience*, 76).

New and exciting ways to transgress social rules. The fact that psychopaths readily transgress social boundaries doesn't imply that they do so at all times, as if driven only by instinct. Usually there's a lot of planning and calculation involved in their harmful actions: which makes them all the more dangerous. Psychopaths are cold and deliberate in selecting their targets, their crimes and the optimal circumstances or timing. As Robert Hare notes, "Of course, psychopaths are not completely unresponsive to the myriad rules and taboos that hold society together. After all, they are not automatons, blindly responding to momentary needs, urges and opportunities. It is just that they are much freer than the rest of us to pick and choose the rules and restrictions they will adhere to" (*Without Conscience*, 78).

By that standard, psychopaths aren't Epicurean. Psychopaths are motivated by positive, intense pleasures. They don't fear repercussions or pain. As Brown elaborates, "Psychopaths are highly pleasure motivated and will excessively seek what they enjoy" (*Women Who Love Psychopaths*, 38).

They sabotage their own futures and harm others in momentary flashes of anger. A psychopath's anger may be intense, but it's as shallow as his other emotions. That's why a psychopath can kill his entire family and go out for a drink with his buddies only a few minutes later. Usually, psychopaths commit cold and calculated crimes. In other words, they don't commit so-called "crimes of passion," even when acting in the heat of the moment. Robert Hare explains, "In general, psychopathic violence tends to be callous and cold-blooded, and more likely to be straightforward, uncomplicated, and businesslike than an expression of deep-seated distress or understandable precipitating factors. It lacks the 'juice' or powerful emotion that accompanies the violence of most other individuals" (*Without Conscience*, 92).

Psychopaths lack such incentives. Robert Hare, among others, explains why therapy can't modify a psychopath's underlying bad character: "To elaborate, psychopaths are generally well satisfied with themselves and their inner landscape, bleak as it may seem to outside observers. They see nothing wrong with themselves, experience little personal distress, and find their behavior rational, rewarding, and satisfying; they never look back with regret or forward with concern" (*Without Conscience*, 195).

"Being in love." Psychopaths commonly experience intense infatuations. But, as we've seen, they're incapable of loving anyone deeply or even of being "in love." They confuse momentarily wanting, desiring or wishing to possess someone with loving that person. As Martha Stout states, "And sociopaths are

noted especially for their shallowness of emotions, the hollow and transient nature of any affectionate feelings they may claim to have, a certain breathtaking callousness. They have no trace of empathy and no genuine interest in bonding emotionally with a mate. Once the surface charm is scraped off, their marriages are loveless, one-sided, and almost always short-term. If a marriage partner has any value to the sociopath, it is because the partner is viewed as a possession, one that the sociopath may feel angry to lose, but never sad or accountable" (*The Sociopath Next Door*, 7).

Psychopaths function like ticking time bombs. Although nothing rattles psychopaths for long, they have poor behavior controls. They can burst into violence at little or no provocation. Being guided by a sense of entitlement and double standards, they're highly insensitive to the feelings of others and hypersensitive to their own. Robert Hare elaborates, "Besides being impulsive—doing things on the spur of the moment—psychopaths are highly reactive to perceived insults or slights... But their outbursts, extreme as they may be, are generally short-lived, and they quickly resume acting as if nothing out of the ordinary has happened" (*Without Conscience*, 59).

Chapter 3. Psychopaths and Pathological Lying

But also they fail to see why lying is wrong. Hare and Babiak observe, "Unencumbered by social anxieties, fear of being found out, empathy, remorse, or guilt—some of nature's break pedals for anti-social behavior in humans—psychopaths tell a tale so believable, so entertaining, so creative, that many listeners instinctively trust them" (*Snakes in Suits*, 50).

Or the false information he gives you, can and will hurt you. Psychopaths lie far more pervasively and with greater malice than non-psychopaths. They lie to manipulate, control, use and hurt others. Hare and Babiak distinguish between "normal" and psychopathic deception: "The difference between psychopathic lies and those told by others is that the latter typically are less callous, calculated, damaging, and destructive to others. They are also far less pervasive than psychopathic lies" (*Snakes in Suits*, 51).

Get the additional thrill of offering a false explanation. Hare and Babiak note that some psychopaths even boast about their capacity to lie. "Some psychopaths are proud of this expertise [to lie], making fun of their victims' gullibility and often bragging about how they fooled this person and that person" (*Snakes in Suits*, 51). Based on my personal observation, I'd definitely say both.

And imagining things that don't exist or aren't true. Because they enjoy the sense of power that deception gives them, psychopaths will lie even when the truth would sound more plausible or when their victim already knows the truth.

Hare and Babiak note, "Surprisingly, psychopaths will lie even to people who already know the truth about what they are saying... Such is the power of psychopathic manipulation" (*Snakes in Suits*, 51).

Psychopaths lie very easily and in a smooth manner. Hare and Babiak explain this facility in terms of psychopaths' excellent oral communication skills and lack of inhibition: "Some psychopaths are so good at this that they can create a veritable Shangri-la view of their world in the minds of others; a view that they almost seem to believe themselves" (*Snakes in Suits*, 51).

Or that humanity in general is. Psychopaths don't accept responsibility for anything they do wrong, which includes their deception. Hare and Babiak note, "Another characteristic of psychopaths is an ability to avoid taking responsibility for things that go wrong; instead, they blame others, circumstances, fate, and so forth" (*Snakes in Suits*, 51-2). Similarly, Martha Stout advises readers not to accept the lie that everyone is sociopathic. She states, "Do not allow someone without a conscience, or even a string of such people, to convince you that humanity is a failure. Most human beings do possess a conscience. Most human beings are able to love" (*The Sociopath Next Door*, 162).

Deceit, manipulation and destruction that psychopaths are capable of. Even when they're obliged by overwhelming evidence to admit their wrongdoings, psychopaths often continue to deny or minimize them. In this respect, they may even be sincere. Their lack of empathy is genuine and nothing short of astonishing. Hare and Babiak observe, "Psychopaths may even blame the victims for their own misfortune, offering convincing reasons why they got what they deserved!" (*Snakes in Suits*, 52).

Fabrication of Details. Jean-François Lyotard illustrates in *The Postmodern Condition: A Report on Knowledge* (Minnesota: University of Minnesota Press, 1984) that offering a lot of details can help make a lie appear truthful. Perhaps this is also why details are a preferred narrative strategy of realist fiction.

As a participant to the website lovefraud.com has eloquently remarked, psychopaths themselves are the lie. In her post on February 28, 2008, M. L. Gallagher states: "When I first got my life back I gave myself a mantra to stop my endless trying to figure out grains of truth from amidst all his lies. Trying to make sense of his nonsense was keeping me sick. Trying to discern the why behind what he had done was keeping embroiled in his crazy-making—and I deserved so much more than that. My mantra was: He is the lie. From hello to good-bye. I love you to I hate you. You're beautiful to you're ugly. It was all a lie. There was no sense in trying to finding a grain of truth amidst all those lies—he wasn't worth my precious breath" (*lovefraud.com*).

Chapter 4. The Psychopath's Antisocial Behavior

The psychopath's antisocial behavior. For further information, see also the *Diagnostic and Statistical Manual of Mental Disorders* published by the American Psychiatric Association, pp. 645-650.

Often, there seems to be no underlying logic to a psychopath's actions. Antisocials enjoy harming others for fun. The *American Psychiatric Association* states that antisocial personality disorder entails a pervasive pattern of disregard for, and violation of, the rights of others that begins in childhood or early adolescence and continues into adulthood. People with antisocial personality disorder (ASPD or APD) are also called "sociopaths" or "psychopaths." Deceit and manipulation are considered to be key symptoms of this personality disorder.

In his own mind, nothing the psychopath does is ever wrong. For more information, see *Psychology Today*'s article on "Antisocial Personality Disorder, 2005 and the Mayo Clinic's article on the same subject, from *MayoClinic.com*, October 9, 2006.

Chapter 5. Psychopaths as Lovers

Psychopaths have low impulse control and are generally highly promiscuous. Not only do psychopaths have a high sex drive, but also they have low impulse control. The result of this volatile combination is that many of them become sex addicts (*Women Who Love Psychopaths*, 168-172).

He's excited by the chase and the "conquest," by the novelty, by the fact that he's (most likely) cheating on other women and on you. Psychopaths are excited by sex primarily because they're stimulated by the prospect of exercising power over others. Seduction, to them, necessarily entails domination. This is because the pathological need for dominance affects all of their actions and desires. As Brown observes, "Rieber and Vetter indicate 'psychopaths are extremely sensitive to power relationships and want maximum power. But they also want to use power destructively... The psychopath's dominance drive is a force behind his pathology" (*Women Who Love Psychopaths*, 39).

What's worse, it becomes normative, since psychopaths enjoy controlling you. After the initial seduction phase, you begin to sense the brutal selfishness of psychopathic lovers. You also notice that sexual relations with such men are about their control of you, not an expression of mutual love and pleasure. Susan Forward elaborates, "Sexual relations with a misogynist are liable to occur only when and how he chooses... One of the first changes that many women report is that sex has become mechanical, the attention and affection that went with love-making in the beginning of the relationship has slipped away" (*Men Who Hate Women and the Women Who Love Them*, 61).

Many psychopaths engage in rape, including spousal rape, and other forms of domestic violence. Because psychopaths seek control over their sexual partners, they become increasingly sadistic and dictatorial in their approach. Susan Forward explains, "I am referring to sexual activities that are unpleasant for the woman but which the misogynist persists in doing, despite the fact that they cause her pain, discomfort, or a feeling of degradation" (*Men Who Hate Women and the Women Who Love Them*, 66).

Of course, they convincingly fake romance and feelings of love in the beginning. Affection, for psychopaths, is purely instrumental. They use it in the beginning of a relationship to attract potential partners. But their real motivation, from beginning to end, is conquest and dominance. Ultimately, Brown notes, "Psychopaths hurt people because power through victimization is much more satisfying to them. They are emotionally rewarded by the harm they case" (*Women Who Love Psychopaths*, 40).

Like some wound-up inflatable doll with holes, always available to that man for his sexual gratification (or else. . .). As mentioned, many psychopaths are sex addicted to sex. Sex enables them to assert dominance over the women they regard as their personal property. Susan Forward elaborates, "If you are involved with a sexaholic, you will eventually begin to feel like an object that exists only for his release; the sexual contact between you will have very little to do with who you are" (*Men Who Hate Women and the Women Who Love Them*, 68). Sexual addiction is never an expression of mutual caring or love. It is, by nature, impersonal.

Chapter 6. Psychopaths and Failure

Psychopaths rarely achieve anything in life. Stout raises the question that if psychopaths are so focused on their goals and so driven to win, then "Why do they not win all the time?" Boredom and the incapacity to pursue any goal for an extended period of time are two of the main reasons why psychopaths usually fail so miserably in life. "For," as Stout pursues, "they do not [win or succeed]. Instead, most of them are obscure people, and limited to dominating their young children, or a depressed spouse, or perhaps a few employees or coworkers... Having never made much of a mark on the world, the majority are on a downward life course, and by late middle age will be burned out completely. They can rob and torment us temporarily, yes, but they are, in effect, failed lives" (*The Sociopath Next Door*, 188).

This logic also applies to their personal relationships. Just as psychopaths tend to fail in their professional endeavors, they also fail in their personal lives. Even their most intimate relationships turn out to be nothing more than empty games of deceit and domination. Stout elaborates, "People without conscience experience emotions very differently from you and me, and they do not experience love at all, or any other kind of positive attachment to their fellow human beings. This deficit, which is hard even to ponder, reduces life to an endless game of attempted domination over other people" (*The Sociopath Next Door*, 155).

Part II. The Process of Psychopathic Seduction

Chapter 1. The Case of Drew Peterson

Many of us followed on the news the story of Stacy Peterson's disappearance. For more details about Drew Peterson, see *Deadly Deception: The Drew Peterson story*, Crime reports, msnbc.com.

In fact, Drew was recently arrested and charged with the murder. See the news story of May 7, 2009 posted on cnn.com.

In his interview with Kotb. See Hoda Kotb's December 21, 2007 *Dateline* interview with Drew Peterson, documented on insidedateline.msnbc.com/archive/2007.

Chapter 2. Red Flags: How to Identify a Psychopathic Bond

This is why psychopaths eventually move from the initial over-the-top flattery to scathing criticism. Psychopaths know that it's much easier to control someone with low self-esteem. Being too willing to "compromise" with the psychopath increases his power over you and decreases your self-confidence. As Susan Forward observes, you begin to feel, and even act, like a doormat: "[W]hen a woman repeatedly gives in to her partner so that her needs take second place to his, she cannot maintain her self-esteem" (*Men Who Hate Women and the Women Who Love Them*, 77).

Psychopaths aim to transform strong and proud individuals into their doormats. According to Françoise Gilot, Picasso was quite explicit about this goal. But it's not unique to him. In their quest for domination, all psychopaths aim to undermine the confidence of otherwise strong individuals. As Brown observes, "Unfortunately, the psychopath only loves himself, and will systematically attempt to annihilate her sense of self-esteem, self-validation and self-worth" (*Women Who Love Psychopaths*, 147).

Chapter 3. The Process of Psychopathic Seduction: Idealize, Devalue and Discard

Not necessarily calculated at every moment in the relationship. Hare and Babiak qualify that the process of psychopathic seduction often "will be more automatic than consciously planned out" (*Snakes in Suits*, 42). Manipulating, deceiving and using people is a natural outgrowth of the psychopathic personality. But a lot of psychopaths' harmful actions are deliberate and calculated, sometimes planned out long in advance.

Hook their victims emotionally and to win their trust. Hare and Babiak note that during the manipulation phase, "Perhaps one of the most effective skills psychopaths use to get the trust of people is their ability to charm them. . . Upon this first impression, they may build an elaborate fictitious character, persona or mask" (*Snakes in Suits*, 48-9).

Observing how they dupe people into believing this fiction. While some psychopaths seem phony, the truly skilled ones have an uncanny ability to lie convincingly. They can pretend to be whatever will get them what or whom they want at the moment. Hare and Babiak state that such psychopaths, "have raised their ability to charm people to that of an art, priding themselves on their ability to present a fictional self to others that is convincing, taken at face value, and difficult to penetrate" (*Snakes in Suits*, 50).

They get bored with you and move on to new sources of pleasure and excitement. As we've observed, psychopaths tend to move from person to person, job to job, place to place and relationship to relationship. They get bored with everything and everyone very easily. Hare and Babiak remark, "In addition to their parasitic nature and lack of empathy, there is evidence that psychopaths *need considerable novel stimulation* to keep from becoming bored. This need, which recent research suggests may be rooted in their brain physiology, often leads them to search for new and exciting opportunities and to move casually from relationship to relationship" (*Snakes in Suits*, 46).

Their loss of interest appears as a devaluation. Which is exactly what it is. It's an indication that the psychopath has gotten whatever he wanted from you and is ready to move on. As Hare and Babiak state, "Once psychopaths have drained all the value from a victim—that is, when the victim is no longer useful—they abandon the victim and move on to someone else" (*Snakes in Suits*, 53).

You suddenly become just an obstacle to their next pursuit. Psychopaths assess each person and relationship in terms of their use-value. They conduct cost-benefit analyses of people and situations, always keeping their selfish goals uppermost in mind. Hare and Babiak note, "People do not exist in their mental world except as objects, targets and obstacles" (*Snakes in Suits*, 46). The same person can suddenly change status, from desirable target to useless obstacle, once the psychopath gets bored with her or has already used up her value.

You accept his implausible excuses. As we've seen, psychopaths lie easily and convincingly. Hare and Babiak explain why their lies seem so compelling to their victims: "Their often theatrical, yet convincing stories and entertaining explanations reinforce an environment of trust, acceptance, and genuine delight, leading most people to accept them exactly as whom they appear to be—and almost unconsciously excuse any inconsistencies they might have noted" (*Snakes in Suits*, 50).

You rationalize his inexplicable absences. The capacity to rationalize bad or suspicious behavior is one of the key reasons why so many good women stay with bad men. Susan Forward explains, "Rationalization is what we do when we smooth over any insight that interferes with our good feelings. It's a way of making the unacceptable acceptable" (*Men Who Hate Women and the Women Who Love Them*, 29).

In fact, he encourages anything that deflects attention from his responsibility. If psychopaths generally fail at everything—relationships, careers and parenting—it's largely because they consider themselves flawless. They therefore do nothing to correct their bad behavior. They always find ways to ascribe blame to others or to circumstances. Brown remarks, "Impulsive psychopaths rarely stop to consider the long term consequences of their actions and repeatedly fail to see that 'their actions=their consequences'" (*Women Who Love Psychopaths*, 42).

The most flattering and pleasant phase of their control. Of course, the flattery itself, however pleasant it may feel, is insidious, phony and used as a means to control you. Flattery constitutes a form of domination. For that reason, it can be far more effective than the psychopath's overt control. If the psychopath eventually switches to more explicit and unpleasant forms of domination, it's because he feels confident enough in his power over his target to put in less and less effort to keep on his mask of sanity. Susan Forward observes, "What makes this so subtle was that initially she may feel flattered. It may appear that her partner is so in love with her that he doesn't want to share her with anyone else. In reality, however, he is gradually making her renounce the people and activities that are important in her life" (*Men Who Hate Women and the Women Who Love Them*, 78).

Once they get bored with you because the spell of the initial conquest wears off. For psychopaths, seduction is a way of getting control over you. Once this goal is accomplished, their control over your life can spread like a bad weed. As

Susan Forward puts it, "The misogynist's control over his partner is like the roots of a plant: it spreads into many areas of her life. Her work, her interests, her friends, her children, and even her thoughts and feelings can be affected by his control" (*Men Who Hate Women and the Women Who Love Them*, 85).

And do whatever you can to regain privileged status. Some women leave psychopaths as soon as they discover their true natures. But, unfortunately, many struggle to save the relationship. In their study, Hare and Babiak note that many of the individuals they interviewed "referred to their psychopathic partners as their 'soul mates' and reported how much they believed they had in common with the psychopath" (*Snakes in Suits*, 79).

Every women's shelter tells abused women that abuse usually gets worse. What may begin with punching the wall or throwing an object, all too often ends with physically harming the other person. Research indicates that very few violent men stop their behavior. Furthermore, practically none of the ones that do so are psychopathic. Sandra L. Brown, M.A. describes as follows the escalation of violence in abusive relationships: "He starts out as very attentive and giving. But then Mr. Hyde appears—controlling, blaming, shaming, harming, perhaps hitting" (*How to Spot a Dangerous Man Before You Get Involved*, 15).

Dr. Jekyll is in fact always Mr. Hyde on the inside. The abandonment phase reveals the real psychopath. By way of contrast, the seduction phase is only a mask or a lure. As Hare and Babiak observe, "To be able to abandon people in such a callous and harmful manner one must be immune to the feelings of those one hurts" (*Snakes in Suits*, 54).

He's gotten everything he wanted out of you. Psychopaths have malicious and predatory intentions when they engage in relationships with others. They're cold and empty to the core. As Hare and Babiak elaborate, "This hollow core serves them well, though, by making them effective human predators" (*Snakes in Suits*, 55).

Chapter 4. Artistic Psychopaths: The Case of Picasso

If you read other biographies of Picasso. See, for instance, Picasso's own account of his compatibility with his long-time mistress, Marie-Thérèse Walter, chronicled in *Pablo Picasso and Marie-Thérèse Walter: Between Classicism and Surrealism* (New York: Kerber, 2004). To find out more about how Picasso eventually devalued and discarded each of his partners, see Arianna Huffington's *Picasso: Creator and Destroyer* (New York: Simon and Schuster, 1988).

I'm the perfect partner or soul mate for you. This message is very compelling to most people, who want to find someone compatible with them who genuinely appreciates them. Hare and Babiak explain: "The first message is that the psychopath likes and values the strengths and talents presented by your persona. In other words, the psychopath positively reinforces your self-presentation, saying, in effect, I like who you are" (*Snakes in Suits*, 74-5).

This process constitutes the "mirroring phase" of the psychopathic bond. The psychopath indicates at this point, directly or indirectly, that he is just like his target. This mirroring effect constitutes a very effective strategy of seduction. As Hare and Babiak explain, "To our great pleasure, we want to believe that this person understands us at a much deeper level than anyone else we have met" (*Snakes in Suits*, 76).

A psychopath will become whatever you want him to be in order to seduce you. Psychopaths become your soulmates for awhile, in order to seduce you. Hare and Babiak state that this gets to the very foundation of a person's identity: "This psychological bond capitalizes on your inner personality, holding out the promise of greater depth and possibly intimacy, and offering a relationship that is special, unique, equal—forever" (*Snakes in Suits*, 78).

He just doesn't stay that way for long. If the psychopath doesn't keep his mask of charm on once he has attained control over you, it's because he doesn't feel it's necessary or worth his while to continue putting in that kind of effort. After all, he's after conquests, not relationships. It's also because the mask itself is fake. Hare and Babiak note, "For one, the persona of the psychopath—the 'personality' the person is bonding with—does not really exist. It was built on lies, carefully woven together to entrap you" (*Snakes in Suits*, 78).

In fact, after the seduction phase, the roles switch dramatically. Once a given target is under the psychopath's control, the manipulation phase begins. The psychopath attempts to bend her to his will, sometimes to the point of annihilating her personality. This is the logical conclusion of a psychopath's entire process of seduction. Hare and Babiak explain, "In summary, the psychopath's psychological game involves analyzing the individual's expectations and desires, and then reflecting them in a psychological mask that is so convincing the person bonds with him or her" (*Snakes in Suits*, 79).

But psychopaths use the power of charisma for predatory purposes. This makes all relationships with psychopaths phony and one-sided. As Hare and Babiak elaborate, "the psychopath has an ulterior—some would say 'evil'—and at the very least, selfish motive... The victimization is predatory in nature; it often leads to severe financial, physical, or emotional harm for the individual" (*Snakes in Suits*, 79).

That momentary sensations, desires and objectives are all that count for him. Because a psychopath can't form real emotional bonds, he also can't engage in any genuine care-taking behavior. His attachments may sometimes be intense, but they're always very shallow. Brown notes, for a psychopath, "None of the attachment has anything to do with emotional intimacy or bonding" (*Women Who Love Psychopaths*, 167).

He demands that her whole existence revolve around fulfilling his every need, yet nothing ever pleases him for long. For a psychopath, no level of power over his target is ever enough. He demands more and more from her, constantly raising the bar. Susan Forward aptly compares the partner's position to having a final exam that she can never pass: "He will constantly invent new ways to test your devotion. It's very much like having a final exam every week for a course you can never pass" (*Men Who Hate Women and the Women Who Love Them*, 55).

The double, triple or even quadruple duplicity. For a detailed explanation of the triangulation of desire and the role of deceit in sexual liaisons, see René Girard's *Deceit, Desire, and the Novel: Self and Other in Literary Structure* (Maryland: Johns Hopkins University Press, 1976).

Chapter 5. The Psychopathic Seducer in Literature: Benjamin Constant's *Adolphe*

In the preface to the second edition, the author vehemently denies any connection between his love life and the characters of his novel. Constant observes, "This scandal was so quickly forgotten that maybe I'm wrong to mention it here. But I felt an unpleasant surprise, which gave me the urge to repeat that none of the characters sketched in *Adolphe* have any rapport with any of the individuals that I know" (*Adolphe*, 26, my translation).

His tumultuous long-term affair with one of the most famous women of the times, Germaine de Stäel. The best biography I read on Benjamin Constant and Germaine de Stäel is Christopher Herold's *Mistress to an Age: A Life of Madame de Stael,* which describes at length the dysfunctional relationship between them. This biography, and several others, leads me to conclude, along with many other literary critics, that there are strong autobiographical elements in *Adolphe*, despite the author's vehement denials.

Which is exactly where Adolphe wants her. Because they seek total control of their targets, psychopaths aren't only jealous of other potential suitors, but also of anything or anyone that can give their victim a sense of meaning outside of their toxic relationship. Susan Forward elaborates, "Anything you do that is out of the misogynist's control or is seen as a threat to him must be abolished" (*Men Who Hate Women and the Women Who Love Them*, 57).

Chapter 6. The Women Who Love Psychopaths

Sandra L. Brown, M.A. published a very informative book on the psychological profile of the women who love psychopaths. This book offers a study of 75 women, worldwide, describing their experiences with psychopaths in their own words (See the Introduction of *Women Who Love Psychopaths*, pp. 7-13).

The bad news of this statistic is that it means there are millions of psychopaths in this country alone who affect tens of millions of lives. Psychologists estimate that there are between 6 and 10 million psychopaths in the United States. Since they're highly sociable and promiscuous, this means that they affect tens of millions of partners.

Beyond the pale of normal experience and comprehension. What people find most difficult to accept is that psychopaths suffer from something like an emotional retardation which is as unfixable as mental retardation. Since psychopaths are often bright, eloquent and well educated, however, most people can't understand why they behave the way they do and why they don't improve. For a discussion of this subject, see Chapter 14 of *Women Who Love Psychopaths*, pp. 231-244)

Brown describes the women who fall in love with psychopaths as successful professionals. Brown notes, "Most of the women I interviewed were professionals. They were intelligent and successful in their fields" (*How to Spot a Dangerous Man Before You Get Involved*, 50).

Psychopaths tend to select strong women at their most vulnerable moments. Sandra L. Brown, M.A. elaborates, "Predators have a natural ability for reading women who are lonely, bored, needy by nature, emotionally wounded, or vulnerable" (*How to Spot a Dangerous Man Before You Get Involved*, 180).

Chapter 7. Coping Mechanisms for Staying with a Psychopath

Thus staying with a psychopath is not simply a case of being masochistic. Susan Forward refutes the theory that women who get involved with bad men do so because of masochistic tendencies. She argues that such women don't generally enjoy the downsides of abusive relationships. Rather, they enjoy the positive sides—the flattery, the romance and the excitement—that they hope, in vain, to recapture. "As I talked more extensively with the couples I was counseling, I found that neither of these terms [masochism and sadism] applied... She did not get any hidden sexual or emotional pleasure from her partner's abusive treatment of her. Instead, it severely demoralized her" (*Men Who Hate Women and the Women Who Love Them*, 7).

A huge incentive. The desire to reform a psychopath is, of course, self-defeating and futile. Even if a woman feels morally superior to the amoral psychopath, the effort to reform him will erode her dignity and moral boundaries. Although her motivations may not be masochistic, the destructive effect upon her life ends up being the same as if they were. Susan Forward, however, distinguishes between masochism and these futile efforts to fix the relationship with a psychopath: "Masochism is defined as a state in which a person gets pleasure from pain. The woman who is hooked in a misogynist relationship is actually trying frantically to avoid being hurt" (*Men Who Hate Women and the Women Who Love Them*, 89).

They foreground all the positive aspects of the relationship and relegate the negative ones, as much as possible, to the background. This strategy, colloquially referred to as "wishful thinking," is quite common when one is in love. Susan Forward explains, "Without realizing it, many women divide the emotional landscape of their relationships into a foreground and a background. In the foreground are all the wonderful characteristics that the man possesses. These are traits that are focused on, maximized and idealized. Any hint of trouble gets pushed into the background as unimportant" (*Men Who Hate Women and the Women Who Love Them*, 23).

Fixing a psychopath and your relationship with him constitutes a self-defeating goal. Every expert on psychopathy I've read draws this conclusion. Yet women involved with psychopaths stay with partners who consistently mistreat them in the vain hope that they can improve. Psychopaths often cultivate their false hopes. Susan Forward notes, "The fantasy is that he'll take her into his arms and say, 'I know I've been terrible to you. Please forgive me. I love you and I'll never yell at you again. From now on things will be different'" (*Men Who Hate Women and the Women Who Love Them*, 91).

Emotional abuse constitutes a pattern of behavior over time that is designed to control another human being. Sandra L. Brown, M.A. defines emotional abuse as follows: "Emotional abuse includes controlling and dominating you by not allowing you to make your own choices; telling you how to dress and behave or whom you can or can't talk to; put-downs that keep you captive and uncertain that you could make it on your own" (*How to Spot a Dangerous Man Before You Get Involved*, 164).

A psychopath derails his partner by constantly keeping her on edge. Alternating between arbitrary "good" treatment and abuse also encourages the victim to blame herself for the abuse. She wrongly assumes that if her partner can be "nice," she must have caused the meanness. This tips their balance of power in the psychopath's favor. Susan Forward elaborates, "Accepting his version of reality means she must give up hers. It's Alice in Wonderland time. She may still know that she is being mistreated, but she invents 'good reasons' to explain it away." (*Men Who Hate Women and the Women Who Love Them*, 94-5)

This unhealthy bonding solidifies when the abuser alternates between the carrot and the stick. Psychopaths commonly switch from being mean to being "nice." This enables them to attain control over their victims and to keep them struggling on the hook. As Susan Forward explains, "Unfortunately, the good times support your mistaken belief that the ugly times are somehow just a bad dream—not the 'real him.'" (*Men Who Hate Women and the Women Who Love Them*, 31)

Such a woman takes each gift, hollow promise and act of kindness as a positive sign. What she's really doing is accepting the high cost of the negative in the relationship for what she mistakenly perceives to be its positive aspects. Over time, however, the negative aspects increase while the positive ones correspondingly decrease. Susan Forward argues that the more abuse the victim takes, the more the abuser will dish out: "Once she accepts an attack on her self-worth and permits herself to be demeaned, she has opened the door for future assaults" (*Men Who Hate Women and the Women Who Love Them*, 32-3).

She wants to believe him even when this pattern of abuse is repeated. Brown concludes from her research that women who love psychopaths generally believe a psychopath's (false) nice words over his (real) harmful actions. She states, "When given the choice between trusting what the psychopath *says* he has done/not done/or will do, or trusting what she has caught him actually *doing*, women who love psychopaths will likely choose the words over the actions" (*Women Who Love Psychopaths*, 141).

Seeing that he can sometimes behave well, she blames herself for the times when he treats her badly. This is based on an irrational assumption, which the psychopath carefully cultivates in her. Susan Forward explains, "The logic goes like this: If he has the capacity to be so wonderful, then it must be something I am doing that's making things go wrong" (*Men Who Hate Women and the Women Who Love Them*, 33).

Exclusively dependent upon his approval and hypersensitive to his disapproval. At this point, she begins to search for what Susan Forward calls "the magic key" that will make the psychopath treat her consistently well. Needless to say, this key doesn't exist. Psychopaths engage in relationships to manipulate, deceive and mistreat others. "The women are convinced that if they could just find 'the magic key,' those 'right' behaviors or attitudes that would please their

partners, they could get their partners to behave more lovingly toward them...
Unfortunately, the misogynist's signals are always changing" (*Men Who Hate Women and the Women Who Love Them*, 35).

Relationships with them are always about control, never about mutual love.
It's as if the abused woman makes an implicit contract with her abusive partner.
She implicitly agrees to give up most of her rights in exchange for keeping him in
her life. Susan Forward describes this unfair agreement as follows: "Your part in
the unspoken agreement is: My emotional security depends on your love, and to
get that I will be compliant and renounce my own needs and wishes. His part of
the agreement is: My emotional security depends on my being in total control"
(*Men Who Hate Women and the Women Who Love Them*, 42).

*Any woman who makes it her life objective to satisfy a disordered partner is
therefore bound to eventually suffer from a lowered self-esteem.* Nothing anyone
can do will ever satisfy a controlling man. He will always require more power
over others. Susan Forward explains why controlling men are like bottomless
pits: "The misogynist must control how his partner thinks, feels, behaves, and
with whom and what she involves herself" (*Men Who Hate Women and the
Women Who Love Them*, 42).

Many become love addicts. Susan Forward stipulates that many women stay
in abusive relationships despite the mistreatment because of a love addiction to
their abusers. She states, "When a woman is in an addictive love relationship, she
experiences intense pain and suffering when she is deprived of her partner; she
feels like she cannot live without him" (*Men Who Hate Women and the Women
Who Love Them*, 87).

Part III. How to Save Yourself from Psychopathic Seduction

Chapter 1. Escaping the Psychopath

*Since any communication with him will leave you vulnerable to his continu-
ing manipulation.* Martha Stout strongly advises "No Contact," or ceasing all
communication with the psychopath. She states in no uncertain terms, "The best
way to protect yourself from a sociopath is to avoid him, to refuse any kind of
contact or communication" (*The Sociopath Next Door*, 160).

Psychopaths are proud of who they are and of what it gets them in life. Martha Stout explains that psychopaths are not only proud of who they are, but also
that they feel superior to the rest of humanity. "If anything, people without conscience tend to believe their way of being in the world is superior to ours" (*The
Sociopath Next Door*, 50).

Psychopaths tend to discourage sharing information. As we've seen, psychopaths foster isolation and secrecy in their intimate relationships. That keeps their victims under their control. Which is why Martha Stout advises victims to share information about the psychopath with others. She states, "Never agree, out of pity or for any other reason, to help a sociopath conceal his or her true character" (*The Sociopath Next Door*, 161).

Want to believe in the illusion of the perfect lover and of the special relationship that he initially created. The illusion of real love is created, above all, by the intensity with which psychopaths initially pursue some of their targets. Yet, as Susan Forward cautions, such whirlwind romances generally offer only the illusion of emotional intimacy. They're usually based on fantasy, not reality and on projection, not real knowledge of the other person. "A whirlwind courtship, thrilling as it may be, tends to provide only pseudo-intimacy, which is then mistaken for genuine closeness" (*Men Who Hate Women and the Women Who Love Them*, 20-21).

Chapter 2. Understanding the Science Behind the Disorder

To understand the physiological basis for this dangerous personality disorder. For more information, see *The Handbook of Psychopathy*, edited by Christopher J. Patrick (New York: The Guilford Press, 2007).

Since it's caused by shallow emotions. The psychopath's lack of emotional depth is wired in his brain. For more information on this subject, see *The Psychopath: Emotion and the Brain* (New York: Wiley-Blackwell, 2005).

Chapter 3. The Two Phases of Mourning: The Rational and the Emotional

Is to attempt to cure him through her love or with the help of professional counseling. Women involved with psychopaths tend to be excessively patient and cooperative with their partners. They try to buy peace at any cost and to mend the relationship by any means. But, ultimately, there are no means to please a psychopath. As Brown observes, "His insatiable need for power and dominance is so nonstop that it feels unquenchable to her" (*Women Who Love Psychopaths*, 40).

Chapter 4. Sharing Information with Others

You need to reclaim their respect by telling them the truth. Page 196. For more information on how to share information about the psychopath with others, see Donna Andersen's advice on *lovefraud.com* and Sandra L. Brown's *How to Spot a Dangerous Man Before You Get Involved*.

Chapter 5. Resisting Family/External Pressure to Stay with the Psychopath

If your psychopathic partner relies upon such allies. For more information on how (and why) to extricate yourself from the psychopathic bond, see Martha Stout's *The Sociopath Next Door*, particularly the chapter "Thirteen Rules for Dealing with Sociopaths in Everyday Life," pp. 156-163.

Chapter 6. Know Your Worth: A Healthy Self-Esteem is the Key to a Good Life

You gain peace and fulfillment from your own healthy self-esteem. For more information on cultivating a healthy self-esteem and why it's important to do so to have good romantic relationships, see Susan Forward's *Men Who Hate Women and the Women Who Love Them.*

Conclusion: Reclaiming Your Life

Sandra L. Brown, M.A. addresses this reasoning. She states, "If so, I would ask you the following questions: How many more years are you willing to invest, now that you know he is unfixable? What is it that you are investing in? What will the next fifteen years look like? What will you be like by then? Why would you want a dangerous man?" (*How to Spot a Dangerous Man Before You Get Involved*, 27).

You have agency. Being a victim of psychopathic seduction doesn't imply that you have no power whatsoever in your life or in the relationship itself. You made a series of choices to be involved with a bad man and to stay with him. But you can also choose to end the relationship. Sandra L. Brown, M.A. emphasizes that it's empowering to assume some responsibility for participating in such a damaging relationship with a disordered partner. "While it may seem easier to believe that you were solely his 'victim,' in fact, it is much more empowering to realize that dating is based on mutuality, not on hostage-taking" (*How to Spot a Dangerous Man Before You Get Involved*, 32).

You willingly stayed with him despite seeing the inevitable red flags early on in the relationship. Sandra L. Brown, M.A. observes that, based on her research, the women involved with psychopaths noticed red flags early in their relationships. They just chose to ignore them because of the supposed benefits of the relationship, which were most palpable during the honeymoon phase, but which decreased over time. "In fact," she states, "not a single woman told me there weren't any red flags" (*How to Spot a Dangerous Man Before You Get Involved*, 47).

They may be strong in other areas of life. How you behave in your personal life says much more about your inner strength and boundaries than the image you project to those who don't know you very well, such as co-workers or acquaintances. Even women who are successful and independent in their professional lives can become weak and passive in their personal relationships with psychopaths. As Susan Forward explains, "Many women who become emotionally dependent on misogynistic partners are extremely independent in other areas of their lives" (*Men Who Hate Women and the Women Who Love Them*, 88).

He has to be "top dog." Sandra L. Brown, M.A. argues that psychopaths, narcissists, violent men and misogynists share one trait in common: they need to be in charge. She states, "Violent [and abusive] men have issues with power and control... They have to be top dog" (*How to Spot a Dangerous Man Before You Get Involved*, 162).

If you regain your sense of identity and boundaries, you become much less vulnerable to psychopathic seduction and control. Being aware of your values and boundaries strengthens your defenses against psychopaths and other kinds of dangerous and controlling men. Such individuals are, by definition, boundary violators. Sandra L. Brown, M.A. elaborates, "If a woman would recognize that each boundary violation pushes her closer to the edge of tolerating or doing all those things she said she would never tolerate or do—things that in the end rob her of her dignity—she might respond to violations as soon as they begin" (*How to Spot a Dangerous Man Before You Get Involved*, 203).

Can give your life a higher, more other-regarding purpose. Martha Stout explains why, overall, it's far preferable to live right and to have a conscience, even if life may be simpler and more carefree without one. Conscience makes us more vulnerable to pain, but it also renders us fully human. If you have a conscience, you may be unable to take advantage of others or to become a dictator. Yet, Stout points out, "Unlike the hollow, risk-pursuing few who are deprived of a seventh sense, you will go through life fully aware of the warm and comforting, infuriating, confusing, compelling, and sometimes joyful presence of other human beings, and along with your conscience you will be given the chance to take the largest risk of all, which, as we all know, is to love" (*The Sociopath Next Door*, 196).

True love bonds with others to live the kind of moral, honest and fulfilling life that you deserve. It's very important not to settle in life for a bad man and a harmful relationship. If you're a decent human being, you deserve genuine love and respect from a nice and caring partner. Don't waste your life on a psychopath. As Susan Forward aptly puts it, "The fervent hope of every woman I've treated in a misogynistic relationship is that somehow something will happen that will make it all better... In truth, your relationship is far more likely to get worse than to get better" (*Men Who Hate Women and the Women Who Love Them,* 174).

Bibliography

Ablow, Keith. *Inside the Mind of Scott Peterson*. New York: St. Martin's Press, 2005.

Arendt, Hannah. *The Origins of Totalitarianism*. San Diego: Harcourt, Inc., 1948.

Arendt, Hannah. *Eichmann in Jerusalem: A Report on the Banality of Evil*. New York: Penguin Classics, 2006.

Babiak, Paul and Hare, Robert D. *Snakes in Suits: When Psychopaths Go To Work*. New York: Harper Collins, 2006

Baldassari, Anne. *Picasso: Life With Dora Maar: Love and War 1935-1945*. Paris: Flamarion, 2006.

Bancroft, Lundy. *Why Does He Do That: Inside the minds of Angry and Controlling Men*. Berkeley: Berkeley Trade, 2003.

Bernstein, Albert. *Emotional Vampires: Dealing With People Who Drain You Dry*. New York: McGraw Hill, 2002.

Bing, S. *What Would Machiavelli Do?* New York: Harper Collins, 2000.

D. Black and C. Larson, *Bad Boys, Bad Men: Confronting Antisocial Personality Disorder*. Oxford: Oxford University Press, 2000.

Blair, James. *The Psychopath: Emotion and the Brain*. New York: Wiley-Blackwell, 2005.

Brown, Nina. W. *The Destructive Narcissistic Pattern*. Westport, CT: Praeger Publishers, 1998.

Brown, Sandra L. *Women Who Love Psychopaths: Inside the Relationship of Inevitable Harm with Psychopaths, Sociopaths and Narcissists*. Penrose, NC: Mask Publishing, Second Edition, 2009.

Brown, Sandra L. *How to Spot a Dangerous Man Before You Get Involved*. Alameda, CA: Hunter House, 2005.

Bullock, Alan. *Hitler and Stalin: Parallel Lives*. New York: Vintage Edition,1991.

Cleckley, Hervey. *The Mask of Sanity*, fifth edition. St. Louis: Mosby, 1976.

Curtis, K. "Scott Peterson: Portrait of a Psychopath." The Associated Press: The Desert Sun, March 20, 2005.

Constant, Benjamin. *Adolphe*. Paris: Folio Classique, 2005.

Conquest, Robert. *Reflections on a Ravaged Century*. New York: Norton, 2000.

Doblert, Duane, L. *Understanding Personality Disorders: An Introduction*. Connecticut: Praegar Publishers, 2007.

Forward, Susan and Torres, Joan. *Men Who Hate Women and the Women Who Love Them: When Loving Hurts and You Don't Know Why*. New York: Bantam Books, 1986.

Forward, Susan. *When Your Lover Is a Liar: Healing the Wounds of Deception and Betrayal*. New York: HarperCollins Publishers, 1999.

Gilot, Françoise. *Life with Picasso*. New York: First Anchor Books Edition, 1989.

Girard, René. *Deceit, Desire, and the Novel: Self and Other in Literary Structure*. Maryland: Johns Hopkins University Press, 1976.

Golomb, Elan. *Trapped in the Mirror*. New York: Harper Paperbacks, 1995.

Hare, Robert D. *Psychopathy: Theory and Research*. New York: Wiley; Gordon Trasler, 1978.

Hare, Robert D. *Manual for the Revised Psychopathy Checklist*, 2nd Edition. Toronto, Ontario: Multi-Health Systems, 2003.

Hare, Robert D. *Without Conscience: The Disturbing World of the Psychopaths Among Us*. New York: Guilford Press, 1998.

Herold, Christopher. *Mistress to an Age: A Life of Madame de Stael*. New York: Grove Press, 2002.

Huffington, Arianna. *Picasso: Creator and Destroyer*. New York: Simon and Schuster, 1988.

Jayne, Pamela. *Ditch That Jerk! Dealing with Men Who Control and Hurt Women*. Alameda, CA: Hunter House, 2000.

Kanton, Martin. *The Psychopathy of Everyday Life: How Antisocial Personality Disorder Affects all of us*. Connecticut: Praegar Publishers, 2006.

Kernberg. Otto. *Borderline Conditions and Pathological Narcissism*. New York: Jason Aronson, 1985.

Leedom, Liane. *Just Like His Father?* New York: Health and Well-Being Publications, 2006.

Lindner, Robert. *Rebel Without a Cause*. New York: Grune and Straton, 1944.

Lowen, Alexander. *Narcissism: Denial of the True Self*. New York: Macmillan, 1983.

Lykken, David T. New York: *The Antisocial Personalities*, Lawrence Erlbaum, 1995.

Lyotard, Jean-François. *The Postmodern Condition: A Report on Knowledge*. Minnesota: University of Minnesota Press, 1984.

Mailer, Norman. *Picasso: Portrait of Picasso as a Young Man*. New York: Abacus, 1997.

Nathason, C., Paulhus, D. L. and Williams, K. M. "The Dark Triad", *Contemporary Educational Psychology*, 31 (1), 97-122, 2006.

O'Brian, Patrick. *Picasso: A Biography*. New York: W.W.W. Norton, 1994.

Olivier, Fernande. *Loving Picasso: The Private Journal of Fernande Olivier*. New York: Harry N. Abrams, 2001.

Patrick, Christopher D., Editor. *Handbook of Psychotherapy*. New York: The Guilford Press, 2007.

Picasso, Pablo. *The Time with Françoise Gilot*. New York: Kerber, 2003.

Picasso, Pablo. *Pablo Picasso and Marie-Thérèse Walter: Between Classicism and Surrealism*. New York: Kerber, 2004.

Reid, William H. *Unmasking the Psychopath: Antisocial Personality and Related Syndromes*. New York: W. W. Norton, 1986.

Richardson, John. *A Life of Picasso: The Triumphant Years, 1917-1932*. New York: Knopf, 2007.

Simon, George K. *In Sheep's Clothing: Understanding and Dealing with Manipulative People*. New York: A. J. Christopher & Co, 1996.

Staub, Ervin. *The Roots of Evil: The Origins of Genocide and Other Group Violence*. Cambridge: Cambridge University Press, 1989.

Stein, Gertrude. *Picasso*. New York: Dover Press, 1984.

Stout, Martha. *The Sociopath Next Door*. New York: Broadway Books, 2005.

Tismaneanu, Vladimir. *Stalinism for All Seasons: A Political History of Romanian Communism*. Berkeley: University of California Press, 2003.

Vaknin, Sam. *Malignant Self-Love: Narcissism Revisited*. Czech Republic: Narcissus Publications, 2001.

Winegarten Renee. *Germaine de Stael and Benjamin Constant: A Dual Biography*. New Haven: Yale University Press, 2008.

Wolman, Benjamin B. *Antisocial Behavior: Personality Disorders from Hostility to Homicide*. New York: Prometheus Books, 1999.

Wood, Dennis. *Benjamin Constant: A Biography*. New York: Routledge, 1993.

Additional Resources: Websites

Psychopathyawareness.wordpress.com

Powercommunicating.com

Saferelationshipsmagazine.com

Lovefraud.com

Drjoecarver.com

Protect.org

Womanslaw.org

Stopfamilyviolence.org

Protectiveparents.com

Batteredmotherscustodyconference.org

Kathleenrussell.com

Thelizlibrary.ogr

Jfc.org

Canow.org

About the Author

Claudia Moscovici has a Ph.D. in Comparative Literature from Brown University. She is the author of *Velvet Totalitarianism*, a critically acclaimed novel about a Romanian family's survival in an oppressive communist regime due to the strength of their love. She also published several scholarly books on political philosophy and the Romantic movement, focusing on psychological interpretations of art and literature. Her publications include *Romanticism and Postromanticism* (Rowman and Littlefield, 2007), *Gender and Citizenship* (Rowman and Littlefield, 2000) and *Double Dialectics* (Rowman and Littlefield, 2002). She taught philosophy, literature and arts and ideas at Boston University and at the University of Michigan. She's currently working on a novel about psychopathic seduction and betrayal, called *The Seducer*.